The
Technical
Writer

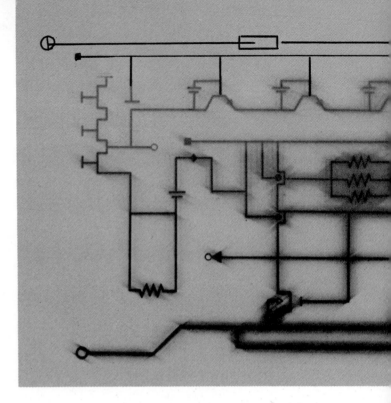

THE TECHNICAL WRITER

ANN STUART
University of Evansville

HOLT, RINEHART AND WINSTON, INC.

New York   Chicago   San Francisco   Philadelphia

Montreal   Toronto   London   Sydney   Tokyo

Printed in the United States of America

8 9 0 039 9 8 7 6 5 4 3 2 1

Library of Congress Cataloging-in-Publication Data
Stuart, Ann.
  The technical writer.

  Includes index.
  1. Technical writing.   I. Title.
T11.S723   1988   808'.0666   87-15028

ISBN 0-03-004579-7

Holt, Rinehart and Winston, Inc.
The Dryden Press
Saunders College Publishing

Dedicated to my husband,
Raymond R. Poliakoff, in appreciation
for his caring, love, and good counsel

Preface

This book includes all traditional topics expected in a good technical writing text; further, it coordinates the use of word processing with the preparation and presentation of technical communication. In so doing, it prepares the student for today's workplace.

Schools differ in the amount and kind of equipment they have for producing computer-assisted information. Teachers differ in their understanding of and experience with word processing programs and other computer-assisted aids. For these reasons, I wrote this book so that it can be used with little or no access to a computer and without reference to particular software or hardware products. Traditional topics are developed just as in any good technical communication text, and wherever appropriate, discussion about the advantages and applications of word processing appears. A visual symbol indicates the beginning and end of these discussions. The benefit of this approach is that teachers can choose how and when they want to integrate computer-assisted methods into the preparation of technical documents. Moreover, students will understand why word processing is so useful and effective in preparing technical information, know what a computer can and cannot do in assisting them to write, and develop standards by which to judge the quality of computer-created work.

The Technical Writer is designed for classroom use in colleges, universities, vocational and technical schools, and for in-house use in employee development programs in the private sector or government. It is suitable for college or university undergraduate or graduate courses and can be adapted for a quarter, semester, or school year.

The following are some of the book's distinguishing features:

1. The writing style is readable, pleasant, free of pomposity, and uncluttered by jargon. It serves as a positive model for students practicing technical writing techniques.
2. Objectives stated at the beginning of each chapter prepare students for the material to be learned.
3. Interesting and practical exercises provide ample opportunity to apply the material discussed in the text.
4. A logical and consistent organization overall and within individual chapters provides a good instruction and learning sequence.
5. Heads and subheads written in plain terms provide a pattern of organization consistent with the principles of good technical writing.
6. Checklists help students focus information and verify the effectiveness of their own writing.
7. A word list of computer terms clearly defines unfamiliar terms.
8. Writing samples provide good models to imitate.
9. A comprehensive index and table of contents make it easy to refer to and find information.

I wish to acknowledge those who helped make this book possible:

My technical writing students who commented on and contributed to the many examples in the text.

My colleagues who shared ideas and offered encouragement: Amir Al-Khafaji, Robert Brooks, Ronald Davaisher, Philip Gerhart, Marvin Guilfoyle, Hans Pieper, Paul Novak, Jerry Seng, Dean Thomlison, John Tooley, Rebecca Van Campen, and William Weiss.

Laura Weaver, who proofread the manuscript and was a supportive friend.

Susan Eno, Director of Medical Records, Welborn Baptist Hospital, who kindly helped with information about on-line user documentation and manuals.

Charline Buente, A.I.A., of Edmund L. Hafer, Architect Inc., who shared her experiences with on-site documentation.

Rick Kallop, of the IBM Corporation, who demonstrated and helped me understand certain graphics capabilities.

Charlyce Jones Owen, my editor, who made this book possible and who cared about the quality of the work.

Kate Morgan, who gave careful guidance and support in the development of the book.

Jeanette Ninas Johnson, who directed with care and good humor the editorial production.

Gloria Gentile, who was responsible for the design.

Annette Mayeski, who saw the book through production.

Reviewers who read and made constructive comments: Richard T. Brucher, University of Maine at Orono; Pat Evenson, North Central Technical Institute; Christopher Gould, Southwestern Oklahoma State University; Joyce Hicks, Valparaiso University; Robert E. Jenkins, Florence Darlington Technical College; James J. Lynch, Virginia Polytechnic Institute; Louis Murphy, Bucks County Community College; Carole Pemberton, Normandale Community College; Nell Ann Pickett, Hinds Junior College; Carol Lee Saffioti, University of Wisconsin—Parkside; David K. Vaughan, University of Maine at Orono; Laura H. Weaver, University of Evansville.

To each of these, I thank you.

Ann Stuart

To the Student

This book covers all the topics expected in any good technical writing book, and it does more. It links preparing and presenting technical communication to the new communication tool—the computer. While you can learn and use all that is taught in this book without a computer, whenever appropriate *The Technical Writer* talks about the advantages of using word processing. You learn how to apply word processing capabilities to the assignments and how to judge whether the writing you or others create is effective.

Your opportunity for hands-on computer experience depends partly upon the equipment available. But even with little or no access to a computer, you will understand, after studying with this book, why word processing is so useful and effective in preparing technical information, know what a computer can and cannot do in assisting you to write, and develop standards to judge the quality of computer-created work. Such knowledge is essential as you prepare for the modern workplace. Most companies already use computer-assisted technology to prepare documents. The future promises more, not less, technology. You simply cannot afford to be ignorant of or disinterested in the modern means of preparing communication. This book is written with you—the student—in mind. It recognizes that many of you have yet to work and to prepare actual working documents. For this reason, documents are clearly defined; audience and purpose considered; objectives, writing tips, and methods of editing given; and formats suggested. The exercises are practical and often involve group work similar to that you will experience in the workplace.

People admire those who can communicate effectively. Since technical communication can be mastered by anyone willing to study and practice, this book offers you the necessary information to plan, create, and present effective technical communication. You must supply the willingness to study and practice the craft of writing and speaking to improve your ability to communicate.

Contents

Part 2   The Writing Process   24

The
Technical
Writer

Part 1

Technical Communication and Its Link with Computers

Part 1 introduces you to technical communication and its link with the new communication tool—the computer.

Chapter One: An Introduction
- justifies your need to communicate effectively
- defines technical communication
- talks about known and promised computer-controlled devices used to prepare and present technical information

Chapter Two: The Student's Guide to Word Processing and Computer Concepts and Language
- discusses word processing and keyboarding
- includes practice exercises for both skills
- provides a word list of computer concepts and terms

Overview

Only you can decide to be a better communicator. It is like going on a diet or quitting smoking. People can tell you how important communication is, or how it will benefit you, or even the dire consequences of not doing it. But you are the only person who can decide that effective communication is worthwhile and apply enough willpower to do what is necessary to make it happen.

It is only natural—particularly if you have yet to work in a technical field—to ask how important effective communication is to your professional future. In my own technical writing classes, I often state that one's success is directly linked to one's ability to communicate effectively. I bolster my own opinion by inviting to the classroom professionals from the "real world." They testify to the importance of technical communication in their own work and consequently in the work and success of students majoring in technical fields. Former students return and detail the types and amount of writing they do in a normal day or week or month; managers come and speak about how good communications are a key to retention and promotion; recruiters visit and explain how a person's letter of inquiry, answers on the application form, and oral communication during the interview are important factors in hiring; co-op students attest to the amount of writing they do on the job and the need to write and speak well. I ask you, as I ask my own students at the beginning of each semester, to believe that anyone in a technical profession must gather and share factual information. Your ability to do this well will affect your own success and that of others who must use your material.

Chapter 1

An Introduction

Why Another Writing Course?

As a result of your schooling, you already have taken and passed with acceptable grades one or more composition courses, so it is perfectly logical to ask: Why another writing course? Why isn't my performance in other writing classes proof enough that I know how to write? How is technical writing so different from other writing that it requires a special course?

These are good questions, but they imply that writing is a subject you take in school until you pass a standard and then you never need to study or practice it again. This is not true. Writing is an evolving activity that you do better as you understand your own ability as a writer and as you work to better your performance. Technical writing in particular can be improved because it requires more skill than talent. Like other skill work, it can be practiced and evaluated, and weaknesses or errors, when discovered, can be corrected. As with other skills, some of you will perform better than others, but everyone can achieve a level of competency that is acceptable now in school and later in business and industry.

Why a Special Course in Technical Writing?

Just as one distinguishes golf from tennis and then separates the particular skills of tennis, such as the serve and return to practice in order to improve one's whole game, curriculum directors make a distinction between technical writing and creative writing or journalism or other types of writing. The specialization allows the writer to prepare reports particular to business and industry and to polish a writing style respected in technical professions.

The Nature and Characteristics of Technical Communication

Its Link to Other Expository Writing

Technical writing is a type of writing that informs and/or persuades. You already know about and have experience in this form of writing because most of what you have written in other composition classes had the same intent. All that you learned in writing those assignments is valid and should be applied to technical writing:

1. Narrow and focus a general subject in order to develop it in detail and be accountable for what you write.
2. Determine the primary audience for your writing. Find out what they know and what they expect to learn. Know if your audience is hostile or friendly; if hostile, decide how you can persuade them to give your work a fair reading.
3. Plan before you begin. Use your outline, jottings, or notes to stay on the subject and go from point to point logically and economically.
4. Use a variety of writing patterns to develop your ideas (comparison and contrast, cause and effect, classification, definition, etc.). Use examples for clarification. Let transitions lead readers clearly through the writing.
5. Write a purpose sentence that makes an exact statement of what you intend to write. Afterward, make every sentence, paragraph, and section contribute directly to the purpose.
6. Proofread for grammar and punctuation errors, good paragraph development, an easy flow of ideas, a consistent tone, the best use of language.
7. Rewrite to improve and refine your work.

Its Own Characteristics

The act of recording technical information is as old as the act of writing itself. Ancient documents from every nationality include writings about architecture, construction, science, agriculture, economics, navigation, astronomy, war, and trade. The writers of such documents intended to record accurately technical information discovered or observed, to direct or inform readers how to perform technical work, or to persuade an audience about a technical subject. Although people have always communicated technical matter, over the past 30 years technical communication has come into its own as an academic specialty, as the subject of textbooks and professional journals, and as the basis for professional associations and societies. This attention has produced a clearer definition of technical writing itself. The following list presents some distinguishable traits you will learn in this book and have the opportunity to practice:

1. Technical writing most often is about scientific or industrial subjects and information from other fields related to science and industry. Recently, however, the subject area has expanded to include precise and descriptive writing about programs, products, theories, and principles from other subject areas.
2. Technical writing contains material that satisfies the specific need of a particular audience. Most read for a practical purpose: to perform a procedure, to understand a process, and/or to gather information in order to make an informed decision. For this reason, technical writing must be carefully accurate, objective, clearly stated, and easy to understand. Ideally, the reader should be able to interpret the information only one way. The dependent relationship among writer, subject, and audience is an identifying trait; a writer of fiction, for example, can choose a subject that only he or she wants to know anything about and to write as a means of self-expression. If others elect to read the work, they may partially understand the subject matter or understand it differently from one another; such eccentricity is not normal or expected in technical writing.
3. Technical writing has a distinctive style. Technical writers care about language as intensely as do writers of other types. Their objectives are to use conventional and exact language and to write rigorously lean prose. Description comes from the perfectly chosen noun, verb, adjective, or adverb within the basis sentence, not from discursive, flowery passages. The beauty of this writing is its clearness and lucidity. It is conservative: most sentences are organized subject-verb-object; the active voice is preferred, and sentences are normally short. It shuns ambiguity and often cultivates redundancy.
4. Technical writing stresses format. Writers of individual reports are expected to present material in a meaningful and easy-to-read fashion. Companies often develop their own formats for in-house writing and expect their writers to use them effectively. Technical readers anticipate that information will be highly organized and have patterns of presentation repeated.
5. Technical writing is designed so that readers can access information easily. Not every reader needs to read, understand, or use the whole document; consequently, parts should be understood by themselves.
6. Technical writing considers visuals an important means of communicating. Writers must know when information can be better understood through visuals, what types of visuals are best for certain information, how to prepare visuals so they are effective, and how to integrate them meaningfully into the text.

Often a Matter of Style

Many subjects can be written about technically and in other ways. For example, a terrible airplane accident occurred in 1985 when a Tri-Star crashed during a blinding rainstorm as it tried to land. Of 163 people on board, 132 died and 31 were injured. The federal investigators determined that the probable cause of the accident was wind shear. In the week following the crash, newspaper and news-magazine reporters wrote about this phenomenon both technically from interviews with air controllers and investigators and personally from interviews with survivors. Some of those comments follow. Notice the unemotional, clearly stated, factual nature of the technical account.

Technical/Objective/Professionals	*Personal/Emotional/Survivors*
Wind shear is a sudden turbulence that can destabilize a plane.	The ride got rougher and rougher and rougher and rougher. The plane was flying apart around me. Metal was going everywhere.
Wind shear is caused by a sudden change in wind direction or speed, causing a strong flow of air straight downward. When the air hits the ground, it flows outward in all directions. As a plane approaches a shear, it meets an increasing headwind that provides the aircraft lift. As it passes through the strong funnel-like down draft, the plane is pushed downward.	The plane dropped suddenly. Everything went haywire.
Finally as it moves away from the funnel, what was a headwind becomes a tailwind, causing the speed of air traveling over the wings to drop and reduce the plane's lift. The sudden loss of lift combined with the force of the downdraft can push a jumbo jet to the ground.	It seemed like we were forced to the ground much faster than the pilot wanted. He kept increasing the engine speed, I guess trying to pull up. I saw the ground and thought we were landing. One bump and the plane came apart. It felt like someone stepped on us when we hit.

The writing in both columns describes what happens to a plane when it encounters wind shear and crashes, but the two differ. The personal comments are descriptive: "One bump and the plane came apart." The remembrance of events is imaginative: "It felt like someone stepped on us when we hit." The comments are personal and about this particular accident. The technical description is factual, dispassionate, and typical of any situation involving wind shear and an airplane. Such characteristics make it useful in a precise analysis of what occurred in this crash on this particular day. Your writing model for a similar purpose is column 1.

The Future Includes Computers

Those of you who are preparing for technical professions, who will graduate in your early twenties, and who will work the normal 40 years before retirement must know how to use computers and computer-based information services. Whether you work in an office, laboratory, hospital, plant, or factory, much of the information you receive and send is going to involve happenings like the following that include use of computers. To be effective, you must know how to interact with computer-controlled devices and be able to talk accurately with others about such devices, as well as understand the capabilities of such equipment:

> You need to understand the capabilities of word processing and be familiar with devices such as mouse pointers, light pens, and touch screens, since many of you will have work stations equipped with terminals and software programs and will be expected to write your own memos, letters, and reports.
>
> You need to be proficient in word processing in order to keep up. Group work is common in technical professions. You may write as a group by passing a diskette back and forth among you as together you develop ideas and write and edit a report.
>
> You need to know the editing capabilities of the software program being used so that you can comment on work in progress while it is still on the screen and offer constructive criticism. Also, you need to understand windowing programs in order to view data from separate programs simultaneously through windows on the same screen and to compare and comment on different aspects of the same report or on different work underway at the same time by the person asking your advice.
>
> You need to understand and know how to use integration programs that allow you to share data between word processing and other programs. For example, if you decide that your report needs a graph, you should be capable of adding it by means of integrated functions on one disk or through separate programs designed to work together.
>
> You need to know how to operate computer-related equipment to receive information and how best to prepare information to be sent in various ways. For example, you may send or receive information on diskettes, by voice synthesizers, through modems, on computer printouts and directly to your computer screen from networks both inside and outside your place of work.

The preceding list mentions what is known and commonplace. The future promises more ways to share ideas technologically and more acceptance of technology in business and industry. You simply cannot afford to be reluctant or refuse to accept such advances. This book helps you become knowledgeable about using computers to write. It introduces you to possibilities and gives standards to judge the quality of the writing produced. Terms you may not know, such as some of those in the previous list, will be defined in the next chapter.

Speaking about Technical Matters:
An Increasing Need

Occurrences requiring effective speaking grow in number and kind. Anyone entering a technical field can expect to present ideas, express opinions, and make recommendations in group work. Some will give presentations at company meetings; others will speak with clients or to the public. All this activity means that you must speak clearly, accurately, and in meaningful sequence, without irritating hesitations or other distracting speech habits. Your posture, gestures, and physical mannerisms must help your presentation. Whatever you have learned about speaking effectively from other experiences or classes applies to talking about technical matters. What you now want to polish is your ability to think and talk clearly and accurately and in a way that will cause people to listen.

Speaking about Technical Matters: The Future Includes Computers

The person who speaks well gains attention and respect. To speak well one must easily handle the tools of oral presentation. These used to be the speaker's own body, the podium, the microphone, the speaker's notes, a variety of visual aids, and any accompanying equipment such as overhead or slide projectors. Today the speaker must also know how computers can assist oral presentations because the following occurrences are becoming common:

Meetings are conducted through conference calls. Many of these include video communications, which means that speakers see each other and the materials used to illustrate information. You need to be comfortable speaking in such circumstances and to know what kinds of visuals transmit clearly and understandably.

It is commonplace to dictate into a machine information that will be typed by either a person or the machine itself. The information may be directly used by someone listening to your dictation. You may also work with voice-activated computer terminals. Both means of communication require you to formulate and speak thoughts in proper sequence.

The computer is a common means of visual support in oral presentations. You need to understand computer graphics: how to create them and how to design ones that can be clearly seen and understood.

Some companies include a video presentation as part of performance reviews. For this reason, you should know how you appear on video. You then can work to eliminate ineffective mannerisms.

Presentations to clients often include a video piece as well as an oral and/or written report. You must understand what makes an effective video presentation in order to help create one or judge what is produced.

This book enables you to learn about your oral presentation needs and creates opportunities for you to practice and become a more confident and effective speaker.

You, Technical Communication, and *The Technical Writer*

The Technical Writer covers the traditional subject matter expected in a good technical writing text. It does more. It includes topics currently being added to the curricula—like documentation for computer users. Most importantly, the book links technical communication with computers, the new communication tool. You will know both the content and standards of common technical documents and modern methods for creating them. You will be better prepared to work effectively in the modern workplace.

Your opportunity to prepare for computer-based information systems depends partly on the equipment available. Some of you have access to very basic computer systems with a meager selection of software programs, whereas others can practice on sophisticated systems with all the latest software. Some of you have your own personal computers, so you can work any time for any length of time; others have unlimited access to computer labs with plenty of terminals and no problem in acquiring time to use them; still others have trouble even finding a terminal to use and compete with many others for both the terminals and work time. These differences matter, but they have more to do with convenience than learning. The important thing for you to recognize is your need to be proficient in creating and using computer-based information, to have hands-on experience with such information, and to have an inquisitive and positive attitude about working with computers. This book helps you gain knowledge and experience. You must supply the right attitude.

Chapter 2

The Student's Guide to Word Processing and Computer Concepts and Language

This chapter is for those who have little or no experience with computers or word processing. It begins by discussing word processing and gives a practice exercise. It continues with a section about keyboarding and includes an exercise. It closes with a word list of computer concepts and terms.

Word Processing

Word Processing Programs Have Common Denominators

 Word processing is a type of software program that lets you type words into the computer, commit them to the computer's memory or to disk storage, and later recall them to read and decide whether or not to rewrite. If you want to rewrite, almost any word processing program allows you to insert and delete words, sentences, and paragraphs; move text within your document; choose a format for margins and spacing; use automatic wordwrap which carries words typed past the right margin to the next line; and search out certain words and replace them with others. Except for automatic wordwrap, you do the same things when you rewrite manually. You add words in margins, above lines, on extra pages that you plan to type into the next draft; you cross through words you want to omit; you circle material you plan to move and draw an arrow to that place in the text where it is to appear in the next draft, or you cut and paste the document together in some new arrangement. The similarity between these actions and word processing is no accident. When word processing was coming into being, software developers studied people writing in order to understand what they did during the writing process. The functions most often performed became the basics of word processing.

You Do Not Have to Understand Computers to Use Word Processing

You can use word processing without knowing how to program or how a computer works. Word processing *IS* a program, and if you can turn the computer on, load the program into it, and know how to use the program's functions, you *can* write using word processing.

You may become an avid user of a computer for technical communication and never use it for anything else. That is what I do. People often assume that because I write books about computers and writing I know a lot about computers. I do not. My present needs do not require that I program, know computer languages, or understand the technical workings of a computer. If my needs change, I shall learn what is necessary to pursue my new interests. You can adopt the same attitude.

Word Processing Will Not Write for You

Word processing ads are so promising you may have the impression that the programs write for you. They do not. The screen is no different from a blank piece of paper rolled into a typewriter or a clean writing pad waiting for your ideas. If you have nothing to say, have not done your homework, and are unprepared to write, the screen will remain empty except for the cursor sitting in the same position blinking its reminder that you are making no progress.

New trends in word processing do help with the formation and expression of ideas. For example, outline and idea processor programs break through writer's block by letting you organize in small segments or in outline format. You can brainstorm or get a start. Later you can expand. These programs help, however, only after you provide the ideas.

Future trends in word processing predict "mentor" or "expert" programs that through artificial intelligence will comment, offer advice, and criticize a writer's endeavors. But until such wonders are available, you must continue to face the blank screen and depend upon yourself to have the ideas, organize them, and get the ideas out of your mind and onto the screen.

Word Processing Can Help You Rewrite

Word processing may not originate documents, but it takes the drudgery out of rewriting. It is the rare person who can write perfect first drafts. Most of us need to begin, write some ideas, add to them, take out material, add other ideas, move text around, change language to suit the tone and audience, and finally, after working the document over several times, decide that it is good enough to call finished. The ability to make changes without having to retype what remains acceptable is word processing's gift to writers. Word processing frees writers to think creatively and critically about their work because they are no longer intimidated by the fact that a change means retyping the whole document.

Word Processing Is Particularly Useful to the Technical Writer

Word processing is particularly suited for anyone writing technical documents. Such documents often call for variable margins, perfectly aligned tables, and different type fonts to underscore separate sections. The technical writer often finds that specifications change during writing, experiments alter information, products or programs require modifications, processes or procedures change, format requirements vary. These conditions require that the writer revise, add text, and reformat. Word processing allows the technical writer to salvage what remains the same and to make necessary alterations without retyping the entire document. Some programs will even automatically renumber pages and footnote numbers.

You Need to Know More Than Which Keys to Strike

This book does not teach how to use particular computers or word processing programs. Too many kinds of computers and programs exist for that to be practical, and new programs appear so rapidly that this text would be out of date before it was published. Your teacher, or the computer lab instructor, other classmates, or the manuals that come with the hardware and software will help you learn how to operate the computer available to you and how to enact word processing functions of the program you are using.

What you will learn is when and why to use a word processing function once you know how to enact it. Being able to push the right keys to eliminate words, move text around, or add new material means little if you do not understand why you are doing so. Revisions must be reasoned out and changes made purposefully. This book gives principles for making good decisions about audience, subject, content, and format. You can combine this knowledge with word processing functions to revise in a meaningful yet easy way.

Check Programs Are No Substitute for Learning

Some students excuse their need to know grammar, spelling, punctuation, and an effective writing style by saying, "My secretary will know what I want to say," or "The typist will make me look and sound good and put in all the commas and things like that." The same type of student says about check programs, "I don't need to learn spelling or grammar; my computer will check my work and correct whatever mistakes I make." These people are in jeopardy. Language skills in America are in a deplorable state, and indications are that many people graduating from high school and even college cannot read and write at expected levels. The chance of having a secretary who knows how to correct and rewrite one's material is not good. The chance of having a check program always available is also a long shot. You must not be someone dependent on others or a machine to edit your work. If people learn that you do not understand the rules of writing well enough to do your own work, they may wonder what else you do not know. Your overall competency can be questioned.

Check programs are convenient and helpful, but limited. Such programs read and "check" your writing for grammar, spelling, punctuation, and even style and language. They work in a variety of ways, but all perform the service of marking errors. Some automatically correct errors; others mark problems and offer choices that you can accept or ignore. If you rely on check programs entirely and do not proofread yourself, you may pass on writing with errors that make you look silly or stupid. For example, most spelling checkers do not distinguish homonyms, so your document can read "to" instead of "too"; some style checkers do not distinguish between a colon or dash, or monitor the use of the question mark, so the sense of what you are saying can be confused; some programs flag all uses of the passive voice, so you tend to eliminate the passive even when it is appropriate; some grammar checks do not spot errors such as subject-verb disagreement, noun-modifier disagreement, and wrong pronouns, or question usage like "it's" or "its," so you appear ignorant of basic grammar.

Good Work Habits Make for Good Word Processing

Some people overstate the delicacy and complexity of computers. As a result, users are afraid to do anything without first checking with someone who understands them. They are terrified to try anything because they might "break" the machine, or they fear that if they hit a wrong key they may wipe everything out. Remember that computers are widely distributed in America's schools; if they can withstand student use and not be destroyed, you should not be timid about trying a software function or striking a key to see what it does.

Like any other machine, computers work better if they are operated correctly. If you follow a few simple rules, you should not be the cause of any trouble your computer may have:

1. Do not eat, drink, or smoke at the terminal or printer. If you must have that cup of coffee, or soft drink, or sandwich, or cigarette with you in order to write, keep everything away from the machine. Then, if a spill occurs or you happen to drop something, it will not touch any of the computer's parts.
2. Be careful with floppy disks—those that you put in and take out of the computer. When not in use, keep the disks in the envelopes they came in. Store them in the original box or in some other container that will keep them from bending or from having things set on top of them.

When you do use a disk, carefully remove it from its envelope; hold it by the top; do not touch the area of the disk that is exposed. With the disk level, insert it into the disk drive. If it balks, remove it and try again or push gently. Do not use main force to thrust a disk into a drive that does not want to accept it.

Keep disks away from extremes of heat and cold.

Keep disks away from anything magnetized. That means you should not put disks on top of the computer terminal, tape recorder, or calculator. You can have this equipment in your work area; just do not lay disks on or near magnetized items.

Do not remove a disk when the red light on the front of a disk drive is on. The light means that the drive is working. If the disk is taken out during this time, both the disk and record can be damaged. It is like dragging a phonograph needle across a record.

If the computer uses a hard disk (one built inside the computer), be careful about moving, hitting, or jostling the computer unit containing the disk. Any movement can damage the disk and potentially cause a loss of data.

3. Static electricity can harm a computer. You may need to place a static-free mat over the carpet where the computer sits. If you conduct a lot of electricity, you may have to spray yourself with an antistatic spray.

4. Be sensible about the computer equipment. When you turn knobs, open disk doors, hit keys, do so with respect. There is no need to be rough.

5. Keep the work area and the equipment clean. Dust and dirt are not good for the equipment.

A Word Processing Exercise

Things you will need:

1. Access to a computer terminal.
2. A disk with a word processing program on it and disk space for you to write or access to a computer with word processing capabilities built into the system.
3. A formatted disk so you can copy (if you want) what you have written on the word processing disk onto the formatted disk in order to save it.

Preparation: Your writing instructor, the lab director, or the manual will tell you how to prepare for writing and how to perform the word processing functions on the computer you are using.

1. Get settled at the computer.
2. If necessary, turn the system on and prepare it for a word processing program.
3. Bring up the word processing program.
4. Adjust the definition on the screen so you are comfortable with the brightness of what is displayed.

Exercise
1. Open a new file named "PRACTICE." Strike the enter key or whatever is needed to cause the new file to appear on the screen.

2. If your program allows you to reset margins, set the left margin at 10 and the right margin at 60.
3. If your program allows, turn off the justification, which will make the right margin ragged rather than even.
4. Type in the following:

> I am excited about writing using word processing. I believe my instructor who says that technical communication is important to my career. I am going to enjoy writing my assignments and look forward to each writing class. If my teacher believes this, the teacher will believe anything, so missing class should be a cinch; I'll say my dog died, and I was too upset to attend class.

Editing
1. Insert "professional" before "career" in line 2.
2. Change "each" to "every" in line 3.
3. Change the "," after "anything" in line 4 to a ".".
    Delete "so."
    Make the "m" in "missing" a capital.
4. Delete everything after "cinch" and change the ";" to a ".".
5. Move the first sentence so that it becomes sentence 3.
6. Scroll the text up and down to see your changes.
7. Reform the paragraph.
8. Save this document.
9. Print the document.

In this simple exercise, you readied the computer; brought up the word processing program; entered text; edited text by inserting, deleting, and moving text; saved the document; and obtained a printed copy. These basic functions allow you to begin word processing. You will learn and master the more sophisticated features available on your program as you use it and are curious enough to try different functions.

A Note to Beginning Users Frustration is a part of learning word processing. If you throw up your hands and quit after the first 15 minutes or the first attempt to create a document, you will not give the program or yourself a fair chance. One of the greatest frustrations is the loss of text. It is important to know that if you do not "save," you will not have a record of what you have written. You can avoid this disappointment by enacting the "SAVE" command frequently as you create text and absolutely when you finish a document. It is also a good idea to make a printed copy of drafts or originals that you reformat. If you do not and decide that you liked the original better, you may have no record of the original and may not be able to reconstruct it.

Early in your learning, practice using features such as indenting, tabbing, and hard spacing because these actions can produce something different from what you had in mind and be a bother when you are ready to edit.

Do not be a quitter. Do not pay to have your paper typed by someone who has been patient enough to learn word processing. Stay with it, and find out that soon you will master the details that are the source of frustration.

Do Your Homework before Selecting a Word Processing Program

If at some time you are in the position to order or purchase your own word processing program, the following guidelines will help you make a good decision:

1. Decide what you want out of a word processing program before you go shopping; do not leave that decision up to the salesperson. To help you decide, make a list of the kinds of writing you do over a month and how often you write each kind. Then analyze what features you need to write and edit these different writings effectively and easily. You may find that all your needs are served by one of the simple and less expensive programs, or you may determine that you need a powerful program with many alternative ways to write, edit, and complete a polished, professional-looking document.

    If you also are purchasing hardware, think about compatibility. Some systems, as well as programs, allow for a lot of interchange among different computers; others do not. If you anticipate moving equipment and/or programs among school, work, or home, analyze compatibility before you buy.

2. Decide how important convenience is for you. Often for less money, but more inconvenience, you can purchase several word processing packages that will do all that you need. But buying several programs is right only if you use one program most of the time and the others seldom. If you analyze your writing and find that you need to change disks often to have all the functions you need, buy one program that will let you write without stopping to change disks.

A Note   Remember that there are hard disks and floppy disks and disks that store programs and disks that store text. If a system uses floppy disks, you may find yourself inserting a word processing disk, storing what you have written to a blank disk, inserting again the word processing disk, writing and saving the text, taking out the word processing disk, inserting a graphics disk, and continuing the inserting and taking out process every time you need a new function. If every program you need is on a separate disk and you use many programs often, you probably need an integrated program or system.

---

3. Realize that no program is going to do everything you want in the way you want it done. Again, analyze what you write in order to determine the functions most important to you, and then purchase a program that effectively and easily produces what you most need.

4. Before you buy, think what you will be writing in the next few years. It makes good money sense to anticipate and buy a program with capabilities that meet your future needs. The difference in money between a simple and complex program may be significant, but if you keep purchasing new programs as your

processing needs expand, the costs can mount until it would have been less expensive to have bought a powerful program at the beginning.

Keyboarding

There was a time when typing was mainly woman's work. That time is no more. In factories, plants, and businesses, men have personal computers in their work areas and enter data themselves. On plant floors, male supervisors, foremen, and workers enter production data. The probability is high, whether you are a man or a woman, that you will use computer keyboards. The better typist you are, the easier it will be to enter information and the fewer corrections you will have to make. Make up your mind to keyboard correctly rather than hunt and peck. This method gets the work done, but you do not look at ease with the equipment. It is easier to type when your hands are positioned correctly.

The following illustration shows the correct position for your hands and which fingers should strike which keys.

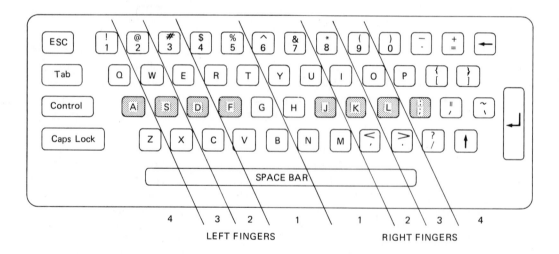

A Keyboarding Exercise

Software programs exist that teach you how to keyboard, but it is not necessary to use such a program or even to take a class. What you want to do is to type using the appropriate fingers, without making a number of mistakes, and at a steady and acceptable speed. You can learn this by typing any material you choose, or by using the following word list that contains all the letters of the alphabet. While practicing, remember:

1. You should type at a speed that you can consistently maintain without a lot of errors.
2. You should keep your hands in the correct position and use the correct fingers.

3. You will increase your speed and accuracy as you practice.
4. You will soon learn to type without looking at the keys.

A Word List for Keyboard Practice

- contour relief topographical mapping stadia scale plat cartology
- refraction elevation curvature level tripod tilting closure
- least-squares monumentation monitoring barometric
- angle horizontal vertical zenith true magnetic declination azimuths compass gyro telescope transit motions theodolites scale-reading digital sight
- length area tape slope alignment mistakes checks accuracy field-notes
- urban survey deed condominium excess deficiency highway street riparian alluvium reliction accretion
- radiation atomic homogeneous absorption amplification electron oscillator susceptibility
- nonlinear second-harmonic parametric frequency electrooptic retardation phase high-frequency beam conjugate holographic waveguide laser
- digital probability random analog channel Fourier transform sampling synchronization vector
- stress bean shear flexural torsion cylinder temperature endurance limit size fatigue
- screws fasteners connections thread bolt joint torque preload fatigue rivet pin
- bearing ball lubrication mounting enclosure welding butt fillet brazed bonded joints spring optimization belt chain shaft rim cone gear
- anatomy physiology cell tissue epithelial reproduction membrane skeletal joint vertebrae thoracic spinal system circulatory immunity
- metabolism homeostasis growth movement responsiveness reproduction adaptation
- carbohydrates lipids proteins nucleic acid bacteria taxonomy catalyst chlorophyll virus nutrition digestive metabolic muscle classify division kingdom system

A Word List of Computer Concepts and Terms

The world is divided between people who know about computers and people who do not. Those who do communicate in a language known as computerese which they never bother to translate when talking with those who do not. So that you will not have a language problem while reading this book, I am going to define basic terms having to do with computers and technical communication.

Boilerplate   A communication technique that allows you to insert previously written text into the document you are now writing.
Booting up or booting the system   Computerese for turning on the computer and putting it in operating condition.
Bug   A descriptive term for an error or malfunction in a program or a computer system.

Cathode ray tube/CRT   The electronic element of a computer terminal screen that produces a picture.

Commands   Actions taken to enact a word processing function. Such action usually involves hitting a key or a combination of keys.

Computer   A machine that enables you to use a word processing program.

Cursor   A blinking character on the screen that tells where the next typed character will appear.

Data   Individual items of information. Computer people call what they type into the computer data. Data is a plural noun and traditionally uses a plural verb, but some recent dictionaries approve usage with a singular verb.

Debug   The action of finding and correcting an error or malfunction in a program or computer system.

Default   A failure of the computer system to perform a task.

Disk/diskette   A thin, flexible magnetic disk storage device.

Disk drive   A device used for reading and writing data. If your system does not have a hard disk, you must insert the word processing program disk into the disk drive before you can begin writing.

Document   Writing that has permanence and can be read by a machine or people.

Error message   Messages that occur when you or the computer makes an error. They appear on the screen and tell what the error is. Some messages tell you how to correct the error.

F-Function keys   Program function keys. Such keys are preprogrammed so that when you hit one, it performs a predetermined function.

File   The designation given each piece of writing you enter into the computer. You name every file and that name is displayed when you start the word processing program. You type in the name to recall it from the computer's memory.

Font   A complete set of printing type of one size and face.

Form feed paper or fan fold paper   A single long piece of paper perforated at intervals so you can easily separate it into individual pages. This type of paper is used in printers to give you a "softcopy" (paper copy / sometimes called "hardcopy") of what you typed into the computer.

Format   A machine function that you perform in order to prepare disks to receive the writing you will do using word processing.

Hardcopy   The printed output from a computer device (*see* Softcopy).

Hardware   The physical parts of a computer system that allow it to enact computing functions.

Help system   Messages on the screen to help users. Some messages are always in view. Others must be called up by simple commands.

Input   All that you type into the computer.

Integration   A trend in word processing that allows you to share data between a word processing program and another program such as graphics.

Justification   Text aligned evenly on the right margin.

Keyboard   A piece of hardware that resembles a typewriter keyboard with additional keys. It is an essential part of the computer's operating system and is essential to word processing, for, through typing, you enter and alter information. Some computers have the keyboard attached to the terminal; others do not.

Light pen   A penlike device that lets you communicate with the computer by touching the pen to certain spots on the screen.

Mainframe   A large general-purpose computer normally having multiple users.

Memory The computer's storage space. The space differs with different computers. What you write and save is stored in the computer's memory until you either delete or retrieve it for review. Different programs require different-sized memory (64K, 128K, 192K, or 256K, etc.). Be sure the computer you are working on has the memory required to run the program.

Menu A list of alternative functions available to the user. The functions become usable by typing the correct symbol or abbreviation.

Menu driven Software programs that offer choices for document handling on the screen.

Merge The word processing capability to combine writing from two or more word processing programs.

Modem A device that allows computer information to be sent over telephone lines.

Monitor A synonym for computer screen. Both resemble a TV screen and display what you enter into the computer.

Mouse A piece of hardware that looks like a small box and plugs into the operating system. It allows the user to interact with information on the screen without using the keyboard.

Network A group of computers that can send information to each other.

Numeric pad The set of numbered keys to the right of the typewriter keys. Most of these keys are preset to perform word processing functions.

Operating system A type of software that makes the computer do its work.

Output Information produced by the computer. In word processing, output is what you type into the computer and either see on the screen or have printed.

Preprogrammed keys or macros Single keys or a limited keystroke combination that is predefined and used to repeatedly insert a word or whole passages into a document.

Printer A piece of hardware that enables you to have a paper/hardcopy of the writing you have done by means of word processing.

Program A computer software package that allows the user to enact a limited number of computer functions. For example, a graphics program may let you create four types of graphs.

Prompt A screen symbol that signals the computer is waiting for a program command.

Random access memory/RAM A method of storing information that allows the user to go right to something stored rather than hunt sequentially through everything stored.

Retrieve To call back from the computer's storage the writing you want to edit. It reappears on the screen.

Save A function that stores what you have written within the computer system. Information can be stored permanently and retrieved for review and revision.

Screen A part of the terminal that displays what you are typing into the computer.

Scroll A function that causes the text on the screen to move in some direction so that part of it disappears and a new part appears.

Softcopy Computer output that is displayed on the screen of a terminal. It is not permanently visible (as is hardcopy).

Software Programs that make the computer work. Word processing is one type of program.

Store To put what you have written into the computer's memory.

Teleconferencing A technique for electronically connecting two or more remote locations visually and audibly for a meeting or conference.

Terminal A piece of hardware containing the display screen, the keyboard similar to a standard typewriter, and the computer's operating system.

Touch screens Terminal screens that when touched cause the computer to enact commands. For example, the screen may have a square on it that reads ''TURN ON.'' If you touch that square, the computer will turn itself on.

User   Anyone who uses a computer system or program.

Voice synthesizer or voice recognizer   The ability of the computer to create or recognize human voice sounds.

Windows   Screen sections that display a part of one computer program. Other sections can display other programs. It is possible to see on the same screen parts of several programs.

Word processing   A software program that lets users see and change text on the screen rather than on paper. Corrections and additions are possible by means of the program and before the document is printed on paper.

Wordwrap   A function that automatically carries the last character of the right margin to the next line. It eliminates your having to hit the return key to go to the next line.

Part 2

The Writing Process

Part 2 applies the writing process to technical communication.

Chapter Three: Preparing to Write
- discusses three subjects common to prewriting:
    - subject
    - audience
    - planning
- offers practical advice about preparing to write
- provides practice exercises

Chapter Four: Gathering Information: A Step toward Preparing to Write
- identifies sources and methods to gather information completely and accurately:
    - the library
    - interviews
    - questionnaires
    - scientific observation
    - field studies
- provides practice exercises

Chapter Five: Writing, Rewriting, and Rewriting Again
- presents ways to begin writing
- gives examples of first drafts
- tells ways to go about revising
- explains readability indexes
- offers ideas and advice about rewriting and word processing
- provides practice exercises

Chapter Six: Final Edit for Style and Format
- talks generally about editing for style and format
- gives proper outline notation
- identifies specific format options available through typewriting and word processing
- provides practice exercises

Chapter Seven: Technical Illustrations
- identifies illustrations common to technical work
- gives standards for preparation:
    charts
    tables
    photographs
    drawings
- talks about computer-assisted preparation
- provides practice exercises

Overview

A decade ago it was popular to talk about writing as a linear activity. The writer was seen as someone who first prewrote an outline and some ideas, then wrote a first draft of the whole work, and later rewrote, correcting mistakes and polishing style. People who wrote about composition saw the writer as someone who performed these steps independently and in an orderly manner.

Today the trend is to talk about writing as a process. The writer is still seen engaging in a series of actions to bring about the finished document, but no longer is it thought that the series is sequential or neatly separated and orderly. Instead, writing is perceived as a volatile activity:

Thoughts whirl in the writer's mind; some hold in the center; others are thrown to the outside and lost; others come to the center again and are used.

The writer thinks about the whole document even while writing a particular part, so a thought suitable for the middle comes while working on the introduction or a better introduction occurs while drafting the conclusion.

The writer works toward a final document in spurts of invention, by writing sections or parts of sections whenever he or she receives information or ideas, and rewrites from the very beginning of the writing process as better ideas or ways of expression occur.

The neatness of the linear approach is lost, but based on my own experience, the process approach is more realistic. For example, I begin by perceiving the whole writing project and seem to hold that whole in my mind even when I am not consciously thinking about it. While I am driving down the street or watching television, a thought for some part of the document will come to mind. While writing one chapter, I will think at the same time how it focuses a future chapter or makes a needed change of something already written. My work progresses, but not in march time. It lunges ahead or hobbles along; sometimes it goes nowhere; other times it makes good progress, but it never advances evenly to a measured beat from beginning to end.

Those of you majoring in scientific or technical fields are familiar with processes and thus should find it easy to think of writing in the same way. In doing so, you lower your expectations of learning to write quickly and definitively and accept the idea of writing as a progression—an ongoing series of actions that bring about the end result of writing effectively.

Chapter 3

Preparing to Write

Technical writing is not written for the writer's exclusive pleasure or as a forum for one's private thoughts. Instead, technical writing presents a specific subject to an understood audience that is reading for a particular purpose. The interwoven dependency of subject and audience is one of technical writing's distinguishing characteristics and one reason technical writers must prepare before writing. Rarely is the wholeness of a good technical document achieved by accident.

No set of rules or formulas guarantees good writing, but at the same time, writing is not so mysterious that little can be said about it or learned. This chapter identifies three subjects common to prewriting: subject, audience, and planning. From what is known about the act of composing, it offers you practical advice. From the given information and exercises, you then can begin to develop your own approach to prewriting.

Subject

In school, finding a subject is often a task. In business, the topic typically comes with the writing assignment. Unless documenting original designs or experiments, you normally will not create new facts or subjects. Instead, you will compile, organize, and relate things and facts as you individually see them and want to report them to readers. Most of what you write will answer an inquiry, report on a project, chart the progress of an experiment, propose a project to a client, or be some other document relating to your work.

The purpose for writing often comes with the subject. For example, a proposal intends to persuade, a progress report to inform, a recommendation to analyze, summarize, and suggest. If the assignment does not clarify the purpose, you must do so before beginning to gather information or write. Without this direction, you gather too much of the wrong material. You muzzle a subject before knowing actually what needs to be said. You have no purposeful way to think about how information should be presented. You have no clue for language choices.

Strategies for Thinking about the Subject and Its Purpose

A variety of problem-solving techniques can be used to help settle the subject and purpose. Those methods that follow are talked about also in other parts of this book. They are mentioned here because they give a structured way to begin your inquiry, and you must inquire. Technical writing is concise and accurate. It makes no sense for a technical writer to begin writing without first understanding why.

- *Know Why You Are Writing.* An environmental impact statement on the effect of the factory's smokestack emissions on the native trees within a 2-mile radius may have as its purpose to foster good will between the factory and the community. The report is to admit some connection between die-off and emission, announce a reforesting program of a type of tree not affected by emission, and demonstrate a quick response to a problem. Understanding the purpose is necessary to show the correct cause-and-effect relationship, to choose the right tone and language, and to organize information in the most effective way.

  Verify the purpose by either doing your own research or inquiring from whoever requests the writing.
- *Never Assume You Know the Focus of a Report Unless You Are Part of the Group Requesting It.* If you are not part of the group, do your homework before beginning to write. If you cannot determine the purpose of the writing from the information given you, ask the people in charge of the project what they want and how your part fits into the whole. Some people hesitate to ask because they are afraid it will make them look stupid. Remember, asking incisive questions reveals an inquisitive mind, one that thinks of problems and seeks solutions. If you cannot directly ask the people in charge, ask their secretaries. Secretaries

know a lot about the business of the company and the people they work for and are usually willing to help.

- *Once You Know the Intent, Suggest as Many Ideas as Possible about the Given Question or Topic.* Do not stop to evaluate; just list the ideas as they come. Afterward, select, order, and eliminate. If you truly free yourself to write anything that comes to mind, a review of the list can reveal creative or seldom considered, but potentially important, information.
- *Know How the Writing Will Be Used.* Will the reader use the information to make a decision? Does the reader expect you to show alternatives and provide a recommendation? Will the reader perform some action from reading the writing? Must the reader understand how something works? After determining how the writing will be used, put yourself in the reader's place and write so that you accomplish the purpose. For example, if the reader must choose among four alternatives, you need to present the information so that similarities and differences can be easily understood and a value judgment made. Perhaps a chart or column format is best. If the reader must do something, you may need an illustration.
- *Assume a Number of Different Perspectives.* Think as management, labor, or owner, as production, marketing, or design. Look at the subject as a thing unto itself, as a thing in context to the organization or other in-house subjects, as a thing outside the organization or in relation to outside subjects. From any given view, define, describe, or consider the subject. Afterward compare the views. Then decide how the expanded understanding is useful in determining what you need to write.
- *Enumerate Characteristics of the Product, Project, or Idea.* From such a list, you can broaden or zoom in on the real essence of a subject. Too often we define something by two or three characteristics we can quickly name. If you take time, you might think of several more. If you think of seven purposes for the writing instead of an obvious two, you improve the chance of fulfilling your purpose.
- *Think of Causes and Effects.* By examining this relationship, you often discover purposes for your writing that you might otherwise ignore.

Audience

In technical writing you want to write specific information for the practical use of readers. If you determine before you write who your readers are and what they know and need to know, you will match message with audience. You also will communicate in a straightforward and sensible way. Most people in business and industry have so much on their minds and are so busy that if they receive a hard-to-read report and can stop reading, they will. If they cannot—because your writing is their only source of the information needed—they become irritated and displeased. You do not want to displease any reader, but especially not someone who has influence over you and your job or who has authority to assign work either to the company you work for or to you.

Ways to Identify Audience

Certain methods help identify audience. Before talking about them, understand that audience analysis is not exclusive to prewriting. What you discover and know about the readers affects later steps in the writing process when you decide on a plan, on information to include, and on style and format. Having said that, the following approaches help you think seriously about audience. They provide structures for collecting information that you later can absorb in an effort to realize who and how many will read your work.

- *Think about Audience in Their Closeness to the Report Writer.* Who in your own technical area; who in closely related areas; who elsewhere in the company, plant, hospital, or business; and who outside the organization will read the document? Listing these different readers causes the writer to see how diverse or alike the audience is. Such determination is immensely useful in knowing what types of information to include, what level of technical language to use, and how much background to include.
- *Make a List of All Possible Readers and Then Prioritize Them from Most to Least Groups You Need to Reach.* Such a grouping lets you see primary, secondary, and other audiences and lets you restrict purpose to the needs of the more important readers.
- *Imagine the People Who Will Read Your Work.* How old are they? How much education do they have? How many are women? What nationalities are they? What part of the country do they come from and live in? What do they do that causes them to read this writing? How much do they know about the subject? What do they feel about the subject? By compiling imaginary identifications of individual readers or groups, you can begin making intuitive decisions. Nothing is certain when we start to guess how people feel, but we have common knowledge about sensitive areas. If you find, for instance, that one-half the readers of the manual you are writing are Mexican women between 20 and 30 years old with a high school or less education, and you are a 40-year-old white male with a Ph.D. in electrical engineering, you certainly have a communication gap to close. You have direction for language and tone.

    You hear a lot about writing "up" or "down." Such terms are not social judgments but signposts to style and need. We all prepare and present differently for meetings with top management, with technical personnel, or with line workers. We sometimes even dress differently. You should be equally aware of differences in your readers before you write.
- *Think about Yourself in Relationship to the Audience You Identify.* How different are you in age, education, environment, values, experience? Learning that you are vastly different does not solve the communication problem, but it at least makes you aware that you have one. You may decide to have someone like

the proposed audience read the text and comment. What he or she does not agree with, understand, or respond to will give you clues about how the writing will be received by a similar audience.

None of these methods used individually or in combination gives definitive answers to the question of audience, but performing such analyses will stimulate understanding and help you avoid oversimplifying the audience or, even worse, writing to people you have not thought about. Remember that the writing process is not complete until someone other than the writer also reads the work. Both parties need to communicate successfully to have effective writing.

The Benefit of Experience

We all learn from our own experience. Sometimes as writers we misdirect information and do not recognize this until someone later tells us. We are embarrassed. Other times we realize too late—the writing had been distributed—that we should have focused differently. Still other times we discover the need to realign the subject in the midst of writing and decide to begin again or foolishly proceed even though we know that the focus is off or the audience is different from the one assumed originally. We need to take time before writing. It may be only an hour to make some phone calls, study again the request, or imagine and list characteristics and categories of the audience. Sometimes students make finishing the assignment their primary objective, so they write without investing time in thinking beforehand. This method may be quick, but it is neither effective nor efficient. If the grade is unsatisfactory, or the reader is unimpressed, or the student is asked to rewrite the assignment, the method fails. Carefully analyzing at first is a better use of time.

A Personal Example

While writing this book, I also received a request from my school to write a proposal for the Consortium for Computer and High Technology Education. Practicing my advice of analyzing subject and audience first proved helpful. Before picking up a pencil, I picked up the phone and called the person at the Consortium in charge of proposals. I asked her how to proceed, and she told me that the proposal subcommittee was meeting the following week and that I should write a letter indicating the University's interest. This letter would be read to the committee and afterward she could advise me of the committee's interest and whether or not to proceed. I did write, and that letter follows on page 32.

The day following the Consortium meeting I called and learned that the subcommittee was interested enough to send two people for an on-site visit. They wished to learn more about the project and would advise us whether to proceed. The meeting was arranged, the visit was made, a favorable report was made to the subcommittee, and the University was formally invited by letter to proceed

October 2, 1985

Mrs. Phyllis Land Usher
Interim Associate Superintendent
Department of Education
Room 229 State House
Indianapolis, IN 46204

Dear Mrs. Usher:

I appreciate your talking with me Monday and your advice about the proposal the University of Evansville and Ball Communications is preparing to present to the Consortium for Computer and High Technology Education.

Both the University and Ball Communications are willing to focus on interactive video. Our present plan is that Ball, a leader in interactive learning in business and industry, will contribute the technology and their experience and the University will design instructional programs that demonstrate the potential of marrying the computer to video discs for elementary, middle, and high school learning. Mr. Ken Quakkelaar, Executive Vice President of Ball Communications, says that while interactive video is not new, no other company in America can do with it what Ball does with group learning. He predicts that our proposed demonstration will be futuristic, impressive, understandable, and feasible for Indiana classrooms.

I look forward to preparing this proposal and to participating in the project if we are funded. As we agreed in our phone conversation, I shall call you after your October 7, Consortium committee meeting for further clarification and advice on how to proceed in preparing our proposal.

Sincerely,

Ann Stuart

Dr. Ann Stuart
Administrative Coordinator
   of Writing Programs

ld

cc: President Wallace Graves
    Mr. Ken Quakkelaar

with the proposal. After receiving the letter from one of the visitors, I called and asked for his help. Some of my questions follow:

1. Is there a standard proposal form that I should use, and if so, would he please send it? (There was no form, so I asked him for a list of topics the committee would expect us to include. He gave those to me.)
2. How much money is available? (I did not want to kill our chances by coming in above the funds that were available. He was not specific, but provided a range for us to stay within.)
3. Who will read the proposal? How much time will readers be given to read it before they vote? What format do they prefer for proposals? (The primary readers were members of the subcommittee, who would make a recommendation to the Consortium members, who would review and vote on the proposal at the same meeting. No particular format was preferred.)
4. How is approval or rejection decided? What criteria are used? (The Consortium normally accepts the subcommittee's recommendation. The criteria were the extent of planning, promise, and value to education.)
5. If the person I was talking to were going to write the proposal, what would he do and not do? (He felt that the proposal would stand or fall on the quality of the critical questions asked.)

I took strict notes and used everything applicable when it came time to write. For example, the list of topics served as a working outline. Knowing that the Consortium members would see the proposal and vote on it at the same meeting caused me to write a synopsis on the cover page. Each voting member could then quickly read it when the proposal came up for discussion and vote. Before beginning to write, I sought advice. I did not assume. How you define and analyze the subject and audience is yours to decide, but remember to do it.

Planning

Once you determine the subject and identify the audience, you can begin to plan the writing. This step, like others in the process, has no magic formula but requires good, clear analysis of what you already know and how you can proceed. Planning involves a number of activities. Some have to do with the writing itself, and others clear the way for getting the writing done. At this point, we are interested in the latter.

- *Schedule Time.* When is the writing due? How much time do you have to gather information, to write, and to rewrite? How long will it take to type the document or to use word processing to prepare it? If someone else is to type, collate, and prepare the document, have you asked for time in his or her schedule? Do you anticipate using visuals, and if so, can they be ready in time? Are other people involved in the writing? If so, when will they have their parts to you, and does that fit your schedule? These decisions do not have to do with putting words on a page but are very necessary for completing writing on time and for having time to write well.

- *Plan Time to Think.* What type of information do you need to satisfy the subject's purpose for this audience? What do you already know, and what do you need to find out? Where can you find information? Do you have time to collect it from sources out of town or through the mail or by the phone? What is the best approach and tone to use to accomplish the purpose with this particular audience?

- *Plan Where You Will Write.* For any involved project, you need space for notes and source material. You may want to leave things spread out, if possible, between writing sessions. You need to keep certain papers, notes, and materials together and in a working order throughout the project. Plan a place where this can happen.

- *Begin to Organize.* You will move text around throughout the writing process, but you need some way to begin. What are you going to talk about first? Where are you going from there? As you gather information, or have the text read by others, or think critically about it yourself, you will shift and eliminate information, but for efficiency, you need an initial plan before beginning. After you complete the writing, you should examine the final plan for consistency, logic, and flow of ideas. Ask yourself, what do I most want to say in this writing? What else do I want to say, and how is that related to my most important idea? Think of the reader as someone who does not understand. It is your job to make things clear. How best are you going to do that?

- *Make an Outline.* An outline is a plan for what you intend to write. The act of outlining forces you to decide about content and its order, but no outline should become a plan set in concrete. The object of good scientific and technical writing is to produce a document that serves the purpose for which it is intended. Do not become so enamored with your beautiful outline that you are unwilling to change it to serve that purpose.

   A few ideas jotted down on a piece of paper are outline enough to decide the order of information and to set some plan to accomplish the goal of the writing task and not leave anything out. This informal outline is the one you know best and the kind most of us use most often. It also is a good guide for gathering information. A sketch of major topics tells you what you need to research and what information you already have available. It also helps you to plan time because it shows how much or how little work you must do before beginning to write.

Practice Exercises

1. The teacher will give a writing topic. Each student will be given a transparency and an overhead projector pen. You will list on the transparency as many ideas as come to you about the topic. Do not stop to evaluate; just write down any and every idea. After 15 minutes, the teacher will call "Stop." Use 20 minutes

or so to evaluate the list, make selections, eliminate, and write a possible purpose. Using the overhead projector, some members of the class will show their "brainstorming" lists. They will illustrate the free expression that occurred using this technique and the direction it provided to give purpose to the topic.

2. You will assume that the writing assignment is to promote a technical or scientific instrument, machine, product, or process. Work in small groups of four or five. Choose what the group will promote. As a group, identify the different perspectives that will help the writer understand subject and purpose (pp. 28–29). Under each perspective, list or identify important considerations. Write a summary of how the expanded view helps identify purpose. The assignment can be handed in or shared with the class orally.

3. The teacher will make a particular assignment indicating subject, purpose, audience, and form, but it will purposely be incomplete or unclear on some points. As homework, use the checklist on pages 28–29 to find out what you know about the assignment and what you need to find out. At the next class meeting, students will ask for clarification. Discover how different your and other classmates' assumptions were from those in the teacher's mind. Learn how to ask clear questions and to take good notes on what is told to you. Afterward, use the checklist again, and for each item write a statement of what you now know about the subject. Later use the statements to write a paper.

4. The teacher will bring to class an item (a pair of pliers, a manual can opener, scissors). Break into small groups, and as a group, decide upon an audience. Describe that audience as completely as possible (pp. 30–31). Together outline a paper for that audience defining the item, orientating the audience to the item as a whole, dividing the item into parts, describing the item, and telling how it is used. (Consult the Index for help in outlining, in writing description, and in defining.) Between class meetings, have one member of the group place the outline on transparencies. At the next class, have a spokesperson(s) from the group identify the audience and explain how that audience influenced planning.

5. You will select an article from a recent scientific or technical magazine. Analyze it from your point of view. How well does it communicate with you as a reader? Consider your education, values, experience, and need or interest. Determine how successfully the writer communicates with you. Share your evaluation and reasons in writing or in class discussion.

6. The teacher will bring to class two or more articles on the same scientific subject by either the same or different authors. In small groups, you will conduct an audience analysis. What does the introduction tell you about the intended audience? What focus does the author assume and what effect does that have on the audience? What is the tone of each article? What are differences between/among articles? What can you say about language and audience? What do format, sentence structure, paragraph structure, and evidence tell you about audience? After the analysis, write a description of the determined reader for each article. Each group will share its assessment with the class.

7. You will write what you think of yourself as an audience. Think about what is

important in composing the self-analysis. Is age important, or education, or taste? What is? Exchange your self-analysis with another student (perhaps majoring in another area). The teacher will give an assignment that is due at a later class meeting. Write the assignment for the person described in the self-analysis given to you. During the class when the assignment is due, the two writers and readers will exchange papers. They will read the work written for each other and will talk as audience to writer of what succeeds and what does not and why.

Chapter 4

Gathering Information: A Step toward Preparing to Write

Gathering information can be exciting, frustrating, rewarding, unproductive, easy, difficult, tedious, challenging—all or a combination of this list. Some people are very good at ferreting out information and enjoy the quest; others have little natural talent and must work earnestly at the task. Both types can be good researchers. It is simply more pleasant for those who have an intuitive sense of where the answer might be found.

Whether or not you have an instinct for research, your choice of a technical field requires you to be able to find information and to be a careful recorder and collector. It is easy to underestimate the time required to do research. You can also be hampered by being unfamiliar with most reference sources, recording information poorly, and stopping too soon. This chapter identifies sources and methods that help you avoid these pitfalls and gather information completely and accurately.

Begin with Yourself

Make yourself and your mind the first source of information. In industry and science, you collect information for a purpose: to solve a problem, recommend a choice, make a discovery, confirm an opinion, or understand conditions. To make the collection efficient and effective, you must understand the audience, know the purpose for writing, and analyze the gathering process:

- Who besides yourself is going to use the information, and do those people need something different from what you are looking for?
- What exactly is the purpose?
- What are the best sources of information?
- How many of the sources are accessible to you?
- How does the time you have to gather information determine or restrict your methods of research?
- How does the budget limit your use of mailing, telephoning, computer searching, photocopying, and printing?
- Are you qualified to conduct the necessary types of research, or do you need assistance? If you require help, who can assist you?

Without making determinations at the beginning of your research, you can waste time, miss opportunities or sources, and gather without focus.

The Library

Developing Good Research Habits

Everyone knows that the library is a major source of information, but not everyone knows how to use the library effectively. The following suggestions help you arrive at the library prepared to work efficiently and guide your research methods.

Go Prepared

Gathering information well requires a disciplined approach. When you set off for the library to work, take what you need.

1. If you are going to enter source possibilities on separate cards, have the correct sized cards. If you plan to keep a running list of sources on a pad or in a notebook, have it with you.

    Do not collect sources on odd pieces of paper, in several yellow pads or notebooks, in different forms, and do not store sources in different places.

2. Take a sharpened pencil with an eraser. It is easy to make mistakes when copying call numbers and periodic references. Be prepared to correct errors and keep the documentation neat and readable.
3. Have plenty of the correct-sized paper or cards you plan to use. Write notes on the same sized paper or card, on one side only, and write about only one subject per page or card. At the time that you take notes, it may seem a waste and bother to record information separately and on one side, but when you work with the information—eliminating what is not relevant, arranging it into an effective outline, and placing like information together—you will thank yourself for recording in a manner that is easy to use.

   Do not record notes on whatever you happen to have with you: an appointment book in your bookpack, old tests or handouts stuck inside some book, or various notebooks normally used for class notes.
4. Have coins available to use in the copying machine when you choose to copy an article or part of it rather than take notes.
5. Make complete reference cards. When you first cite or use a reference source, document it completely. Too many people get in a hurry or decide they will go back and fill in source information needed for footnotes and bibliography after they determine what sources will be used. Such a practice is foolish. It makes more sense to lose a little time by completing cards you may not use than to return to reference materials later. Many who have written term papers share the experience of finishing the paper and being ready to type the last page—the bibliography—only to discover missing information. Often such projects are completed late at night when the library is closed, which makes the problem more aggravating.
6. Take good notes. The copier may make note-taking a forgotten art. Copying is easy and lets you take material with you, but it often is a waste of money. Copying whole articles only delays what you ultimately must do—select particular information to work into your own text.

   Whether you copy onto note cards or work information directly into your text from primary sources available to you while writing, you will make three kinds of notes—quotations, paraphrases, and summaries:
   a. *Quotations.* Copy exactly what is printed. Enclose the passage in quotation marks. If you omit a part, use an ellipsis (three periods . . .) each time you make an omission. If you want to add a comment, place it in brackets [   ].
   b. *Paraphrases.* Say, in your own words, someone else's facts or ideas. People sometimes borrow and do not give the proper credit. Be fair. If you use someone's information, say so either by a comment in the text or a citation.

      Two problems commonly occur when paraphrasing: (1) The writer changes only a word or two and then takes credit for having expressed the idea in his or her own words. This really is cheating. (2) The writer is not careful and in the rephrasing changes meaning through language. A good paraphrase restates the passage in different words, yet retains the same meaning.
   c. *Summaries.* State, in a few sentences, the main idea or meaning of

what you have read. If you use words or phrases from the original, put them in quotation marks.

The following excerpt illustrates the correct use of others' material into one's own work:

The ellipsis indicates the quotation is cut off before the period or at the end of the sentence.

Sir Philip Sidney's defense of the poet could be the defense of a good technical writer: "the skill of each artificer standeth in that Idea or fore-conceit of the work, and not in the work itself. And that the poet hath that Idea is manifest. . . ." In this context it is significant that not surface features, "rhyming and versing," but rather imaginative projection, "feigning notable images of virtues, vices, or what else, with the delightful teaching," is "the right describing note to know a poet by" (108–09, 112). Adapting the Sidneian definition to the technical writing classroom is not difficult. While technical writers rarely feign images of virtue and vice, Sidney's "what else" could include the technical writer's created illusion, vital to all technical communication, that the raw facts of a given experiment, investigation, or case happen somehow of themselves to form a pattern. Behind this illusion, of course, is the technical writer, shaping and synthesizing the inchoate stuff of experience into reports designed to inform and enlighten an identified audience, and thus engaging in a fundamentally poetic process. Science and technology are far more poetic than some of their practitioners and, ironically, most humanists seem to realize. (Rutter, R. 1985. Poetry, imagination, and technical writing. *College English* 47: 705.)

Quotation copied exactly including unusual spelling and capitalization

Rutter summarizes Sidney and incorporates some of his own phrases. When Rutter does use Sidney's words, he indicates as much by quotation marks.

Explore the Library

Most libraries have certain basic works and services in common, yet each is different. If you are not familiar with the library available to you, visit it to discover what it offers and where things are located. Look for the following areas:

1. The information desk—the place to ask general questions and often to check out materials.
2. The periodical area—the place to find current issues of magazines and journals.
3. The archives—the place that houses historical materials on the institution or locality.
4. The rare book room—the place where valuable or delicate materials are stored securely and under the right conditions of light, temperature, and use.
5. The multimedia area—the place to find information stored on tape, microfilm, microfiche, etc., and the equipment necessary to read such materials. This area is staffed by library personnel, so someone can help you learn to find and use the equipment and to handle the information source correctly so you do not damage it.

6. The oversized shelving area—the place where materials are stored that are too large to be shelved in the standard bookcases. Not every library has a separate area for such items, so find out how oversized materials are housed.

7. The reference area—the place that houses reference materials. Such materials cannot be checked out. A reference librarian is usually located nearby to assist you.

8. The vertical file—the place (usually a bank of filing cabinets) where all kinds of unbound materials—pamphlets, brochures, circulars, booklets, and clipped newspaper and magazine articles—are stored. This source is not for in-depth information but for brief material on popular topics. The files are normally purged at set intervals; for example, at a local library, nothing remains in the file more than three years. Normal procedure is to divide the file space alphabetically and to place materials in labeled folders and arrange these alphabetically in the appropriate file space. For example, in the "B" drawer of the vertical file at one library I consulted, the individual files read in order:
   Baby Doe
   Baby Fae
   Baby Sitting
   Back Ache
   Baldness
   Banking, etc.

9. The card catalog—the facility that houses index cards listing what books and certain other materials the library has and where they are stored.

A walkabout through the library will give you a sense of its stature and let you come upon specialized services and collections. For example, a person or family or business can leave an individual collection to a library and stipulate that the collection remain together, so it will be housed in a separate room or area. Your walkabout will let you discover what is unique to the library you are working in and give you a bearing of the building so you can work in it more efficiently.

Devise a Search Strategy

The number of sources and services available for research in technical fields is varied. You must take it upon yourself or work with the reference librarians to find everything available. Look for such aids as specialized encyclopedias, specialized bibliographies, handbooks, and government publications. New sources become available all the time. The task of keeping up is ongoing.

If you develop a step-by-step process of collecting and evaluating information, you will save time and be able to find more useful and relevant information. Work from the general to the specific:

1. Begin by using relevant indexes and abstracts, annuals, handbooks, bibliographies, the card catalog, newspapers, government documents, encyclopedias, dictionaries, general books, or summary articles on the subject. Read for an overview—to learn the terminology, to recognize important people or works on the subject, to identify a time frame for further research. If a discovery made in 1979 altered everything on your topic after that date, you need to know that. When finished with this scanning of lots of general information, you will

have a feel for what is most important and available and will be better able to select and narrow a subject.

2. Once you have an overview, define the research topic. Write questions you want answered. Know exactly what information you need and what is possible to find, given the time and resources available.

3. Return to those references useful to your narrowed topic and record only relevant items. This method uses a slow start and causes you to return to references after a general reading, but it is ultimately efficient because it saves copying every initial reference.

Standard Library Sources

Catalogs

1. *The Public Catalog.* Most libraries place the information/checkout desk and public catalog near the library entrance. Remember when you use the catalog that some libraries use a dictionary system that places author, title, and subject information in a single catalog in their respective alphabetical listings and other libraries have individual catalogs for subject, author, and title entries. Notice how your library organizes its holdings before beginning to search. You also need to determine what the public catalog does and does not cover. For example, some do not include periodicals; if you do not know this, you can miss good sources.

   Some people fail to make good use of catalog entries for research purposes. They copy the author, title, and call number and ignore other information that might lead to valuable references. Items (4), (5), and (7) of the following author entry are examples of information often overlooked.

Author Entry

```
①  TK
    7888.4  ②Davio, Marc.
    .D38       ③Digital systems, with algorithm
    1983       implementation / M. Davio, J.-P.
               Deschamps, and A. Thayse. -- Chichester
               [West Sussex] ; New York : Wiley,
               c1983.
               ④xvii, 505 p. : ill. ; 24 cm.
               ⑤"A Wiley-Interscience publication."
               Bibliography: p. 490-497.
               Includes index.
               ⑥ISBN 0-471-10413-2
               ⑦1. Computers--Circuits.   2. Logic
               circuits.   3. Algorithms.   4. Computer
               architecture.   I. Deschamps, Jean-
               Pierre, 1945-       II. Thayse, André,
               1940-         III. Title

                              ◯

⑧  InEU     29 JUN 83      8282197   IUEUat        82-2710
```

(1) *Call Number.* The call numbers indicate the book's precise location on the library shelf and are your key to finding the work. Copy the total combination of letters and numbers in the order and format they appear.

(2) *Author(s).* The last name appears first, followed by the first and middle names and sometimes additional information such as titles or birth and death dates.

(3) *Title.* The title appears as it does on the title page of the book; notice the names of two other authors. The city of publication, publisher, and publication date follow.

(4) *Technical Information.* This book has xvii (17) pages of front matter, has 505 pages of text, has illustrations, and is 24 centimeters high.

(5) *Special Features.* The department within the Wiley publishing company responsible for this book is identified. The book includes a 7-page bibliography (490–497) and an index.

(6) *International Standard Book Number.* This number is used when ordering the book from the publisher.

(7) *Tracings.* The run-in list identifies other headings under which this book is entered in the public catalog: 4 subjects (Computers—circuits, etc.), 2 other authors (Deschamps and Thayse), and the book title.

(8) *Codes.* The codes pertain to computer cataloguing and are not pertinent to you.

Notes on Often Ignored Items:

Item (4) *Technical Information.* Even if the author, title, or subject entry suggests that this book is not on your particular reference topic, the front material may give clues to other information. If the book is on a closely related subject, it is worth a glance. Sometimes illustrations include more than the book's subject, so they too are worth looking through.

Item (5) *Special Features.* This information can be a gold mine for the researcher. Bibliographies included within books are specialized and can save you hours of looking for materials on the same subject. Such bibliographies can also suggest auxiliary research to pursue. A good index will not only tell if a topic is included, it will also cross-reference the reader to supplementary topics, so you harvest ideas for other lines of inquiry.

Item (7) *Tracings.* This item lists other subjects under which this book is entered in the public catalog. You may not have thought of looking under "Algorithms," but when you go to this subject area, you will find that it reveals other applicable materials.

The same information that appears on the author entry appears on the title and subject entries; the only thing that differs is the order of presentation.

---

2. ***On-Line Catalogs.*** The on-line catalog is becoming more common in libraries. Every catalog has its own personality, but all on-line systems have the same access points to materials as manual catalogs—author, title, and subject. Terminal screens are often formatted the same as standard catalog cards, so what you *see* is familiar.

Instructions for using the catalog usually appear on the terminal that remains up and ready to use. Help is available on the terminal by typing a simple command, usually "H." If something happens that halts your search, printed instructions are usually nearby or the librarians are willing to help.

   a. *Tips for Using On-Line Catalogs.* The following conventions are common to most on-line systems. Knowing about them beforehand will make your search easier and faster.

- Enter author's name, last name first.
- Omit the initial article (a, an, the, la, el) of titles.
- Send information to the computer by pressing the "Enter" or "Return" key.
- Correct typing mistakes by using the backspace key and typing over the error.
- Do not substitute the letter "O" for a zero or an "L" for a one.

   b. *Convenience of On-Line Catalogs.* Typing in an author's name and having every book written by the person that the library owns appear on the screen is much more convenient than shuffling through cards, but the greatest convenience is having on-line catalog terminals placed throughout the library. A user can be in the stacks, have a question about sources or the information copied down, and not have to return to the central catalog. A terminal is always nearby.

Locating Catalog Materials within the Library

Once you copy the call numbers for the books you want to locate, you must find them in the library. If the library has closed stacks, fill out a request slip for each book and take them to the proper desk where a staff member will go, retrieve the works, and bring them to you. If the stacks are open, you must locate the books yourself.

Libraries organize materials one of two ways: by the more common Library of Congress system or the Dewey Decimal system. Signs are usually posted throughout the library stating which system is used and showing the method of classification. The major classes for each system are as follows:

Library of Congress: materials arranged by letters of the alphabet to represent various subject areas:

A	General Works	H	Social Sciences
B	Philosophy, Psychology, Religion	J	Political Science
C-D	History & Topography except America	K	Law
E-F	America	L	Education
G	Geography, Anthropology, Sports & Games	M	Music

N	Fine Arts	T	Engineering & Technology
P	Language & Literature	U	Military Science
Q	Science	V	Naval Science
R	Medicine	Z	Bibliography & Library Science
S	Agriculture, Forestry		

Dewey Decimal: materials are arranged by numbers representing subject areas:

000–009	General Works	600–699	Technology (applied sciences)
100–199	Philosophy & Related Disciplines	700–799	The Arts. Fine & Decorative Arts
200–299	Religion	800–899	Literature
300–399	Social Sciences	900–999	General Geography & History &
400–499	Language		Their Auxiliaries
500–599	Pure Sciences		

Notice that both systems shelve books by subject; that arrangement can be helpful to you. When you locate the book you are looking for, look around at other books nearby as they may also prove useful.

Periodical Indexes

Newspapers, popular magazines, and scholarly journals are important reference materials because they report current information. Books take months or years to write, more time to publish, and even more time to reach the library and be processed for use. In technical fields, information can change rapidly; periodicals can help you stay informed.

The primary source for periodicals is a number of general and selected subject indexes. All indexes serve as alphabetical guides, listing names, titles, and subjects, and telling you how to find each item. Your task is to find out what indexes the library has and to recognize their peculiarities. The quickest and probably the best introduction is to ask the reference librarian to identify those applicable to your particular subject.

1. **A Sample of Indexes.** The following indexes are common to engineering; they illustrate the kinds of differences that can appear among indexes and identify information important to research.

   a. *Applied Science and Technology Index* (published monthly and cumulated annually). Articles are indexed by subject only. The example on top page 46 is representative; the reference information is marked.

   b. *Engineering Index* (published monthly and cumulated annually). Each monthly issue has an author index. The monthly issues are superseded by the annual volume. Each index is arranged in an alphabetical subject format with short summaries. Journals in all fields of engineering are indexed, as well as selected books and papers of conferences and symposia. Sometimes bibliographic/reference information appears. See example on page 46.

   c. *SHE: Subject Headings for Engineering/Index and Supplement.* SHE tells what headings are and are not used in *Engineering Index*. It is

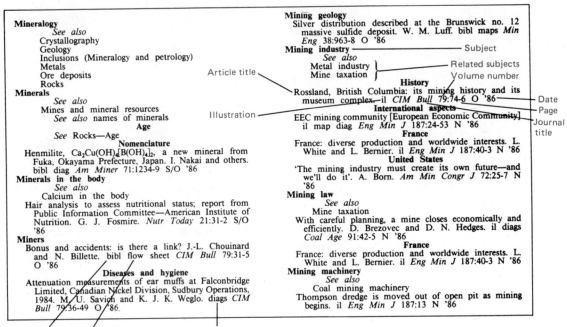

Mineralogy
 See also
 Crystallography
 Geology
 Inclusions (Mineralogy and petrology)
 Metals
 Ore deposits
 Rocks
Minerals
 See also
 Mines and mineral resources
 See also names of minerals
   Age
 See Rocks—Age
   Nomenclature
Henmilite, $Ca_2Cu(OH)_4[B(OH)_4]_2$, a new mineral from Fuka, Okayama Prefecture, Japan. I. Nakai and others. bibl diag *Am Miner* 71:1234-9 S/O '86
Minerals in the body
 See also
 Calcium in the body
Hair analysis to assess nutritional status; report from Public Information Committee—American Institute of Nutrition. G. J. Fosmire. *Nutr Today* 21:31-2 S/O '86
Miners
Bonus and accidents: is there a link? J.-L. Chouinard and N. Billette. bibl flow sheet *CIM Bull* 79:31-5 O '86
   Diseases and hygiene
Attenuation measurements of ear muffs at Falconbridge Limited, Canadian Nickel Division, Sudbury Operations, 1984. M. U. Savich and K. J. K. Weglo. diags *CIM Bull* 79:36-49 O '86.

Mining geology
Silver distribution described at the Brunswick no. 12 massive sulfide deposit. W. M. Luff. bibl maps *Min Eng* 38:963-8 O '86
Mining industry — Subject
 See also
 Metal industry — Related subjects
 Mine taxation
   History — Volume number
Rossland, British Columbia: its mining history and its museum complex. il *CIM Bull* 79:74-6 O '86 — Date / Page / Journal title
   International aspects
EEC mining community [European Economic Community] il map diag *Eng Min J* 187:24-53 N '86
   France
France: diverse production and worldwide interests. L. White and L. Bernier. il *Eng Min J* 187:40-3 N '86
   United States
'The mining industry must create its own future—and we'll do it'. A. Born. *Am Min Congr J* 72:25-7 N '86
Mining law
 See also
 Mine taxation
With careful planning, a mine closes economically and efficiently. D. Brezovec and D. N. Hedges. il diags *Coal Age* 91:42-5 N '86
   France
France: diverse production and worldwide interests. L. White and L. Bernier. il *Eng Min J* 187:40-3 N '86
Mining machinery
 See also
 Coal mining machinery
Thompson dredge is moved out of open pit as mining begins. il *Eng Min J* 187:13 N '86

Labels: Article title · Illustration · Bibliography · Flow sheet · Diagrams

Applied Science and Technology Index example.

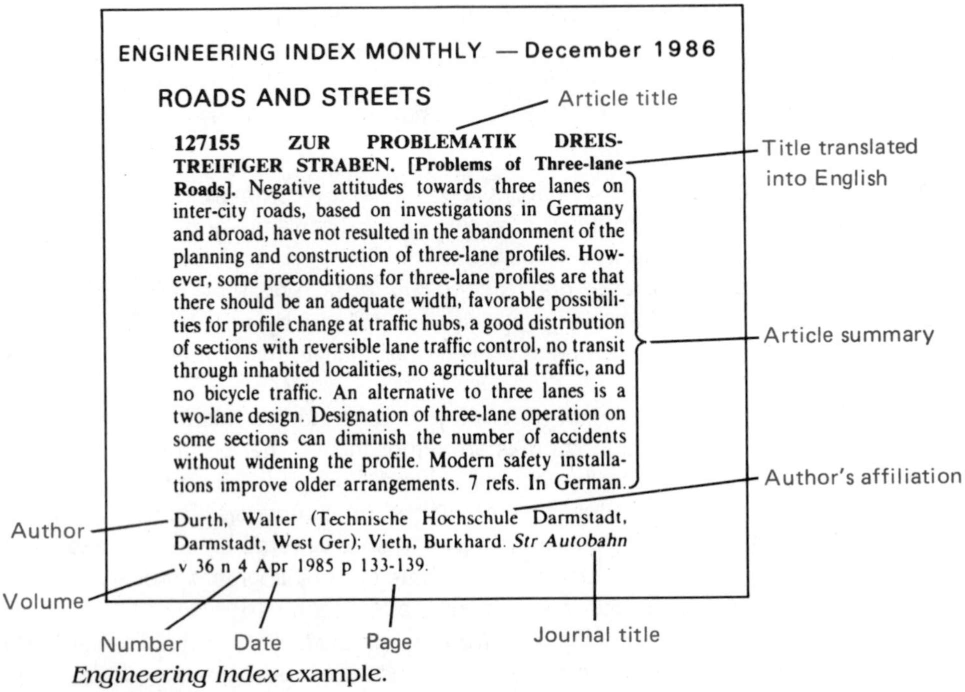

ENGINEERING INDEX MONTHLY — December 1986

ROADS AND STREETS — Article title

127155 ZUR PROBLEMATIK DREISTREIFIGER STRABEN. [Problems of Three-lane Roads]. Negative attitudes towards three lanes on inter-city roads, based on investigations in Germany and abroad, have not resulted in the abandonment of the planning and construction of three-lane profiles. However, some preconditions for three-lane profiles are that there should be an adequate width, favorable possibilities for profile change at traffic hubs, a good distribution of sections with reversible lane traffic control, no transit through inhabited localities, no agricultural traffic, and no bicycle traffic. An alternative to three lanes is a two-lane design. Designation of three-lane operation on some sections can diminish the number of accidents without widening the profile. Modern safety installations improve older arrangements. 7 refs. In German.

Durth, Walter (Technische Hochschule Darmstadt, Darmstadt, West Ger); Vieth, Burkhard. *Str Autobahn* v 36 n 4 Apr 1985 p 133-139.

Labels: Title translated into English · Article summary · Author's affiliation · Author · Volume · Number · Date · Page · Journal title

Engineering Index example.

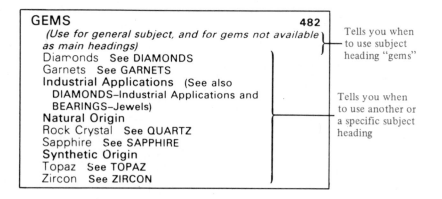

```
GEMS                                                482
    (Use for general subject, and for gems not available)      Tells you when
    as main headings)                                           to use subject
    Diamonds   See DIAMONDS                                     heading "gems"
    Garnets   See GARNETS
    Industrial Applications   (See also
       DIAMONDS–Industrial Applications and
       BEARINGS–Jewels)                                         Tells you when
    Natural Origin                                              to use another or
    Rock Crystal   See QUARTZ                                   a specific subject
    Sapphire   See SAPPHIRE                                     heading
    Synthetic Origin
    Topaz   See TOPAZ
    Zircon   See ZIRCON
```

a separate paperbound volume usually shelved next to the volumes of Engineering Index:

d. *Energy Index* (published annually). Each annual volume provides a narrative review of the year's events in energy as well as related information on legislation. A statistics section with graphs, maps, and tables illustrates trends. The index's primary function, however, is the Index Section which gives extensive listings by subject of energy-related information found in journal articles, government documents, conference proceedings, and so forth. See example on page 48.

Every discipline has its own set of indexes. Become familiar with them, for they are valuable resources. Consider also newspaper indexes. The *New York Times Index* and *Wall Street Journal Index,* for example, are excellent references for announcements and major news stories. The *New York Times Index* even prints the maps, graphs, and pictures that appeared with the stories.

2. **Tips for Using Periodical Indexes.** Some disciplines have their own indexes. For others, you may need to look for information in a related field index.

- Remember, when using an index, do not stop with one issue. Look in the index of the previous year and of the year before that.
- Of indexes that have cumulative volumes, find out how they accumulate, so you know when to start looking if you want to search earlier periodicals.
- Be careful when looking for subjects. What you think of as the subject term may not be what is used. If you do not find what you are looking for, ask the reference librarians; they have used the indexes so often they may know other terms to use.
- Remember to copy all bibliographic information.

3. *Locating Periodicals.* Every library has a periodical holdings list. If the library is of moderate or small size, you might want to glance through the list before beginning to collect references. The problem in doing research in a modest library is that most indexes list the world's publications, so most of the works cited will not be in the local library. Besides telling you if the library has the periodical you seek, the list will also tell what dates of the periodicals the library has and whether they are on microfilm, microfiche, or in paper copy.

OIL USAGE

OIL SUPPLY, INDUSTRIAL

Perspectives on the Appropriate Role for the Federal and State Governments During Petroleum Supply Interruptions, Natural Resources Lawyer, 1984, v16, n4, p613 (27)   *02-84-23023

OIL TANKERS ————————————— Subject

see also oil spills-tanker; supertankers ——— Related subjects to research

Exxon's Taking of Hudson Water Leads to Inquiry , New York Times, Oct 5, 83, pB5
12-84-20337

Cities Service Develops System to Monitor Petroleum Losses , Oil & Gas J, May 9, 83, v81, n19, p95 (5)   12-84-20713 ——— Article title

Oil Transport and Storage , OPEC B, Oct 83, v14, n9, p55 (7)——— *12-84-20714 —— Journal title / Date

Marine Offshore Outlook 1983 , Texas A&M Univ Report TAMU-SG-83-504, Jun 83, (29)
*07-84-21050

— Number of pages/ length
— Beginning page
— Number
— Volume

Petroleum Logistics: Movement of Oil to California , California Energy Commission Report P400-82-065, Sep 82, (144)
*12-84-21270

Multivariate Analysis of Worldwide Tanker Casualties , API/EPA/USCG Oil Spill 8th Conf, San Antonio, Feb 28-Mar 3, 83, p553 (5)   *12-84-21773

Annual Statistical Bulletin 1981 , OPEC Report, 1982, (248)   *17-84-21881

Innovative Offshore Engineering in the Arctic, Marine Technology Society/Oceanic Engineering Society/IEEE Oceans 83 Conf, San Francisco, Aug 29-Sep 1, 83, v2, p1013 (7)   *07-84-22555

OPEC Annual Statistical Bulletin 1982, OPEC Report, undated, (235) *17-84-22906

Oil Economists' Handbook 1984, Applied Science (Elsevier) Report, 1983, (282)
03-84-23033

Exports of Domestic Crude Oil, US Library of Congress Congressional Research Service Report 83-622 ENR, Dec 8, 83, (68)
*17-84-23426

January 1984 Market Review and Crude Oil Spot Prices, OPEC B, Mar 84, v15, n2, p51 (11)   *17-84-23453

Better Safety, Lower Costs Result from New Technology, World Oil, Apr 84, v198, n5, p62 (5)   *07-84-23547

Spain, OPEC B, Jun 84, v15, n5, p34 (13)
*03-84-24031

Energy Index example.

Some libraries keep current periodicals separate from back issues. Some shelve back issues with the book collection; others shelve them separately. You need to find out how the library handles them. If you are working with open stacks, be persistent when you attempt to locate an issue. People do not always replace periodicals in sequential order. If you do not find the day, week, month, or quarter you seek, look among other issues. You often find that what you are looking for is incorrectly shelved.

Reference Librarians

Day after day this group of people answer questions—sometimes ones that are obvious or not well thought out—and get up from their desks to go with people and show them source materials and explain how to use them. The amount of information they know or can figure out ways to find is amazing. When alone at their desks, they mostly read (probably gathering more information that most of us never heard of), but do not let that turn you away. Reference librarians are trained to teach others how to use libraries effectively. When approached, they will be some of the most helpful people you will meet in your educational career.

I asked one reference staff what they wished students would do before coming to them for help. Collectively they answered that students should be able to tell the librarian in plain English the subject of their research, what questions they are attempting to answer, and the name of the teacher directing the project (school librarians often know a faculty member's prejudices). If students take this approach, rather than cause librarians to pull this information from them, assistance can be given more quickly and effectively.

Interlibrary Loan Services

If you are working in a modest library, you can borrow books and obtain photocopies of articles not available locally from other libraries. Procedures differ, so ask someone at the checkout desk about this service. Waiting time varies (allow at least two weeks), copyright laws limit the number of requests you can make, and costs for the service are set by individual libraries. But when you locate the perfect source document and learn that it is not in your working library, an interlibrary loan can be a godsend.

Computer Database Searches

A search is not automatically good just because it comes from a computer, but the use of computer searching techniques permits the retrieval of literature citations on specific topics with a speed and precision far surpassing manual methods. To decide wisely about using computer database searching, you need to understand the advantages and disadvantages.

1. ***Pros and Cons of Computer Database Searches***
    a. *Advantages*
        - *Quick.* Minutes can produce what it may take you hours and/or days to search.
        - *Variety of Concepts Searched.* The computer can combine and simultaneously search by subject, time, language, and document type. You would need to search individually for the same results.
        - *Current.* Some databases are updated daily; others are made current weekly or monthly. Printed sources are not updated as efficiently.
        - *Printout.* The printout eliminates having to copy the source matters.

- *Accurate.* The computer does not grow tired. You can begin to skip or make mistakes after hours of manual searching.
- *Variety of Databases.* The databases include materials from a number of libraries. Your search is not limited to your local library.

  b. *Disadvantages*

- *Cost.* This factor stops most of us. Paying for every second you are in a database is standard. You can also be charged royalty fees for listings. This fee can vary between $.10 and $2.50 a source. Weigh time versus cost. The reference librarian in charge of searching should be able to give you an estimate.
- *Databases Limited.* A database is just another source. It is limited by what has been entered into it just as other sources are limited.
- *Only Recent Information.* The prior fifteen years is probably the most time that will appear on the database. Some are limited to the past two years or some other relatively short time. Be certain the time searched is appropriate for your research.
- *Irrelevant Citations.* You can pay for minimally related citations. Research on "wood" may produce five articles by a person named Wood.
- *Partial Documents.* Like other indexes or abstracts, a computer search does not produce the whole document. You still must acquire it through normal procedures.

2. **When and When Not to Use Computer Searching.** Knowing when to use a computer search is also helpful in deciding whether or not to make the investment. The following guidelines help you decide when and when not to use computer searching.

  a. Searches that may be appropriate

- When you are looking for very specific information or a specific topic.
- When money is no object and the references need not be focused or limited. A large "smorgasbord" of sources is acceptable.
- When you need to know *everything* published on the topic.
- When you want to search for materials that discuss two or three ideas together.
- When you search topics stated in so many ways and with so many synonyms that manual searching will take too much time.
- When you are looking for materials so new they may not be indexed in published form.
- When you have manually searched and can speak specifically about what you are looking for and ways to find it.
- When you need to search databases that are not available in printed form.

  b. Searches that are not appropriate

- When the topic is general. The cost is prohibitive because the retrieval is huge.

- When the question is hypothetical ("What if . . ."). The literature is there, but it is difficult to express specific commands for a meaningful search.
- When the question is of an ethical or moral nature. The problem is the same as the one stated previously.
- When the search involves ranges or comparisons. It can be difficult finding terminology to search the relationship you are investigating.

3. **Search Request Form.** The following form is typical of those used to request a computerized search. The better it is filled out, the better the staff person performing the search can help. Clearly define the topic. State the purpose of the search. Say if you expect an overview or comprehensive search of the topic. List known relevant journals, authors, etc. Tell how the search can be narrowed if too much information is found. How can it be broadened if too little is found?

Some staff people request the user be present during the search so he or she can assist in making decisions when alternatives are given or different lines of pursuit must be followed. Others do not offer the user this option. Costs differ depending on the system being searched, but all are fairly expensive. Be sure to understand your financial obligation before requesting a search.

Computerized Search Request

NAME: _____ DATE: _____

ADDRESS: _____

TELEPHONE: _____

STATUS: _____UG _____GRAD ___FAC ___OTHER

THE SINGLE MOST IMPORTANT ELEMENT OF YOUR REQUEST IS TO COMMUNICATE AS ACCURATELY AS POSSIBLE TO THE SEARCHER THE SUBJECT IN WHICH YOU ARE INTERESTED. In the space below describe the subject of your search in your own words. Be sure to indicate synonymous or alternative words and consider pointing out any aspects that are *not* of interest.

It is very important to maintain a balance between including all essential and important elements of a subject and leaving out minimal and unimportant elements. Asking yourself these questions may help: If I were to read an article pertinent in all respects to my subject, how would I summarize it? In one paragraph, what does this article discuss?

How many references do you *expect* to receive?
_____5-20 _____20–50 _____over 50
How many references do you *hope* to receive?
_____5-20 _____20-50 _____over 50

If at all possible, list a particularly relevant article on your topic: _____

_____

_____

Standard Search Restrictions: (check only those that apply)

Time period covered   all available years   ___
by search: selected years   ___
                                   (specify:_____)

Languages:	*Demographics:*	*Publication types:*
English only ___	Human subjects *only:* ___	Journal articles ___
Selected languages ___	Animal research *only:* ___	Books or monographs ___
(specify:_____	*Specific age groups *only:* ___	Dissertations ___
_____)	(specify:_____)	Conference papers ___
All languages ___	Geographic limitations: ___	Gov. or tech. reports ___
	(specify:_____)	

*ERIC users see separate listing.

A FREE TEXT SEARCH
["Free text" means that any place the term "Aids" appeared in the
record, a reference was retrieved.]

10/5/12 Record number
1995024   86212024 Ignore
Predictive value of a screening test for antibodies to HTLV-III Article title
Sivak SL; Wormser GP Authors
Section of General Internal Medicine, New York Medical College.
Valhalla 10595 Corporate affiliation of two authors
Journal title Am J Clin Pathol (UNITED STATES) , Jun 1986,   85 (6) p700-3.
Ignore ISSN 0002-9173   Journal Code: 3FK Journal date Vol. No. Page
Languages: ENGLISH Language of printed article
Journal Announcement: 8608
Subfile: AIM; INDEX MEDICUS

A test for the detection of antibodies to HTLV-III is available
and will be widely used to screen donated blood to prevent
transfusion-associated acquired immunodeficiency syndrome (AIDS).
Based upon the sensitivity and specificity, the authors
calculated the expected predictive values for different groups of
asymptomatic individuals using Bayes' theorem. The prevalence of
HTLV-III infection has great impact upon the positive and
negative predictive values of the test. For a member of the
general population there is a less than 3% chance that a positive
test represents a true positive. High-risk patients, such as
hemophiliacs, with a positive test will have a greater than 95%
chance of actually having antibodies to HTLV-III, but the
negative predictive value of the test in this group is less than
ideal. The authors recommend that all positive tests for HTLV-
III be confirmed by more specific methods when obtained in low-
risk people. Members of high-risk groups for AIDS should
continue to refrain from donating blood, despite the availability
of the screening text. Article abstract

Tags: Human; Male Categories for searchers to use
Descriptors: Acquired Immunodeficiency Syndrome--Prevention and
Control (PC); *Antibodies, Viral--Analysis (AN); Enzyme-Linked
Immunosorbent Assay *Hemophilia--Immunology (IM); Homosexuality;
*Human T-Cell Leukemia Virus--Immunology (IM); Mass Screening--
Standards (ST) Subject headings useful to searchers

4. ***Example of Computer Database Search.*** All printouts vary in format. (See example on facing page.) Look for generic elements that you will recognize such as journal title, author, language, etc. Some information given is helpful only to the person doing the search. Ignore it.

Bibliographies or List of References

Writers who use information from another document, another person's data, a conversation, or interview must identify the source in whatever they write. Such references are collected and presented at the conclusion of a chapter, article, or book. The references give credit for ideas or quotations used in one's writing, and they provide readers with sources to consult if working on a related subject.

A bibliography or list of references An alphabetical listing of sources used in the research, preparation, and writing of a document. The authors' surnames are the basis of the alphabetizing. The list may include sources critical to understanding and writing about the subject but not specifically referred to in the writing.

Preparing a Bibliography or List of References

Each major discipline has its own stylebook for presenting the details of documentation. Certain publications and companies issue their own style manuals. Each will differ on minor points such as where to place the date of publication or how to punctuate between entries, but agree on major items to include: the author's or editor's name, the title, and facts of publication. It is impossible to give a guide or example that will satisfy a universal style, so before you begin to write, ask the company or journal or professor of your particular discipline which manual you should follow.

A popular style manual accepted by many technical and scientific journals is *The Chicago Manual of Style,* 13th ed. (Chicago: University of Chicago Press, 1982). It lists the following items to be included in references to books and periodicals:

Books

Author:	Name of individual or group of individuals, editor or editors, or institution that wrote the book
Date:	Date of publication
Chapter or Essay:	Full title
Title:	Full title including subtitle. If title follows a chapter or essay title, introduce by "In"
Series:	If part of a series, the series title and volume or number in the series
Volume:	Volume number
Edition:	Number of edition used beyond the first edition
Page:	Starting and ending page numbers
Publication:	City of publication and publisher's name

Articles

Author: Name of individual or individuals who wrote the article
Date: Date of publication of periodical
Title: Full title of article including subtitle
Periodical: Name of periodical
Volume: Volume number and issue number
Pages: Starting and ending page numbers

Examples (in the style of *The Chicago Manual of Style*, 13th ed.):

Book with single author:

> Puotinen, C. J. 1983. *Using the IBM personal computer: WordStar.* New York: Holt, Rinehart and Winston. (Notice the book title is given in small letters except for the first capital.)

Book with two authors, a chapter title, an editor, and an edition:

> Smith, Thomas E., and Sally J. Horn. 1988. Charts and graphs. In *Communicating with graphics.* 3d ed., ed. M. J. Hodor, 68–79. New York: Holt, Rinehart and Winston. (If the editor is named on the title page and his or her name follows the title, capitalize the "e": Ed. Jane Medley. The Chicago style requires that every author's name be given.)

Book with editor only (no author named on title page) and chapter or essay in book or collection:

> Poliakoff, R., ed. 1987. The story of oil. In *The history of minerals*, 123–132. New York: Harper & Row. (Notice italics.)

Article with two authors:

> Rutter, Roberta, and Patrick Bonner. 1988. Poetry, imagination, and technical writing. *College English* 47: 698–712. (Notice the use of small letters in the article title but standard title capitalization for periodicals plus italics.)

Another respected stylebook favored by those in the sciences and humanities is the *MLA Handbook for Writers of Research Papers* by Joseph Gibaldi and Walter S. Achtert (New York: Modern Language Association, 1984). It lists the following items to be included in references to books and periodicals:

Books

Author: Name of individual or group of individuals, editor or editors, or institution that wrote the book
Chapter or Essay: Full title
Title: Full title including subtitle
Editor: Name of individual(s) who edited the book
Edition: Number of edition used beyond the first edition

Volume: Number of volume used
Publisher: City of publication and publisher's name
Date: Date of publication
Page: Starting and ending page numbers

Example of citing a chapter in a book using the MLA style:

> Smith, Thomas E., and Donald J. Horn. "Charts and Graphs." Communicating with Graphics. Ed. M. J. Hodor. 3rd ed. New York: Holt, Rinehart and Winston, 1986. 68–79.

Articles

Author: Name of individual or individuals who wrote the article
Title: Full title of article including subtitle
Periodical: Name of periodical
Volume: Volume number and issue number
Date: Date of publication of periodical
Page: Starting and ending page numbers

Example of citing an article in the MLA style:

> Rutter, Ruth, and Peter Bonner. "Poetry, Imagination, and Technical Writing." College English 47.5 (Sept. 1985): 57–68.
> (If a day is given in the date, it goes before the month: 12 Sept. 1985. Abbreviate the name of the month except May, June, and July.)

The differences between the Chicago Manual and MLA styles are minor but represent the distinctions made about different items. For example, the date is positioned differently in the two styles of citation. The titles of books and journals are printed in italics in the Chicago style; they are printed in regular type and underlined in the MLA style. Every word after the first word in a title is printed in small case in the Chicago style; all major words in titles are capitalized in the MLA style. Titles of journal articles or essays are not placed within quotation marks in the Chicago style; they are in the MLA style. None of this means that one style is right or preferred over another. It simply means that you must know which is the appropriate style manual for your discipline and follow its conventions. It also means that you must proofread carefully to ensure consistent attention to minor stylistic conventions.

Citing Other Types of Sources

Some style manuals give instructions for documenting other kinds of sources, others do not. If yours does not, develop a consistent form closely following what you use for books and articles. For correspondence, include the name and location of the organization or person sending the correspondence, the name and location of the organization or person receiving it, and the letter's date. For an interview or speech, give the name and location of the speaker, the name and location of the listener, and the date. Other sources you may need to document include government documents, computer programs, patents, conference proceedings, abstracts, and audiovisuals.

Identifying Sources within the Text

In place of formal footnotes, source citations can very simply be made within the text by referring to the bibliography or list of references. Place a parenthetical reference at the end of the material you are documenting, on the same line with the text, and inside the end punctuation. Possible citations in the MLA style can be:

(Stuart 89)	(Refers to the entry in the bibliography or list of references with the author Stuart, page 89.)
(Stuart, "Computers" 123–25)	(If more than one work by an author appears, use a short form of the title.)

If the work has two or three authors, include the last name of each. For more than three authors, use et al.: (Stuart et al. 123–25).

If in the list of references or bibliography two or more references are listed for the same author or authors, the author's name is given only in the first entry. In immediately succeeding entries, the author's name is represented by a short line followed by a period. Chicago style:

Stuart, A. 1984. *Writing and analyzing effective computer system documentation.* New York: Holt, Rinehart and Winston.

———. 1986. *Linking technical writing with computers.* New York: Holt, Rinehart and Winston.

Example of citing sources within text:

The goal of poet and technical writer alike is "by the power of the written word, to make you hear, to make you feel—it is, before all, to make you see" (Rutter 705). Is this not the goal of any writer?

Understand that you do not need to document every idea that you read somewhere else and also include in your writing. You know when you are directly using someone else's idea or data. When you are, give credit. A good rule of thumb is to use a quotation or credited paraphrase to cite expert or controversial opinion, to present statistics or little known facts, or to provide interpretation of commonly known facts.

You also need to give credit for ideas, theories, and opinions that you received from someone or someone's writing that directly contributed to the development of your work. Sometimes you can indicate a general obligation with a statement in the text.

The following example of crediting ideas within the text appears later in this book on page 60. The person's name and affiliation are identified within the sentence. It is perfectly acceptable to paraphrase, but you must clearly indicate that the ideas are not your own.

> A person who successfully manages and conducts telephone interviews is Susan E. Scarlett, president of Insight Services, Inc., a market research company specializing in health care issues. I asked her what she would tell a group of students to help them better prepare and gather information via the phone. Her advice is the basis for the following discussion.

Sources Other than the Library

Interviews

Other people are a major resource. If the information is not publicly available, someone usually knows something about the subject. If you can interview a person who has first-hand knowledge or a number of people who know a bit of what you need, you can piece together the whole from among several interviews. Interviews do a number of things; they collect several viewpoints on the same subject, teach the history of a problem, or fill in missing information. You will conduct them either face to face or on the phone. To be a good interviewer, you need to develop certain habits. Helpful suggestions follow:

The Personal Interview

1. ***Be Certain You Are Interviewing the Best Person.*** Do not waste both your and the other person's time by assuming he or she has the information you need. Remember that a job title is no guarantee that you have the right person. If you set up the interview by the job title alone, you may discover after you arrive that the person in charge of the project you are interested in left the company three months ago or now has another position in the company.

   The time to check if you have the appropriate person is when you set up the appointment. If possible, talk personally with the person you want to interview. Explain briefly the reason for the interview and why you want to talk with him or her. If the person cannot help you, he or she can say so and probably direct you to someone who can.

   Sometimes you cannot get through to set up the appointment with the person you want to interview. In large organizations, secretaries or administrative assistants act as shields for those they work for and will not let anyone speak to their employers without knowing what it is one wants to discuss. If you say you want an interview, the secretary or assistant will check and let you know or will go ahead and give you an appointment but will not put your call through. When you run against this situation, fit into the system. Explain to whoever will talk to you what you need and why you think the person you want to see can help you.

2. ***Conduct a Structured Interview.*** Plan and write out questions before the interview. Those who are inexperienced at interviewing, often wing it; such an approach is not good. When interviewing more than one person, you are not likely to ask the same questions each time in the same order or with the same language, and the disadvantage increases if you have only one opportunity to interview a person. If in your off-the-cuff interview you forget a question or do not ask exactly what you intend, you have no second chance to rectify the omission. This condition is less important, of course, if you see the person who is being interviewed every day at work or in some other regular way. Regardless of this, you should be prepared to capture information correctly the first time.

   Before you go to interview, prepare the interview sheets: write one question per page, the name of the person interviewed, the person's position or relevance to your research project, the date and time of the interview, and anything else important. Ask the same questions, in the same order of everyone interviewed. This procedure not only prevents gaps in responses but also makes the data reliable for evaluation.

3. ***Be Prepared.*** When you arrive, have the interview sheets in order, in a folder or some other appropriate container, and have pencils or pen available. The person being interviewed has granted you time. Do not waste it getting yourself organized.

4. ***Establish Rapport and Acquire Consent.*** The person being interviewed may not understand why you are interviewing or know anything about you. If so, introduce yourself and state your purpose. In every case, say why you are doing the interview and how the results will be used. Ask if the person has any questions and answer them honestly, even if it means the interview may be canceled.

   Clearly ask for consent. At the outset, find out if you may use the collected information. A written release is not always necessary, but you should record that you spoke with the person about using the information and record any reservations. Some people will not want their name or any other names used; some will ask that the company remain anonymous; other stipulations may be made. If both of you agree about the conditions, ask the person being interviewed if it is acceptable to proceed.

5. ***Maintain Rapport during the Interview.*** As the person talks, give positive reinforcement for verbalization. Smile; shake your head in a positive movement; comment, "Yes," or "Do you want to elaborate?" or "I appreciate that," or "I had not realized that." If you do not respond, the person being interviewed has a conversation with himself or herself and often that conversation becomes less and less verbal.

6. ***Stay in Control.*** Keep the interview moving. Compare the number of questions to be asked with the time granted. If your appointment is open-ended, ask before you begin how much time the person can give; then quickly calculate how many minutes you can allow for each question. This does not mean you should take your watch off and set it in front of you or bring out a stopwatch. Be subtle but keep track of time. If the interview is dropping

behind, say that in order to complete the questions, you need to move along. The person granting the interview may respond that if you need more time he or she can stay with you, or the person may acknowledge the time restraint and pace answers so the interview can be completed.

7. ***Consider Carefully before Taping Interviews.*** Weigh the disadvantages and advantages of taping your interviews. One disadvantage is that some people are restrained when they know their words are being taped, which can restrict the gathering of information. The real disadvantage is to you, however, who must listen back to audio material—through pauses, trivia, and asides. You give double time: time to conduct the interview and time again to listen and transcribe.

   On the other hand, taping captures exact language, phrasing, and ideas, and for certain information, can be the best method. Taping also frees you to give your whole attention to listening.

8. ***Write Responses.*** Develop an accurate and personal shorthand to use during the interview. As soon as possible following the interview, go over your notes and fill in what needs to be explained so they will make sense a week or month later.

   It is all right to ask the person being interviewed to wait so that you can gather information completely and accurately. Simply say, "Can we hold up a second until I get that down?" or "I'm sorry, can we wait a minute while I write," or "Will you please repeat that?" Naturally you do not want to do this continuously, so develop the ability to recognize what needs to be written as said and what can be summarized.

9. ***Guard against Prejudices.*** Resist making judgments about a person's knowlege by the way he or she looks or acts. You may dislike smoking, fat people, men who wear polyester suits, or people who will not look at you, but put those feelings aside and hear accurately what the person has to say.

10. ***Recognize the Limitations of Interviews.*** Realize that anyone interviewed tells what he or she considers important or the truth. Just because you get to talk to someone is no guarantee that you are receiving indisputable information. We all are biased by our own experiences, our education, our background, and our survival. Listen to sift for facts, for the truth.

Telephone Interviews

The telephone is an efficient means of gathering information from other people. It saves time and money in that you do not have to travel to the person you are interviewing, but it is not an easy source to use. Some people hate to talk on the phone; some say "no" more easily on the phone and cut you off; others resent calls breaking into work; some are so irritated by telemarketers calling to sell at all times of day and night that they react negatively to anyone calling; some are turned off by the intelligent computer that phones to ask questions; people are also suspicious of giving information over the phone if they do not know or cannot verify the legitimacy of the caller. All of this makes successful calling difficult, but it may still be your best means. The good news is that you can learn to deflect some prejudices and ask questions and treat respondents in ways that will produce the best results.

One person who successfully manages and conducts telephone interviews is Susan E. Scarlett, president of Insight Services, Inc., a market research company specializing in health care issues. I asked her what she would tell a group of students to help them better prepare and gather information via the phone. Her advice is the basis for the following discussion.

1. ***Collecting a Database for Calling.*** If you plan to call only a few people or those you know or have an introduction to, it is simple to make the interview arrangements, but sometimes you need to gather information from a large sample or from a random group, all of them strangers. People are in the business of selling other people's names, so calling lists are available (companies selling lists even appear under "Mailing Lists" in the Yellow Pages of the phone book), but for the most part you will construct your own database of people particularly related to the research project. To recruit people who will talk to you, Susan Scarlett feels you need to write and send a letter of introduction to prospective people to interview.

   The letter itself should do the following:

   • Introduce the company or project and explain its purpose or the individual and the individual's reason for the interviews.
   • Offer an honorarium and state the amount.
   • Explain the method of conducting the telephone interviews.
   • Describe the ways in which the information gathered from the interviews is used.
   • List examples of the sponsors of studies or research projects.
   • Ask that a preaddressed, postage-paid form be completed and returned by mail.
   • Conclude with a clear, strong message about why the addressee should respond.

Susan pays attention to detail to increase the chance of her letter's being opened, read, and the enclosure returned. Good quality stationery and a hand-stamped envelope with a commemorative rather than regular issue stamp makes the letter look like it is worth reading. She uses a personal computer with a data merge facility to merge the list of names with the primary document and make both the letter and envelope appear personally addressed. Mailing labels are not used because they give a "mass mailing" impression. Her printer is letter quality. Everything about this first contact is designed to make a good impression. Susan feels that if one's material is sloppy, casual, or unprofessional in any way, the sender is wasting time and money because the letter will not be seriously considered.

The form that Susan suggests you include and have returned gathers information about the person to be interviewed:

Who will connect the respondent with the interviewer?
What is the best time to call?

What are some facts about the professional to be interviewed?

For example, if the person Susan is soliciting is a cardiologist, she might ask:

---

1. How many prescriptions per week does the doctor write for the following drugs?

    1–10   11–20   21–30   30–above

    Drug A
    Drug B
2. What pacemakers are used?

    Brand A _____
    Brand B _____
    Others _____

Susan believes the form should be simple and able to be filled out quickly without much thought. It should be designed so that it is addressed to the company or interviewer and stamped, or a stamped, addressed envelope should be enclosed. Do not expect the receiver to stamp material you wish returned. If the number of pieces to be returned is large, you may want to open an account at the post office that will allow you to use "Postage to be Paid by Account xx" envelopes. Only those pieces returned will be charged against your account.

2. *Making the Call Itself.* The very first contact is the point at which you do or do not succeed. Susan advises that you seize the opportunity at hand. For example, when the secretary answers the phone, Susan tries to get a reading on the secretary's personality. Is this person formal and rigid? dumb and not too smart? young, bouncy, and informal? With only a few syllables to go on, she makes a decision and goes with her instinct.

   If the call is being placed from the data base, then the interviewer can use an opening such as, "I'm calling to follow up on a letter which Dr. ____ sent to me." The secretary is more inclined to forward the call to the respondent upon realizing that the caller and the person being called have already corresponded.

   If the call is not to a prerecruited respondent, begin by telling your name and where you are calling from. Susan feels that if you will not tell, you betray the secretary's trust. Be very professional, but make a friend out of the first contact. If you do, you will have better success: that person will go to bat for you and put your call through or tell you when the person you want to interview will be back or when he or she will be available.

   Your investment of time can be tremendous. In one study recently completed by Insight Services, Inc., Susan and her callers talked to 1600 doctors' offices—these calls were not busy signals or "no" answers, but rather conversations with someone in the office who told the interviewer that the doctor had just gone to lunch, or was in with a patient, or when to call back—to get 200 interviews. You may not be making this many calls, but you still need to anticipate and set aside time.

3. ***Conducting the Telephone Interview.*** Susan places great emphasis on the need to feel confident and comfortable with what you are doing. If you are curt, rude, or do not understand the subject matter, the respondent may either stop the interview or respond very poorly to you. She advises that you be well versed on the subject of the interview. Know the buzz words and how to spell them, but do not fall apart when the respondent says something you do not understand. Ask the person to explain or to spell a word. People like to be appealed to, asked for help. As long as you present yourself honestly and professionally, you will be successful. Know the goal of your interview, so that when the respondent goes off the track, you can bring the interview back.

   Make the interview enjoyable. Do not fire questions at the respondent but encourage the person through conversation to expand comments. Listen to what is said. If it does not make sense at the time, it will make less sense later on. So ask questions so that you understand what is being said.

4. ***Using Structured and Open-Ended Questions.*** Most interviews are a combination of two types of questions. The design of the structured question is such that answers fall into stated slots (with "others" always available), therefore making tabulations easy and efficient. Open-ended questions generally lead to an in-depth exchange between the interviewer and the respondent. Answers are often subjective in nature, and the interviewer is called upon to probe and clarify to obtain complete, clear answers.

   a. Examples of structured questions used by Insight Services are as follows:
      • What brands are you aware of? (The preposition at the end of the sentence is intentional. The question is stated informally to reduce the stiffness of the interview.)
      • Have you ever heard of (brand name)?

		Aided Aware	
	Unaided Aware	yes	no
Brand A	X		
Brand B	X		
Brand C		X	
Brand D		X	
Brand E			X
Other (specify)			

The answer to the first question tells you what the respondent mentions without being prompted; the person has heard of (and mentioned spontaneously) Brands A and B. Before you ask question 2, always ask, "Any others?" When you are satisfied that the respondent cannot think of any others without being prompted, you can then ask question 2. Upon prompting, this respondent recalls that he is also aware of Brands C and D but that he has not heard of Brand E.

- What are the drawbacks of X? (Do not read response options until respondent has stopped talking. Then ask the ones not mentioned.)

Not effective	
Takes too long to work	
Expensive	
Difficult to use	
None	
Don't know	
Other (specify)	

b. An example of an open-ended question follows:

- How do you decide that this type of wound requires X? If this open-ended question does not elicit a specific response, it could be followed by:

   What does the wound look like if you are going to do X?

   What is it about the nature of the wound that makes you decide to do X?

   What are the characteristics of a wound in which you would do X?

Only if the respondent does not offer any information at all will you ask leading questions. Examples follow:

- What about color?
- Tell me about the size.
- Tell me about the depth of the wound.

Most respondents talk better when they feel as though they are not being quizzed but being appealed to for an opinion about something, so you often gather more information with an open-ended question. Design your questions to suit the goal of your research project.

5. ***Learning How to Listen Well.*** To interview well, we must listen well. When asked, most of us will say we are good listeners. The facts are that most of us are not; we are not even aware that we are not, and we receive little or no formal training in developing this skill. Probably the main skill to acquire in order to be a good listener is to use effectively the time left between the time we hear an idea, absorb it, and wait for the next idea. We listen faster than most people speak. The poor listener thinks of other things during the lags; the good listener makes good use of the time to evaluate the information, form questions, relate it to other information, or commit it to memory. The next time you conduct an interview or attend a lecture or presentation, become aware of the time available after you hear a sentence or idea and the next sentence. Practice concentrating on processing what you have heard rather than wasting the lag time.

Our prior expectations also hinder good listening. We decide before or while the person speaks that the subject is uninteresting, or too complex for us to understand, or too simple. Sometimes we listen only for the main point. In doing so, we become impatient for the speaker to get to the point and fail to absorb developmental information. When we become too annoyed, we often stop listening and begin thinking our own thoughts.

The following are some good listening habits to develop:

- Ignore a speaker's personal or speaking habits that irritate and distract you from listening well.
- Do not stop listening after the speaker says something with which you disagree. Push aside the desire to think about a rebuttal. Continue to listen for information important to you.
- Shut out distractions—noise, other people, temperature, etc. Recognize them and will yourself to ignore them.
- Listen for supporting information as well as main points.
- Overcome the desire to stop listening when the subject becomes complicated. Make understanding it a challenge and use lag time to study and comprehend better.

Questionnaires

The questionnaire is a popular means of gathering information and the form most people think of when a survey is needed, but first you should ask yourself if a questionnaire is your best means of gathering information. It is appropriate when you want to gather a very shallow level of information such as numbers and frequencies, when you need to question a large number of people, and when you require an inexpensive method.

Questionnaires appear deceptively simple to construct, but unless you know something about writing questions, they can yield worthless answers. Anyone who plans to do research on a regular basis should take a methods course or do some self-study. Many readable books on research methods are available in college or large city libraries. If you plan to use the questionnaire method only occasionally, the following procedure is a guide:

Define the Problem

About 70 percent of your time should be spent defining the problem. Have a clear vision of what you want to know. Write the main questions; what information do you need to make the answers to the questions usable? For example, a question may require demographic data (age, sex, and the like) to be interpreted correctly; if it is not collected, the information may be useless.

Select the Best Sample

The final study is only as good as the sample that is drawn. The same books on research techniques that help you form questions teach sampling principles, but the basic rule is to gather from people whose response is meaningful and reliable and from a distribution that reflects all opinions. The population need not be representative in all respects, only in those relevant to the substantive interests of the study.

Write the Questions

Before you begin to write questions, make an outline of the report that will result from the questionnaire. Plan each section and subsection. Afterward, go through the outline to decide what information is needed to write each section. Use this understanding to write meaningful questions. The report outline will also cause you to see if the questionnaire is complete. You can check it against what is needed to write the report. If you construct good questions, the report practically writes itself. You just plug in the collected data and flesh out the outline to full sentences.

If you know nothing about posing valid questions, go to the library and look under the subject headings "Methods" or "Methodology"; you will find books that can help you. You should study the best way to word and structure the questions. Without knowing how language and form can prejudice or invalidate a question, you can write a questionnaire that is practically useless. Some very basic tips include the following:

1. Use words the respondent will understand and interpret the same way you do.
2. Construct questions so answers are clear, brief, and include all possible answers. Possible types of questions follow:

Multiple choice:	Choose between several possibilities. Include the choice "others."
Dichotomous:	Choose between two answers.
Rating:	Rate on a scale (e.g., 1 to 10) the importance of several items to the respondent.
Ranking:	Rank several possibilities in order of personal preference.
Fill-in-the-blank:	Write a short answer.
Essay:	Write an extended answer.

3. Ask only one piece of information per question. Avoid asking for a single answer to a combination of questions.
4. Avoid using negatives (not, never, no) in questions. They make for easy misinterpretation.

5. Format the questionnaire so questions are spread out and uncluttered. Use white space generously. Avoid squeezing several questions on a single line. Do not abbreviate questions.
6. Provide a structured method of response—boxes, brackets, or parentheses.
7. Order the questions carefully. Realize that subsequent answers can be influenced by what goes before. Place the most interesting questions first, the dull demographic ones last.
8. Give clear instructions.
9. Number the questions.

Conduct a Pilot Study

Select 10 to 15 people who are not part of the research or the sample group. Ask them to answer the questionnaire and note problems. One good way to do this is for each person to meet with you personally. Ask the person to read each question aloud and to say aloud whatever comes to mind in answering: Does the person not know what a word means? Is the question confusing? If so, how? Are there multiple meanings to the question? Are instructions not clear? Whatever the person says, you record. At the end of this exercise, you know which are problem questions, and you know the problems to correct.

Mail the Questionnaire

Write a cover letter to accompany the questionnaire. Explain the purpose. Ask for a prompt response. When possible, hand address the letter and always pay for the return postage.

Gather the Returns

You may need to call or write a follow-up letter asking those who have not responded to do so. If 50 percent return the questionnaire, you are doing well. But recognize that it is not the number, but the representativeness of the returns that is the critical variable. Check the returns to see if the sample is still random. Look at the last ones returned; it is likely that those who fail to return are from the same group as those who return last. You may find that you need to collect more information from this and other groups of your sample who are not fairly represented.

Personally Interpret the Data

Once you receive the questionnaires, you must make sense of the data. It often is easier to administer the questionnaire than to figure out what it means. A good research course or some reading will help. You need to understand about the application of statistics to human behavior, to business, or to whatever it is that you are trying to interpret. All kinds of things can influence data. For example, studies show that prior questions can set up responses for subsequent questions. Your understanding of such conditions will make you cautious of snap judgments and aware of how complicated and difficult it is to gather reliable data.

Scientific Observation

The best scientific researchers ask the simplest—not simple—questions. Those posed by Nobel Prize winners are elegant, beautifully structured, sweeping in scope, and can be answered by a clear "Yes" or "No." Sometimes scientists ask Nature questions that she must answer, "Maybe" or "Sometimes." The results are imprecise not because Nature did not know, but because the scientists asked poor questions. Your first duty as a research scientist is to learn to ask good questions.

Scientists must record what they observe, and the validity of the information is often linked to the quality of the reporting. Gregor Johann Mendel became the father of genetics because he wrote *everything* down. Others had done and were doing similar work, but without documentation, they lost their place in history. Students can also document poorly. Either they judge something to be unimportant or too much trouble to record, or they are embarrassed to document their own variations in procedure. For example, in an experiment depending on daily injections in mice, a student may pick up a dirty syringe, fill it, discover the error, and think, "Oh gee, I'll empty it, wash it out, refill it, and no one will know; I won't write this down because it makes me look dumb." The experiment may fail or have unusual results, and the difference may be related to the solution that was in the syringe prior to being filled or the solution that was used in washing, but answers will not be found and time will be wasted because no one but the student knows of the abnormality.

Record scientific, experimental data in a notebook with nonremovable pages. Each notation should be dated and the time given. Whenever possible, data should be entered in the same format. Report everything, but interpret nothing. It is correct to write, "The solution turned green," but unacceptable to add, "I think it did so because. . . ." Remember that the scientist's most important quality is to be open to the evidence. Do not let pet theories or expectations or wants color what you do, see, and record. The time for conclusions or speculations is after all data are collected and analyzed.

For every experiment, define and state in the documentation an endpoint, the way to tell if the experiment works. For example, in an experiment with chickens where you want to determine the results of removing a certain organ, the chickens may die every time the experiment is performed, and you may state—partly because you want it to be so—that the removal of the organ results in the chickens' deaths. But without an endpoint, you cannot be sure. The control could be another group of chickens that receive incisions, but each is sewed up without removing any organ. If that whole group or part of it dies, it is not clear whether the chickens that had an organ removed died from the loss of the organ or from the trauma of the incision.

Field Studies

Field research is most likely to be used by people interested in studying naturally occurring interaction in a particular context. It attempts to make sense out of an ongoing process that cannot be predicted in advance. Examples might be studies of plant life, weather conditions, construction footing subsidence, and so on.

Field researchers must do their homework before beginning to observe. They should know everything available about the subject prior to entering the field. Once there, researchers need a systematic method for making and recording observations. If possible, they should write in a field journal as they observe. They should record both what they *know* happened and what they *think* happened. Full field notes should be written as soon as possible after observation. The date, time, condition, and any other significant data should be noted.

Summary

Using the Computer to Gather Information

The computer is marvelous for compiling information because you can add or delete at will. As you discover additional facts or need to alter others, you can easily do so. When collecting information that needs to be tabulated or sorted, you must think about how to enter the data into the computer. You want to be able to retrieve information in ways that are meaningful to the experiment. In certain cases, security must be built into the program so that you can be certain the data cannot be altered either by mistake or intention.

Apply Good Research Methods to Any Gathering of Information

This chapter identifies some standard research sources, but more importantly, it makes the point that gathering information requires discipline. The approach to the research, the search for information, the documentation of the research, and the analysis and interpretation must all be performed in a thoughtful and mannered way. Whatever you are out to find, allow enough time, and prepare yourself to collect data that are accurate, usable, and in a form that applies to the eventual written or oral presentation of the information.

Practice Exercises

Bibliography Exercise:

1. You will use your working library to obtain information and insert on worksheet on the facing page. Its accuracy and completeness will be checked by either the teacher or the librarian.

2. Your instructor will assign a technical term or theory. In the library, locate the reference sources listed here. Look for the assigned term or topic in each source, and after examining the type of information found, answer the questions following the list:

The public catalog
Reader's Guide

Worksheet for a Preliminary Bibliography
Specify the topic of your research precisely:

List the subject heading in the subject catalog related to your research. Do not guess. Use the catalog and list *all* the headings.

List three promising books: author, title, publisher, date of publication, tracings, other relevant information. Look for recent works.

List two indexes used, the years searched, and identify an article from each. Document completely.

Applied Science and Technology Index
Engineering Index
New York Times Index
The Harper Encyclopedia of Science
McGraw-Hill Encyclopedia of Science & Technology
Oxford English Dictionary
Civil Engineering Handbook
Magazine Index
Chemical Abstracts
Biological and Agricultural Index
Biological Abstracts

- Identify the kinds of information you can get from these sources (title, author, year, language, pages, illustrations).
- Group sources that give like information. Explain your criteria for the grouping. Make appropriate headings and list the sources under the various headings.

Listening Exercise

3. The teacher will determine a time in class when he or she will present a short lecture (5 or 10 minutes). The teacher will set up a listening exercise for the presentation. Each student will consciously keep track and make notes of how much lag time he or she had during the presentation. When did it occur? What did the listener do with this time? What distractions threatened listening? What habits of the speaker (the teacher may choose to create some for this presentation) did the listener have to put aside?

    Afterward the class will discuss what individual class members discovered and how many noted similar things.

    Near the close of the class, the teacher will give a quick, but very careful, quiz of the essential points in the lecture. The quiz will include minor or developmental information as well as main points. The teacher will read the answers, and class members will score themselves to see how well they comprehended what they heard.

Interviewing Exercises

4. For role playing, the teacher will have two class members sit in chairs facing away from each other. (The purpose is so that neither one can see the other's facial or body movements.) Pretend one person is telephoning the other to acquire information through a telephone interview. The number of possibilities is endless.

    - The person calling can have trouble getting the secretary to give an appointment or let the call go through. The caller must deal with this.
    - The person being interviewed may give one-word answers and not elaborate. The caller must deal with this.
    - The person being interviewed may talk on and on and get off the track. The caller must deal with this.
    - The interviewer may ask vague questions. The person being interviewed must respond to this—get disgusted, help the interviewer, and so on.
    - The interviewer may do all the talking. The person being interviewed can respond to this.

    The exercise also lets class members practice a good telephone manner and being polite. The interview questions and situations can be worked up by the individual teams in class work prior to the role playing.

5. The teacher will divide the class into teams of two or three. Each team will decide topics on which each person could interview the others. (People often interview more than one person at a time.) Each person will work up a set of interview sheets. (These may or may not be collected and commented on by the teacher.) The teacher will schedule the interviews over a number of class periods so the exercise does not become dull by repetition. By the time the exercise is finished, every student will have played both the interviewer and the person being interviewed. The students should role-play the interview. The students should be as creative as they wish—use props, costumes, set the stage! Whatever they choose, however, should be to make the role playing more real,

not silly. If possible, videotape the interviews and arrange for those participating in the interview to view the tape at their convenience. Have a class discussion after a day's presentation of two or three interviews. What did others see to imitate—to avoid?

Summarizing Exercise
6. In class, each student will summarize the Rutter paragraph on page 40. After 10 minutes or so, break the class into groups and have the members of a group read their summaries to each other. Have them decide together what the major differences are. Have them speculate why they exist. Bring the class back together and have each group report its findings to the class. What similarities or differences exist among the groups' findings? What makes a good, accurate summary?

Questionnaire Exercise
7. Break the class into groups. Have each group decide on a topic about which a group of students can be questioned. The group could be students who are of a certain major, live on one floor in a dorm, or eat in the school cafeteria. Each group should research the methodology of writing reliable questions and of selecting a reliable population to sample. Each group should write a questionnaire, distribute it, collect the returns, tabulate the results, report the findings of the questionnaire to the class, and determine what the group learned about collecting information in this way.

List of References Exercise
8. You will write a paper using five or more references. Cite correctly in the text whenever a source is used in writing the paper and compile correctly a list of references, using a style manual (*Chicago Manual?*) designated by the teacher.

Computer Search Exercise
9. The teacher may arrange a demonstration of a computer search for the class. Often librarians will work with the faculty, and when a search is to be conducted and paid for by the library or some other department, the librarians will arrange to do part of the search during the time of the technical writing class. Students go, watch the librarian do the search, and listen to the explanation of the good things and problems with the method and the information she or he has to work with.

Chapter 5

Writing, Rewriting, and Rewriting Again

A Task Made Easier with Word Processing

At some point you have studied, researched, and outlined enough, and it is time to write. This realization turns most of us into instant procrastinators. I often decide the laundry cannot wait another day, or notice the dogs need to go for a walk, or take a nap. You may do all other homework including assignments for next week or find you cannot possibly begin writing without something to eat—preferably something you can get only by leaving campus. Regardless of the activity, the shared goal is to stall having to write.

I am not sure what it is about writing that makes us dread beginning. Maybe it is knowing that if the project is of any importance, length, or complexity, it will take time, mental discipline, and a commitment to do something to the best of our ability. We do not always relish the challenge. Nevertheless, people in the technical professions must write, and given this fact, you need to develop methods that produce good writing in an effective and repeatable way. Much of how we write is influenced by what we read, what we see someone else do, or what we hear when discussing writing with other writers. We imitate what seems effective and later make it our own. This chapter presents ideas about writing and rewriting for you to imitate and make your own. It also shows how to make the task easier with word processing.

Outlining and Drafting

At this stage in the writing process, you understand the subject, have analyzed the audience, gathered information, and sensed it is time to quit the preliminaries and begin writing. Your reputation will be built on both the thoroughness and accuracy of your research and your ability to get things done. Therefore, develop a feel for when to stop the research and begin writing.

The assignment brings the subject, and the research produces ideas, so you know what to say. It is how to say it that remains a question. One habit that prepares you for writing is to review the assignment and to plan how to begin.

Think Again about Purpose

Some people, after doing research, want to tell the reader all they have learned. Your job is just the opposite. Study until you have an in-depth understanding of the whole subject, then cut away everything except the particular information necessary for the reader of your report, given the report's objective.

Hone the subject to a sharp focus so that you can relate every sentence, paragraph, and section directly to the purpose.

Check the Form of the Original Request

Note or listen well when you receive the assignment. Did the person asking you to write mention "short report" or "memo" or "summary" or "outline"? Such words suggest the expectations of the requester. If you were asked to submit an outline and you write a ten-page report, or you were asked to write a formal report and you prepare a memo, then the person who made the request is not receiving what was requested. This may not be bad, but it could give problems. First, you did not do what was asked. Secondly, you could annoy the receiver because the writing is not what was expected. Why run this risk? Check what was said to you. If you decide there is a better way to present the information, ask the person who requested the writing if your way is all right.

Decide upon an Order

Let the purpose of the writing help you eliminate everything unrelated. Whatever information is left, map out its placement. You will make changes as you write, but it is important to sense at the beginning how the parts of the report relate to the whole and how everything contributes to the purpose.

The order you choose should provoke interest, be logical, be the simplest to understand, and make referencing easy.

Outlining

Decide Whether to Outline

The act of outlining forces you to decide about content and its order, but no outline should become a plan set in concrete. The object of good scientific and technical writing is to produce a document that serves the purpose for which it is intended. Do not become so enamored with your beautiful outline that you are unwilling to change it to serve that purpose.

1. *The Informal Outline.* If you are to write a memo or short report, a few ideas jotted down on a piece of paper are enough of an outline to decide the order of information and to set some plan to accomplish the goal of the paper. The informal outline also is a good guide for checking information. A sketch of major topics tells you what information you have available. It shows how much or how little work you still must do.
2. *The Formal Outline.* When the writing project is large and complicated, the outline becomes something quite different from a list of a few words jotted down on paper.

   A formal outline for a large writing project identifies the subject and content for *every* major section and *every* subsection within the report and places information where it will make the best sense and impact. It is the means by which the writer tightens the subject and ties down ideas so no loose matters rattle around in the report to distract the reader or cause a breakdown in the report's performance. Such outlines are not produced without the same amount of planning, writing, and rewriting that is associated with writing the actual report.

   A formal outline is also a guide for the writer. No one can keep all parts of a large writing project currently in mind and remember relationships that have occurred at various times to the writer. A good and detailed outline captures such relationships and lets one add or subtract ideas as they come to mind or are discovered. It frees the writer to think about the isolated writing task at hand or even to put aside the writing and work on another project. When the writer returns to the writing project later, the outline is a reminder of purpose, ideas, and their connections. It is a diagram of how the parts make up the whole.
3. *Tips for Outlining*
   a. Know the purpose and function of your report, your audience, and your facts before setting the order of presentation. All reports are organized, but not all are organized well. Remember that you can help the reader understand by the way you arrange information. Think about what you want to communicate and then organize in a way the reader can best understand. Help the reader see the

organization by words like "first," "second," "therefore," "consequently," "nevertheless," "furthermore," etc.

b. Make the words, phrases, or sentences of the outline meaningful to you. At the time you write down a word, you may understand what it means in light of the report. Four or five days later, however, when you go back and review the outline, what you wrote may not be clear enough to reconstruct the idea or its relationship to the function of the report.

c. Be willing to change the outline as you work through the report. Some writers make a commitment to the content and organization of the outline and, because a lot of work has gone into planning the outline, they are unwilling to think critically about the organization as the report progresses or as new information affects outcomes or relationships. Such obstinateness is unreasonable and not compatible with scientific investigation.

d. Share the outline with co-workers or with people working on other parts of the same project to receive ideas and constructive criticism. If possible, show the outline to the person or persons who are to receive and work with your writing. Ask if it reflects what they need or want. If not, ask for their suggestions.

e. Use patterns of organization learned in other writing classes to arrange information:

Chronological. Organize information by days, weeks, months, or years, as it appears in the time sequence of the subject, beginning with the first time important to the subject and proceeding in sequence to the latest time.

Problem/Solution. State the problem and present the solution(s). If there is more than one, organize by the most economical, efficient, and accurate means.

Spatial. Use the physical form of the subject as a means of organization: top to bottom, side to side, front to back, around the edges, or whatever other form is used.

Comparison/Contrast or Similarities/Differences. Use to discuss two subjects.

• By Subject

Subject A

Point of comparison
Point of comparison

Subject B

Point of comparison (Must be the same point discussed first under Subject A.)
Point of comparison (Must be the same point discussed second under Subject A.)

- By Topic

    Point of comparison

        Subject A
        Subject B

    Point of comparison

        Subject A
        Subject B

    And so on.

Simple to Complex. Begin with what is easy to understand or what is necessary to understand the more complex information that appears later in the outline.

Cause and Effect. Begin with the cause and show the effects or vice versa.

Pro and Con. Arrange by points for the subject followed by points against.

Most to Least. Begin with the most important or economical or safe or whatever and progress to the least of whatever point you are making.

  f. Be complete. Include all information necessary to accomplish the report's purpose.

4. *The Use of Word Processing to Outline.* Outline processing programs like ThinkTank (Living Videotext, Inc.) let writers make better use of outlines. When you write a formal outline of any length, it is not easy to see main headings or just subheadings because the outline is written over several pages. Unless you copy parts of the outline into different lists, you cannot isolate major headings or list subheadings under a certain topic; however, the outline processor enables you to see any combination of the outline.

  a. You can collapse the outline so that you see only major topics (I, II's, or 1.0, 2.0's) or a list of subtopics under A or B's or 1.1 or 1.2's. This facility allows you to check at any time the sequence of ideas, their logic, and completeness.

  b. You can "hoist" a particular topic and all its subheadings so that you can isolate and evaluate a section of the outline without having the rest of the outline in view to distract you.

  c. You can move the entire outline to any other location in the document file. All submaterial moves also, so you can quickly reorganize at all levels and between levels or try placing ideas at different positions in the outline to best communicate relationships and be accurate and effective.

  d. You can "clone" the outline, which means you can have identical elements of the outline appear in more than one place. When you change a clone, all the other clones change too.

    e. You can print the whole outline or just a section of it and move text from document to document and from word processor to word processor.

Writers can literally see their thoughts in any combination. This visualization helps writers see clearly the flow, connection, and sense of what is being written.

Drafting

Writing the First Draft

Few people write publishable first drafts. Most first attempts just get words on paper. There is nothing wrong with doing this. It breaks the resistance to writing and frees the flow of ideas from the mind to paper.

    For me, the first writing is the most difficult. Before beginning, I want to stop the whole project—hate writing—can be cross with people—all because I cannot get hold of the whirl in my mind. Then I see a way to begin. I sit down at the word processor and compose directly onto the screen by looking at space and typing what I say to myself. If I think of two descriptive words, I type both without choosing between them. My goal is to capture ideas before I lose them. Writing is not easy for me. I work at it, but when I do it effectively, it gives great satisfaction. You will find your own sense of accomplishment from your individual successes in writing well.

Student Example 1

In this example, the student was to write about a technical subject to a lay audience—someone intelligent and capable of understanding but not informed on the subject. In the first draft, the student Micheal Bennett presents information straightforwardly but piles facts upon facts. The material is dense and hard to understand.

First Draft:

Molecular motion is the basis of all matter and life in the universe. Without it neither could function or even exist. If one could imagine an atom, with all of its electrons spinning endlessly around its proton and neutron filled nucleus, that suddenly stopped moving around in space and ended its routine of joining other atoms to form molecules and from molecules compounds, or if one could imagine life and all of its components and processes ceasing to operate, then one could imagine what the universe would be like without molecular motion.

    Molecular motion is a fascinating and probably the most vital principle in all of the sciences. It is the foundation that supports all the concepts and theories of the physical sciences, yet it is also one of the least known and understood.

    The theory of molecular motion states that all matter in the universe is constantly vibrating. It is as though every atom, which composes everything in the universe, is lying in a "mass" of particles; these particles are smaller in a sense than the individual atoms themselves, yet larger as a whole, than the universe, and this "mass" is always vibrating. This motion is the initial source of energy which enables atoms to move around and form different molecules and compounds and thus is the reason the universe can exist as it does today....

Writing the Second Draft

Realizing that he had no audience in mind, Micheal decided to write to a young person who likes science but has no formal scientific learning. His method is to teach the unfamiliar by relating it to the familiar. The rewrite is organized, clear, and tightly held together. It exemplifies well the value of rewriting. In the first draft, Micheal unsuccessfully communicated, but he did succeed in getting thoughts out of his head and onto paper. Afterward, as this draft shows, he reworked the material and produced a very nice piece of writing.

Second Draft:

Have you ever wondered why planets, stars, rivers, steam, or living creatures exist in our universe? Have you ever wondered why they are held together or just how they first appeared or began? What were they before they became what they are today? If you have ever puzzled about such fascinating miracles, then you have also wondered, either knowingly or not, about atoms and even more importantly about molecular motion. Molecular motion is the basis for all matter and life in the cosmos.

Try to imagine a large plate. On this plate are placed hundreds of small beads packed together in a manner that completely conceals the bottom of the plate. On the surface of these beads are placed three or four large foam balls. If the plate is then vibrated, the larger foam balls begin to move randomly about the surface of the tiny beads. The foam balls seem to obtain the energy needed for this action directly from the plate. This seemingly obvious deduction is misleading. Actually, the foam balls are moved by the vibration of the smaller beads below them. These smaller beads are using the energy of the vibrating plate to move the foam balls. Thus the beads, being more tightly packed and smaller, transfer the energy from the plate to the freely positioned, larger foam balls. This action makes the foam balls "appear" to move on their own. If one can imagine this example, then one can also imagine the principle of molecular motion.

Molecular motion is defined as the vibration of tiny bits of matter, called particles, that are densely packed. These particles cause larger, more complex pieces of matter, called atoms, to move around in space.

Molecular motion relies basically on the same principles as the beads and foam ball example. The particles which move the atoms act like the beads which move the bigger foam balls. In the case of the beads, however, the initial source of energy is known to be the vibrating plate. In molecular motion, no one knows the initial energy source. Nevertheless, it is an accepted law of nature that the particles involved in molecular motion transfer their energy to atoms that use it for locomotion.

Molecular motion is the basis for other laws of nature. It is the foundation for other principles which govern our universe. It is extremely vital to our understanding of the cosmos and of life upon our planet....

Student Example 2

Senior engineering students at the university where I teach conduct an engineering design project co-sponsored by an area industry. Part of that project is to document in a style acceptable to business and industry. The student begins by writing a proposal that states a problem, explains the need for a solution, proposes a solution, presents a plan of work, and formally asks permission to proceed. Terry Beck, a mechanical engineering major, agreed to share his work in progress. The following excerpts are from his proposal to investigate a backup source of child-resistant closures for a local pharmaceutical company.

The Student's Preparation For Writing

Industries willing to sponsor projects submit to the School of Engineering project descriptions, and on a day when representatives from the industries can be present, seniors and the representatives meet to discuss and assign the work. Once Terry had signed up for his project, his industrial advisor arranged three hourly meetings for them to explore and define the project. Terry admits he was surprised at how much time the sponsor gave and how carefully he defined the background, need, and purpose of what was to be done. Many times in their meetings, the sponsor, to be certain that Terry's understanding was accurate, asked him to explain back what had been said. Terry had never before planned so carefully and admits that he probably would not have analyzed the subject as well without guidance.

Terry also began to sense his audience through these meetings. When he arrived at the company, everyone he saw was dressed professionally; the offices and labs looked efficient; the documentation he was shown was articulate, precise, and well expressed. He knew that his standards were going to have to match the company's and that the company's standards were high.

The School of Engineering gives each student a handout of the proposal format. The following excerpt sets forth expectations for the discussion of the "Technical Approach."

> *Technical Approach.* This section serves to show that you understand the problem and have a solution (or a program for finding one). It also sets the stage for a clear understanding of your subsequent work statement. Included in this section are two major technical discussions:
>
> (1) *Problem Definition (or Background)*—Summarize the pertinent information for understanding the problem as you see it. Do not simply play back the information the client gave you, but select from it, interpret it, and add to it as necessary for a clear understanding of your position. Depending on the complexity of the problem, you may want to add a separate section on "technical discussion."
>
> (2) *Proposed Solution (or Approach to Problem)*—Present your solution or approach to solution in conceptual terms; define the major tasks, their interrelationships, and the operations under them. This segment spells out what you think needs to be done; however, you are not at this stage committing to do it all.

Terry readily admits that he never considered another way to present information or questioned the items to be included. He was happy to have the help. His first writing effort follows. The comments I wrote to him appear superimposed on the text.

Student's First Draft:

TECHNICAL APPROACH

II. PROBLEM DEFINITION

At the present time, Company A is supplied child-

resistant closures by a single company, Company B,

be specific

out (east.) Having only one source for child-resistant

closures puts Company A in a potentially hazardous *correct language?*

position. If their current supplier would have to

stop production   *including?*

(shut down their operation) for any reason, (such as) a

the needed

strike, Company A would not receive closures from

Company B or anyone else. For this reason,

an alternate

does not appear accurate or to be the right sense

Company A is looking for (another) company to

design and supply a closure for their containers. *if company B ever shuts down*

This new closure will serve as a backup to the

Company B closure if it is found to be acceptable.

has been selected as a possible alternate

~~Company C's design has been chosen to be this~~ *supplier*

~~backup, provided that it meets Company A's~~ *depending upon whether it can meet Company A's requirements*

~~requirements.~~

Why am I reading this? How is it a definition of the problem? The whole paragraph needs to be reworded in content and focused.

The Company B number × closure, currently

used by Company A, is 33 millimeters in diameter

and 14 millimeters in height. This is the largest

closure size used by the company. It is made up of

two different parts, the inner section and the outer

shell (see Diagram 1). The inner section fits inside

the outer shell. The Company B closure uses a top

lug system for removal from the container. To

remove the closure, one must push down on and

twist at the same time. When one pushes down on

the closure, the lugs of the outer shell engage the

lugs of the inner section (see Diagram 2). Friction

between the two lugs drags the inner section along

with the outer shell when a twisting motion is

applied to the outer shell. When the closure is

twisted but not pushed down upon, the lugs of the

outer shell simply skip over the inner section lugs.

This accounts for the clicking sound heard when

only a twisting motion is applied.

Company C's alternate closure is very similar to

Company B's closure except that ramp sections are

used in place of lugs in the outer shell (see Diagram

3). Pushing down on the closure locks the inner

section lugs to the vertical sections of the ramps

(see Diagram 4). Otherwise, the inner section lugs

only slide along the contour of the ramps.

How is this a problem?

The student coordinating this project ~~approves~~ *will perform tests. Based upon the data found, the student will* ~~of or disapproves of Company's C's closure being~~ *recommend whether or not Company A should* ~~submitted to Company A for their analysis. This~~ *consider Company C's alternate closure for* ~~decision is based on data produced from an~~ *further testing.* ~~assembly line test, a protocol test, and interaction~~

~~with the purchasing and marketing departments of~~

~~Company A.~~

Editorial Comments on First Draft

The draft has problems common to many first drafts—inaccurate wording, awkward sentences, unclear statements, material that is either not relevant or stated in such a way that the relevance is not seen, but it is a good beginning. Terry's task now is to rewrite, correcting language and style and making ideas more clear and accurate. (See Final Draft, pp. 89, 90.)

In our conversation about the first draft, we discovered that Terry felt he had been clear. This perception is a common writer's problem. As writers, we know what we want to say. We understand what appears on paper because in our minds we know about background, relationships, and a lot more about the writing topic than appears on paper. The communication gap occurs because the reader does not have the same understanding. It is the writer's job to write fully and clearly so readers have the same understanding. No formula assures this will happen. You must imagine yourself as the receiver, distance yourself from what you know, and read to catch those places where you have assumed the reader will understand. Ask yourself questions: When was the experiment performed? Where was it performed? Were there any unusual circumstances? Were the results expected? What is being done with the results? Did the experiment come in at cost? What else does the reader need to know in this section of the paper to understand?

Rewriting

To be able to rewrite is an opportunity. Sometimes writers have no time between the writing and the sending of a report. Other times the writing is not important enough to merit revision time. When you have the time and the report warrants the time, rewrite. Use the opportunity purposely. Mold the text to the purpose and audience of the paper. Make it a display of your ability to organize and think clearly—to be direct—to see precisely the point and to support your opinion or belief with suitable information.

Some rewriting is academic. It requires that you recognize the need to improve language choices, to make corrections in grammar or punctuation, to alter sentence structure, and to improve style. Other rewriting is less governed by rule. It requires knowing about the memory, thinking processes, and what decisions to make in order to arrange words and text to register effectively with the brain. The following discussion presents guidelines for approaching academic revision, suggests ways to revise for best comprehension, and touts the benefits of using word processing to rewrite.

A Checklist for Revision

Set high goals for the degree of resolution in your revision. Make the prose economical, even imaginative; make the presentation of the concept mind-catching, but obvious. The following checklist will probe you to keep working on the text—to make more than cosmetic changes:

1. A feeling of relief is natural after completing the first draft. The trained writer has this feeling because the labor of creating is over and the act of refining can begin. Go beyond the word or sentence level in revision. Evaluate texts in their entirety. Measure what the text says against what you mean to say.
2. Revise first for larger issues of meaning and then change words and phrases.

If you spend a lot of time at the beginning on language and then decide to change meaning, you have wasted time. Deception is also possible when you pick through the text correcting a lot of little mistakes. You fool yourself into believing that you have done a serious revision.

3. Review the purpose of your report. Is every idea, part, section contributing to the purpose?

4. Would the purpose of your report be better presented by reorganizing information? How can you better organize?

5. Have you made clear the organization and the relation of ideas by the use of outlining—headings—transitional phrases and words such as "therefore," "as a result," "consequently," "in contrast," "in addition"?

6. Put yourself in the reader's place and read the introduction. Read it aloud. Does it both tell the purpose of the document and catch the reader's attention? Does the reader understand what this document has to do with his or her work or responsibility? Is it to provide information—provoke a decision—cause an action?

7. Have you supported opinions and explained ideas? Would examples make an idea easier to understand? Would an explanation of how you arrived at an opinion make it more acceptable or reliable? Have you included the figures or theories that lead to your deductions? Have you taken time to make the reader as well informed as you or have you assumed too much?

8. Does the conclusion add or do something new, or does the report just stop or ramble to an end? Relate the conclusion to the purpose. Bring into focus what the report has done and provide ways for the reader to use it as intended. If the reader must make a recommendation based on what you have presented, summarize the findings in a way to help do this.

9. Realize that rewriting does not occur in a neat series of revisions: one for continuity and flow of ideas, one for vocabulary, one for grammar and punctuation, and so forth. Rather, the whole is altered many times. You go back through a text as often as time or need allows. Each time you interact with the whole document.

The Relationship between Reading and Writing: Its Application to Revision

A lot is being learned about how people read and how this knowledge can help writers write effectively. This active area of research is one you will want to follow. The reference librarian can identify educational, communication, or writing journals that publish in the subject area or can direct you to other fruitful sources. By the time you are writing in the workplace, many writers will recognize the relationship between reading and writing and be applying it to produce better writing. You need to be competitive.

The following theories are some that are already known and illustrate how this understanding can help you write better:

- Writers have as a goal getting information into the reader's head—into memory. Readers take in information through two faculties: short-term memory and long-term memory. Short-term memory can only hold small units of information for short periods of time. Long-term memory accepts information which it integrates with whatever else is stored through a process of combining the old and new and making a new understanding.

- Writers need to omit needless words and place related words together, in order to compose units of thought appropriate for short-term memory.
- Writers need to compose sentences in particular ways, in order to facilitate an easy transfer of information from short-term to long-term. For example, in a sentence that contains a known fact and a new one, place the new at the end. The known information links to facts already held in memory and brings the new information along with it. The mind can then refigure understanding including the addition. Writers can also similarly link sentences, paragraphs, and sections of reports by having the beginning refer to the same topic as what preceded.
- Writers can facilitate understanding by repeating key phrases in ideas and using parallel structure to present similar ideas. When information moves out of short-term memory and into long-term, it can move about and align itself with any related bit of stored material. Such techniques help the memory make meaningful connections.
- Readers encounter difficulty in understanding when they cannot easily understand the text. For example, if a pronoun antecedent is unclear and can possibly refer to two different nouns or seems not to have a reference, the reader stumbles. A number of stumbles impairs understanding and can drive away the reader.
- Readers make meaning from their own emotional, experiential, and intellectual backgrounds which will not match those of the writer. Therefore, the writer needs to explain and illustrate plentifully so that the reader can understand what is in the writer's mind. The reader then compares and makes meaning out of what is received by processing it with his or her own prior knowledge and background.
- Readers comprehend faster information that is logically organized. Writers, therefore, should consider using patterns of organization like comparison/contrast, cause/effect, least important to most important/vice versa, and chronology to aid understanding by having readers recognize the order and afterward be free to think about meaning. Format can announce organization. A report can use type sizes or kinds to establish a hierarchy of context. An organized presentation of heading can do the same thing. Well-organized documents make for efficient and effective reading.
- Readers also comprehend better when writers correctly signal connections between ideas. Transitions like "in addition," "on the other hand," "consequently," "therefore," "besides," and "nevertheless" prepare the reader to accept correctly what follows. Headings in large reports can do the same thing. Words like "introduction," "background," "experiment," "recommendation," and "summary" signal what the reader should expect. The reader prepares his or her expectation and can more quickly understand information.

Much of the research about writing and reading is very sophisticated and involves a discussion of cognitive thinking, linguistics, and semantic memory. It is obvious that application will take careful composing and will not be realistic for most of what anyone writes every day. For very important writing, it can add to the writer's potential to affect understanding. How interested you become in this subject is yours to decide, but you certainly need to be aware that this research is occurring and that some technical writers will be using it to write more effectively.

To think in a more simple way how reading affects understanding, consider how you read, or do some simple observing of those around you and notice how many of the following habits are practiced:

People begin by looking to see how much has to be read.
Many stop to look at anything in visual form.
Some begin by looking at the beginning of each section and then at the conclusion.
Others pick up a document and start at the beginning and never look ahead to see what is included in the appendices, and so on.
People tend to read first and last entries whether or not they are the first and last paragraphs of the section, the beginning and end of the report, or the first and last sentences in a paragraph.
Most readers, when asked, react negatively to pages crammed full of words with no white space or headings to indicate subject topics.

Such simple observing proves that you cannot write expecting the reader to move sequentially through the text from beginning to end. You recognize the value of presenting information in visual form; know that you need to make first and last entries strong, accurate, and comprehensive; understand that you cannot assume readers will look ahead and discover an illustration or an appendix; and need to format information so pages are easy to read and reference.

Readability Indexes: Another Aid to Revision

Ways exist to measure the reading level of your writing. Readability procedures can be performed manually or by using the computer. *Gunning's Fog Index* is a popular method for manually determining the years of formal schooling required to read information comfortably. It uses the equation $(X + Y) \times (0.4)$. Take any 100-word passage. Determine the average number of words per sentence and enter that number for X; count the number of three-syllable words (exclude capitalized nouns, word combinations like "repairman," and verbs made into three syllables by adding "ed" or "es") and enter that number for Y. Add X and Y and multiply by .4, which gives you the approximate years of schooling and lets you know if the intended audience will be able to understand your writing.

You can also use the computer to determine readability. Writer's Workbench, an AT&T's Unix-based program being tested and refined while this book is being written, has a statistics-gathering component that can tell you what percentage of your sentences are simple or complex and what the length of your average sentence is, as well as compare your vocabulary with its list of familiar words and use these statistics to determine approximately how much education a person needs to understand your writing. IBM's Epistle program has a style component that provides similar checks. At this writing both of these mainframe-origin programs need extensive memory, but the developers expect that to change. It is likely that by the time you read this book, one or both programs will be available on personal computers. If you do not have the opportunity to experiment with such programs, you should at least know about their existence and potential.

A Word of Caution about Using Readability Indexes

Some applications of readability indexes are sensible. For example, you may need to write a manual explaining how to perform a technical procedure to a group who have been tested and whose known reading level is eighth grade. With this knowledge, it would be very helpful, before writing the whole manual, to have the means to test the reading level of a sample you have written. Once you test and know you are writing at the correct level, you can use the sample to imitate and maintain the required style—to sense language limitations and effective sentence structures.

You should, however, use readability indexes cautiously because they tend to reduce writing. Simple sentences become better than complex ones; words of few syllables become better than words of many; short sentences become better than long ones. Writing does not become clearer or easier to understand just because it is simpler. Good and accurate writing comes about when writers say exactly what they intend without the possibility of multiple interpretation and use language that is grammatically correct, precise, and interesting. For the most part, who cares if words have five or two syllables if the language captures the meaning and the reader's imagination? Who can stand the thought of reading an endless string of simple, short sentences? If you think about it, people in science and technology deal with the mysteries of the universe, the future of machines, and the relationships of the earth and man; certainly such thoughts deserve expression that equals their significance.

Certain types of technical writing such as specifications for machinery or procedure manuals rightly require straightforward, simple expression, but consider the larger corpus of technical writing. For the most part, you should use readability indexes sparingly. Be sensible about matching subject matter, expression, and audience. Do not kill an exciting idea by a simple-minded presentation or let the axiom touted so often in technical writing—less is better—cause what you write to be deadly dull.

Rewriting and Word Processing

 From talking with students and other writers and from my own experience, I collected the following thoughts about rewriting and word processing:

1. Rewriting lets people recognize their own thinking processes and sense of options. They gain a sense of their potential as thinkers. Because word processing makes rewriting easier to do, writers try more things than they might manually and thereby stretch themselves mentally to see just how fine they can tune what they are writing.

2. Meaning does not just come. We make it. Word processing assists the writer to make meaning by providing a way to create, combine, rearrange, and revise ideas and collect materials.

3. Learning to rewrite well is an acquired skill. The word processor will not help students who cannot recognize errors or flaws in their writing. It does not by itself discover errors or make people better writers. It is a convenient tool only for those who have ideas about what they want to change in their writing.

4. Screening offers only a limited view. Writers rush to turn thoughts into words before they are lost, and the keyboard is a good facility for doing this. However, one difficulty with composing on a screen may relate to a habit of writers going back and reading what they have written. Scanning is not the same as being able to look back at the same time as writing ahead. Being able to see only a small section of text also makes it difficult to retain control over the developing ideas.

5. Word processing helps develop or expand ideas. When the teacher or another critic marks a draft or says in a conference that an idea needs to be expanded, word processing allows you to go back and add, leave the text for a while, go back and say a bit more, wait, go back and insert some more. It is always possible to reform and cause the document to accept the additional text without having to retype from the start each time.

Word Processing Functions Useful in Rewriting

The following functions are common to good word processing programs. To find out which ones are available in the program you are using and how to enact them, consult the user's manual, the program's help screens, or the lab instructor.

1. *Scroll.* Rewriting means rereading. In order to read what you have written, you need to "scroll" or move the text forward or backward. Think of what you have written as appearing on a continuous roll of paper. The scroll command rolls the text past the screen so you can read it. Different programs have different options:

   - You can move up or down manually through the text one line at a time.
   - You can set a command for continuous scrolling and have the program automatically reveal text, a line at a time, the new lines appearing at the bottom of the screen.
   - You can scroll at different speeds so you can read very slowly or rapidly.
   - You can scroll back and forth a screen at a time. The continuous scrolling command will continuously move the text a screen at a time until you decide to stop.
   - You can scroll horizontally in order to read wide documents.

2. *Delete and Insert.* A lot of rewriting has to do with crossing out and adding words or figures. The word processing commands of *delete* and *insert* allow you to do so with less trouble than ever before. You can delete a letter, a word, a part of a line, an entire line, or a paragraph. You can add the same. In fact,

you can add as much as you need, wherever you need it, as long as you have disk space.

3. *Print or Copy a File.* Your written document is called a "file." When you begin to rewrite, what you delete is gone forever unless you make a printout of the original or make a backup copy of the file. Having a backup is a good idea because you do not always like what you have rewritten. You may prefer the first way of saying something. Be sure you have a way back to it.

   To see the whole, you need a printout. With word processing, you see only a screen of text at a time. For long documents, you need to see the text together to check for transitions, logic, completeness, continuity, consistency, and format.

4. *Move Blocks of Text.* We all know about cutting and pasting as a way of rewriting. We decide that a sentence or group of words will fit better somewhere else, so we cut the text apart and paste or tape it together in a new order. Word processing makes moving blocks of text easy. Depending on your program, you can move a block of text from one place in the file to another and either delete the text from its original place or leave it there for comparison. After you decide exactly where you want the text to be, you can delete the unwanted block.

   Some programs allow you to move text from the file you are using to a different file or move text from a different file to the one you are now in. Since files are usually no longer than 20 pages, this function allows you to "cut and paste" text anywhere within a document written on several or many files.

5. *Find and Replace Commands.* Sometimes in rewriting, you will decide to replace, with a better term, a word often used in the text, or you may discover that an often-repeated term is misspelled. Word processing lets you make such a change easily. Given the right command, the computer will ask what word you want replaced, what word should be substituted, and then search the file in order to find and replace all occurrences of the term.

6. *Reform Paragraphs.* Rewriting with a typewriter means retyping because the text gets out of line—individual lines and pages become too short or long; the page numbers are no longer correct. Word processing takes care of all that and more. Depending on the program, you can reform from single spacing to double spacing, from a justified right margin to a ragged one, and from narrow columns to wide lines without retyping.

7. *Format.* Part of rewriting involves arranging information on the page and deciding what will be capitalized, underlined, centered, and so forth. Once you make these decisions, the delete/insert command lets you move through the text and make items alike that should be alike. Other commands center text, underline it, print in boldface or italics, or give a number of other options.

Knowing When to Use Word Processing Functions for Rewriting

You use the same principles to rewrite whether you use a pencil and paper, a typewriter, or a word processor. You cut out unnecessary material, add where ideas are not fully expressed, reorganize because something is difficult to understand—is not in the correct order—is not presented logically. Everything you know about writing from taking other courses and experience, you apply to writing with a word processor. The writing process is no different. Only the technology has improved.

Student Example

This draft is number four of the example you read on pages 80 and 81. In the second and third drafts, Terry and I worked together on language and style, but mainly on saying things completely and clearly. The convenience of word processing occurred in several ways:

1. *Made Multiple Copies.* Multiple copies could be printed so that each of us could have a copy to edit.
2. *Reformed Paragraphs and Renumbered Pages without Retyping.* Terry did not mind trying something new because if we chose to change or eliminate it later, word processing allowed him to reform paragraphs and pages and to renumber pages without having to retype. He also made a copy of his original file, so that he could go back to that version if he wanted to later.
3. *Removed and Reformed Pages without Retyping.* If we could not decide between two words or ideas, we could leave both in because later we could remove one and reform the page without retyping.
4. *Flagged Words, Ideas, and Sentences.* We could flag words, ideas, and sentences we were unhappy with or unsure of by typing ... or /// before and after them. Again, we could do this because Terry would not have to retype a whole page or pages for the final document.
5. *Made Revisions without Retyping.* With the proposal typed into the computer, Terry did not have to start from scratch every time he sat down to type a revision. He was making only those changes that he had agreed should be made, and so he did not resent the time. Without word processing, a lot of time would have been wasted retyping sections that had no changes.
6. *Skipped over Sections without Affecting Pagination and Spacing.* Terry was free to skip over sections he was not prepared to write or could not improve at the moment. He could type an * or leave a couple of lines. He did not worry about how this would mess up pagination or space within the document. Once he went back and wrote the section, he could use the reform command and the document would be reshaped correctly.

Final Draft:

TECHNICAL APPROACH

II. PROBLEM DEFINITION

At the present time, Company A is supplied child-resistant closures by a single company, Company B, in Covington, Kentucky. Having only one source for the closures is a potential problem for Company A. If their current supplier stops production for any reason, including a strike, Company A will not receive the needed closures and will not be able to continue processing products requiring child-resistant closures. Sales will suffer, and losses will occur. For this reason, Company

A is looking for a company to design an alternate closure that will be available in case Company B does not or cannot deliver.

The problems in selecting and approving an alternate company and closure are that the company must demonstrate reliability to match Company B's, and the closure must be comparable to Company B's and pass both federal and Company A's standards.

To be comparable, the alternate closure must be 33 millimeters in diameter and 14 millimeters in height. It must be comparable in design. Company B's closure is made of two different parts, an inner section which fits inside an outer shell. This closure is removed by a top lug system. One pushes down and twists at the same time. When one pushes down, the lugs of the outer shell engage the lugs of the inner section. Locking the two sets of lugs causes both sections to move together, allowing the closure to be removed. When one twists but does not push down, the lugs of the outer shell skip over the inner section lugs, producing a clicking sound but no locking. The closure is not removed.

Terry Beck, project coordinator, will run Company C's closure through a series of performance tests. Based upon the data found in these tests, he will recommend whether or not Company C's closure should be submitted to Company A's Product Development Department for further testing.

Comments On Student's Rewriting

The final draft is better stated than the first and is better organized. For example, the opening paragraph is more accurate and gives more information than the first draft. Paragraph 2 clearly states the problem. Paragraph 3 sets specifications. The paragraphing and topic sentences signal content and make the section easier to read than the first draft.

Practice Exercises

1. Use the checklist on pages 82 and 83 to guide your revision of a document you are now revising or will revise in the future.

2. Keep all the writing (from beginning to end) that you do for a certain paper, including the notes you scribble at first—everything. After your final revision, analyze the stages of rewriting. How many steps were involved in writing this paper? What was accomplished in each step? What kinds of changes occurred at each rewriting? How do you actually revise? As you read from the beginning to the end of the paper, do you look for one thing? Do you revise some other less organized way? How much better do you think the paper is as a result of rewriting? Hand the analysis in with the paper, or bring it to a teacher/ student conference and use it as a basis of discussion about the value of rewriting, or use it to contribute to a class discussion on the value of rewriting.

3. If you have a word processing program available that will check style, run such a program on one of your papers. Write a summary of the kinds of stylistic problems flagged by the program. What is your main problem according to the program? Do you find places where you disagree with the style checker? If so, where and why? If you have available grammar check or spell check programs, do the same analysis with them. Use the summary to learn

about your writing and/or to be the basis of a discussion with your teacher. How can problems be corrected?

4. If you have word processing available, write a paper using it to build a text and make revisions throughout the writing, rewriting process.

5. After the first draft, try rewriting first for content and organization and later for language, punctuation, and grammar. What does this do for the quality of your rewriting? Does it keep you from believing that you have rewritten just because you have changed some words? Does it force you to make larger, more serious revisions?

6. If you have word processing available, sometime in the quarter or semester after you have used it to write and rewrite several times, write an analysis of how you believe word processing affects your writing process. What does composing directly onto the screen do for your writing? What problems does it give you as a writer? Ignore the obvious like being able to insert and delete. Tell if word processing actually causes you to try more things and therefore stretch yourself as a writer. Use the analysis for class discussion.

7. Select a paragraph from a recent technical paper you have written. Write the grade level of people who you think could understand the writing. Use the *Gunning's Fog Index* (p. 85) to check the difference between your expectation and what the index shows.

8. Choose a reading level for a writing assignment. For example, write a procedure that could be performed correctly by anyone with a sixth-grade education.

9. Try to guess the reading level of a paragraph in a scientific or engineering journal; in a popular science magazine; in a newspaper article about a technical subject; in your college textbook for science, engineering, computing science, or another subject. Check your guesses with the *Fog Index*. After determining the levels of each paragraph, decide what makes the difference. Go further than just saying vocabulary or sentence length. What particularly is different about language? Is it merely short words or more than that? What about organization?

10. If you have access to an outline program, use it to plan a future technical assignment. Practice filling in major steps, going back and writing ideas to develop those steps, collapsing the outline to see only the major steps. Explore the program's capabilities. See for yourself how being able to call up the major outline helps you to concentrate and stay on the subject. It serves as a map of both what you have written and what you are going to write. See the advantage of being able to fill out or subtract from the outline and yet keep it neat and readable. Hand in your work with the outline program as one example of your steps in writing.

11. If you do not have an outline program available at school, go to your favorite computer store and ask for a demonstration. Ask if you may try the program yourself. You may be able to try several different programs and compare their features. While there, inquire about the latest trends in word processing. What is new and exciting?

Chapter 6

Final Editing for Style and Format

Options Increased with Word Processing

No one waits until the final rewrite to make all decisions about style and format. Many decisions are determined by organizational choices made early in the writing process. Others, such as deciding how to present headings within a chapter, deciding how to handle paragraphing, whether to use standard tabs, are properly made as the writing develops through drafts. To delay choosing style and format means having to retype many similar items to make them appear alike. But the time comes when either you have worked the document over to your satisfaction or the schedule demands that you stop rewriting and prepare the document for presentation. Before starting to type the final draft, stop and consider what you can do to make the document attractive and easier to read and more accurate. Your options are more limited with a typewriter than with a word processor, but make the best use of whatever equipment is available. This chapter talks generally about style and format edits, then specifically identifies format options commonly available through typewriting and word processing.

Editing for Style

Anything you do to make your text not dull but inviting increases the chance of catching the reader's attention. It is a blow to the writer to think that after working hard to research, organize, write, and rewrite a substantial document, the reader is not eagerly looking forward to reading it—perhaps even dreads having to go through it—or, more commonly, needs and wants to understand the information but sees the report as just one more thing to work into an already impossible schedule. As a technical writer, you must expect this. People in business and industry are busy. Their day begins early, is filled with phone calls, meetings, and tasks to be completed. Make the report as accurate and error-free as possible. The reader will read with less resistance.

Check Content and Language

When you check the content and language of your document, the goal is to divorce yourself from it and read as if you were the reader. Where are you confused? bored? turning back and forth to put ideas together? asking yourself questions? Read aloud if possible. Cut unnecessary words and sentences that are redundant. Reword to avoid sexist language. Substitute other words for ones overused. Select words carefully. They are not interchangeable, even if they have similar meanings. Each word has its own peculiar and distinctive shade of meaning. Your writing will have force and lucidity if you choose exactly the right word from the wide range of possibilities our language offers. A sound editing approach is to look for or choose plain, simple words rather than long, ornate ones. As a reading public, we admire plain language. We find it more direct, persuasive, strong, and beautiful.

Check for consistency in verb tenses, person, and pronoun references. Writers normally write a section of a report at a time. They rewrite throughout the whole writing process. This approach refines, expands, and improves the quality of content, but often throws style out of kilter. A final reading to evaluate how the parts make a whole and to "hear" the language for elegance, simplicity, clarity, and correctness will add to the effectiveness of your work.

Write concisely. Call objects, actions, and results by their proper names. A cell is not a "thing." The failed experiment is not a "flop" that went "haywire." It failed because an element of the experiment did not work. Identify precisely the element and the condition.

Most of us use shortened forms of words or terms particular to our professions when we talk with other professionals or write informally, but avoid such jargon or slang in formal writing. When using jargon, you assume, often incorrectly, that readers understand the language in the same way you do. This is not always so.

Pay attention to paragraph construction. Every report should have a stated purpose. Every paragraph in the report should be about that purpose. Check each paragraph. Does it have a clear topic sentence? Does the paragraph relate to the report's stated purpose? If it does not, then delete it or rewrite the purpose to include all that you write about. After checking to see if every paragraph is related to the paper's purpose, check that *every* sentence in each paragraph relates to the paragraph's topic/purpose sentence. Are there sentences on other subjects? Are there sentences on the subject, but they do not add to the topic? Remove all such sentences. Either place them in a new paragraph with an appropriate topic/purpose sentence or delete them entirely. Such precision makes writing sound like a mechanical activity. It is not, but neither is it loose, carefree, or impulsive. You cannot go wherever your thoughts happen to wander. Good technical writing needs to be disciplined and to the point. Only careful proofreading will guarantee nothing extra or unnecessary.

Whenever possible, use the active rather than passive voice. Active is more direct and economical; it clearly identifies the person or thing responsible for the action.

Active Voice

actor   action   recipient of action (It is clear who did what.)

I   made an error in your estimate.

↑   ↑   ↑

subject   verb   object

Passive Voice

recipient action

An   error   was made in the estimate. (It is not clear who made the error.)

↑   ↑

subject verb

Combine sentences to tighten your writing, to connect independent and dependent clauses so sentences establish correct relationships and read more easily. Four strategies are used to combine sentences: adding, deleting, embedding, and transforming. Examples of each follow:

1. *Addition.* Connect sentence elements with commas or semicolons and either coordinate or subordinate conjunctions.
   Original sentences:

   The dimples are much smaller than those of most golf balls. The dimples are cut much shallower than those on any other balls. These two features allow the Pinnacle to cut the wind and help the ball to carry farther.

   Sentences combined and sentence elements connected:

   The dimples on the Pinnacle golf ball are much smaller and shallower than those on other balls; these features let the ball cut the wind and travel farther. (semicolon)

   The dimples on the Pinnacle golf ball are much smaller and shallower than those on other balls, but these features let the ball cut the wind and travel farther. (comma and coordinate conjunction)

   The dimples on the Pinnacle golf ball are much smaller and shallower than those on the other balls; however, these features let the ball cut the wind and travel farther. (semicolon and conjunctive adverb)

Original sentences:

The quality of the set made the play. It gave the play realism and warmth.

Sentences combined and sentence elements connected:

The quality of the set gave the play realism and warmth; it made the play.

2. *Deletion.* Eliminate unnecessary or repetitious words or phrases.
   Original sentences:

   Until 1968, there were two high schools serving the aforementioned communities. There were Thebes High School and, of course, Tamms High School.

   Sentences combined and unnecessary elements deleted:

   Until 1968, two high schools, Thebes High School and Tamms High School, served the aforementioned communities.

   Original sentences:

   Titleist, one of the biggest names in golf equipment, has produced a product that has become far superior to the competition. This product, known as the Pinnacle, has been very profitable for the company.

   Sentences combined and unnecessary elements deleted:

   Titleist, a big name in golf equipment, has produced a product called Pinnacle that is very profitable for the company and competitive with the competition.

3. *Embedding.* Place elements of one sentence within another sentence.
   Original sentences:

   There is a bill before the Congress that would raise the speed limit across the nation. The bill is being supported by the trucking industry and consumers who are pressuring the legislators and Transportation Department to increase the speed limit.

   Sentences combined and elements of one sentence embedded in another sentence:

   A bill, supported by the trucking industry and many consumers, is before Congress to raise the speed limit on the nation's highways.

4. *Transformation.* Change the form and order of words, phrases, even clauses.
   Original sentences:

Micheal realized he had no clear audience in mind. He decided to write to a young person who likes science but has no formal scientific learning.

Sentences combined by changing the form and order of sentence elements:

Realizing he had no clear audience in mind, Micheal decided to write to a young person who likes science but has no formal scientific learning.

Writing Samples

The following excerpts from student writing illustrate various principles of good writing. They can suggest patterns for development or ways to organize or express yourself.

Sample 1: Relates the unfamiliar to the familiar for better understanding:

Organelles, called mitochondria, act as power plants providing all the energy the cell needs in order to function properly. In real cities, many power plants burn coal in order to make electricity. In mitochondria, a substance called APT (a complex chemical produced by cells called adenosine triphosphate) is burned to provide energy that the cell can use. If a cell were without these little powerhouses, it would be much like a city in the middle of a blackout. Nothing could be done because there would be no power for the rest of the city to use. (Karie Dasenbrock)

Sample 2: Uses narrative and a dramatic tone to involve and interest the reader:

Imagine yourself in a classroom on the day of a big test. You get out two pencils, walk to the front of the room, and take your place in line at the pencil sharpener. When it is finally your turn, you put a pencil in the slot and find that the sharpener is full of shavings. You instinctively remove the container portion and empty the shaving into the trash can. The container is replaced; you sharpen your pencils and start this whole wasteful process over again.

After watching this dreadful occurrence again and again, in classroom after classroom, I feel I can hold my tongue no longer. I must tell of the incredible injustice going on around the world. Beautiful trees that are totally defenseless are giving their lives only to end up as shavings in a trash can. I ask you, must this meaningless killing go on? I say no! This is why after great consideration, I have come up with a few ideas to end the massacre or at least keep trees from dying in vain. (Troy Coker)

Sample 3: Uses effectively the pattern of comparison and contrast to make a point:

A long time ago in a galaxy far, far away, a great adventure took place. Not so long ago in Washington, D.C., an interesting proposal was brought forth. By coincidence, both of these items have the same name, "Star Wars." In the adventure, Luke Skywalker and his friends battled forces beyond comprehension. In the proposal, Ronald Reagan and Congress outlined a defense system that was fantastic in its scope. The futuristic weapons of science-fiction fantasies have been or may soon be realized.

In "Star Wars," the Death Star is a weapon capable of destroying entire planets. Weapons of this type are not uncommon to our world. Ever since World War II, we have had weapons that could end life as we know it on this planet. Since we do not have a Luke Skywalker, who will come to our rescue? That's right! Ronald Reagan will.

The threat of the Death Star was brought to an end by a laser bolt from Luke Skywalker's spaceship. Ron has his lasers too which are equally capable of ending the "Death Star-type" threat of nuclear weaponry. The first is a chemical-based laser which focuses beams of light by using chemical gases such as hydrogen fluoride. Ron's lasers created by this process would punch through steel walls faster than Luke's could cut through Imperial Stormtroopers. (Kevin Kent)

Sample 4: Uses a clear topic/purpose sentence to begin a tightly developed paragraph:

A solution to the loose mold problem is important to Company X. The varying widths of the ingots means that the molds will have to be changed when an ingot of a different width is needed. For this reason an easily accessible and safe means of changing and tightening the mold is needed. A loose mold can result in casting an ingot with a hump, one that is bowed, or one that is cracked. An ingot with any of these flaws will have to be scrapped, melted down, and then cast again. Company X has estimated that the problems associated with the present clamp cost the company almost $7,000 a week, or about $350,000 a year. These figures illustrate the importance of solving this problem. (Kevin Sexton)

Sample 5: Communicates through example:

Besides the characteristic of being "wet," water also has a very high heat capacity (the ability to hold a high level of heat). Water's ability to hold heat is a positive factor that contributes to the life of organisms as well as to the environment. All organisms contain water which enables them to function in hot climates without being continually burned by the heat of the sun. For example, it is possible for a person on a hot summer day to place one's hand on a black car and not be burned. Two main factors prevent this from happening: heat and molecular motion—the theory that all particles of matter are in constant motion. Imagine that the tiny particles in motion are like the bumper cars at an amusement park. They buzz around in every direction, constantly colliding with all of the other cars they meet. When the driver adds power to the car by pushing down on the accelerator, the car goes faster. Consequently, the driver is able to have more collisions in a shorter period of time. When heat is added to the particles, they move faster. In the example of the person putting one's hand onto a hot car, the heat is added to the person's hand causing the particles to move faster. They bump into each other and into the hydrogen bonds holding the water molecules together. Eventually the collisions cause the hydrogen bonds to break. Most of the heat absorbed into the person's hand is used to increase the molecular motion and break the hydrogen bonds of the water instead of raising the temperature of one's hand. This does not mean that one will not feel heat in his hand, nor does it mean that people can go around touching hot objects without being burned. But without the presence of water in our bodies to absorb heat, we could not so much as walk outside on a hot day, for the sun would raise the temperature of our bodies to an extent that could be fatal. (Cindy Weiss)

Sample 6: Uses comparison and humor to make a point:

I feel that people should take any kind of music for its real purpose: to be enjoyed and appreciated, not analyzed and digested. For example, two lovers go walking in the woods late one November night. They look up at the sky and see the sparkling of the stars and the comforting flow of moonbeams to earth. They sense the beauty of the moment and the heavens above them. Then out of nowhere, the young man begins to explain the reason the moon reflects the sun's light rays, that stars are actually sources of hydrogen and helium fusion which cause the solar winds, that the galaxy we live in is nothing but a normal-sized mass of stars rotating outwardly in the cosmos due to some law of astrophysics. No longer would the night sky be relaxing and beautiful to the two lovers. It would become a confusing mass of data, frightening in its presence. Such is the same for modern music. If people could just take the songs for what they really are and not analyze them, maybe the music could fulfill the "true" purpose it was written for: to ease and relax the people who listen to and enjoy its sound. (Micheal Bennett)

Check for Proofreading Errors

Your writing and your image as a writer can be marred by mistakes that you fail to discover and that consequently appear in the finished document.

The good advice on the facing page from Carolyn Boccella Bagin, managing editor, and Jo Van Doren, production coordinator, of *Simply Stated* is a guide for both proofreading and developing good habits that will reduce future errors.

Editing for Format

To format is to arrange information on the page. Margins, spacing, indentation, typeface, headings, enumeration, paragraphing, capitalization, punctuation, page numbering, graphics, illustrations, white space, and division of report sections are elements you can order. No format standard exists. Companies often issue their own requirements. Writers often develop their own preferences and become known by their style. Notice what pleases you in others' work. Imitate, alter, become visually aware of this nonwriting aspect of revision.

Why Bother to Format? Isn't Good Writing Enough?

Teachers used to answer this question by talking about the benefit of showing pride in your work and explaining that a well-presented document reflects a care-

How can you produce error-free copy?

- Never proofread your own copy by yourself. You'll tire of looking at the document in its different stages of development and you'll miss new errors.

(If you must proof your own copy, make a line screen for yourself or roll the paper back in the typewriter so that you view only one line at a time. This will reduce your tendency to skim your material.)

- Read everything in the copy straight through from beginning to end: titles, subtitles, sentences, punctuation, capitalizations, indented items, and page numbers.
- Read your copy backward to catch spelling errors. Reading sentences out of sequence lets you concentrate on individual words.
- Consider having proofreaders initial the copy they check. You might find that your documents will have fewer errors.
- If you have a helper to proof numbers that are in columns, read the figures aloud to your partner, and have your partner mark the corrections and changes on the copy being proofread.
- If time allows, put your material aside for a short break. Proofreading can quickly turn into reading if your document is long. After a break, reread the last few lines to refresh your memory.
- Read the pages of a document out of order. Changing the sequence will help you to review each page as a unit.
- List the errors you spot over a month's time. You may find patterns that will catch your attention when you proofread your next document.
- If you can, alter your routine. Don't proofread at the same time every day. Varying your schedule will help you approach your task with a keener eye.
- Not everyone knows and uses traditional proofreading marks. But a simple marking system should be legible and understandable to you and to anyone else working on the copy.

Where do errors usually hide?

- Mistakes tend to cluster. If you find one typo, look carefully for another one nearby.
- Inspect the beginning of pages, paragraphs, and sections. Some people tend to skim these crucial spots.
- Beware of changes in typeface—especially in headings or titles. If you change to all uppercase letters, italics, boldface, or underlined copy, read those sections again.
- Make sure your titles, subtitles, and page numbers match those in the table of contents.
- Read sequential material carefully. Look for duplications in page numbers or in lettered items in lists or outlines.
- Double-check references such as, "see the chart below." Several drafts later, the chart may be pages away from its original place.
- Examine numbers and totals. Recheck all calculations and look for misplaced commas and decimal points.
- Scrutinize features that come in sets, such as brackets, parentheses, quotation marks, and dashes.

April 1986. *Simply Stated* (Document Design Center, American Institutes for Research) 65:1–3.

fulness that prompts readers to anticipate a well-written one. Such thoughts are still valid, but the simple truth is that the electric typewriter and the word processor have made an attractive and neat document expected. Anything less is unacceptable. Furthermore, today's readers are visually sophisticated because of television, movies, advertising, and magazine layouts. To be impressive, you must go further, do things better, or be more creative than others. When preparing a document with desktop technology, you can benefit from developing the eye of a good typesetter and designer.

The following discussion is limited to the layout of information. To read about the preparation and use of graphics and illustrations, see Chapter 7. To learn the formal elements of particular reports, see Chapters 9, 10, and 11.

Format Tips

1. Set up 1-inch margins all around unless the report will be bound. If so, leave a 2-inch margin on the left.

2. Format to reflect organization. As the writer, you see in your mind the logic and flow of the report and understand relations among its parts. The reader does not bring to the report the same understanding. If the report is of any length, it can be particularly difficult to keep the whole and its parts in mind. Headings and enumeration are two effective elements that both break up and relate parts of the document. It may not be a compliment, but it is a fact that many readers do not effectively concentrate on and absorb long passages. Knowing this, you increase your chances of being read and understood if you visually disrupt the regularity of line after line of text.

Headings

- Keep headings short and informative. Later in this chapter, I have two headings: "To Format with a Typewriter" and "To Format with a Word Processor." If I had said just "To Format" for both or introduced the first with "Typewriter" and the second with "Word Processor," the reader could not glance at the page and know the content of the paragraph or that I had divided format possibilities by the equipment used.
- Make headings inclusive. Headings are helpful in the first reading but equally important as references. When the reader first goes through the material, headings are like signposts telling where one is and is going. If a section covers drilling and completion of oil wells and the heading mentions only drilling, you have not adequately informed the reader. Such a heading is also not helpful for referencing. Readers often need to find information they read earlier in a report. They search a text by glancing at chapter titles, headings, and subheadings. If these are misleading or missing, the document is not easy to use. Technical documents especially should be simple to reference.
- Arrange headings by rank and use enumeration, capitalization, different types, or other elements to indicate different rankings. To subordinate by visualization, you could make major topics in full capitals, sub-topics with only the initial letters capitalized, and sub-topics to sub-topics in lowercase but underlined.
- Make headings of like value parallel. For example, if you write the first major heading—action verb, object, modifier—write all major headings grammatically the same. If you make the first heading of a certain rank a noun, make all other headings of that rank nouns.

Enumeration

- A numbering system visually displays the structure of the paper. A glance at the table of contents or through the report itself lets the reader sense the organization and plan. If the work appears well thought out, the reader is more willing to enter into the reading. A jumbled, unsystematic structure or no indication of structure discourages the reader from going further unless one absolutely must.
- An outline notation is one enumeration system used for marking divisions of your paper. Two systems exist, the Roman numeral-letter-Arabic and the decimal. One is as good as the other, but you should not mix the two. If your readers will refer often to different parts of the report and ask others as well to turn to or read certain sections, then the decimal system is probably the easier to reference.

The Roman Numeral-Letter-Arabic Numeral System

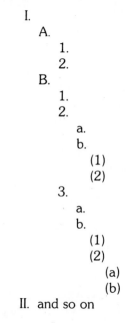

I.
  A.
    1.
    2.
  B.
    1.
    2.
      a.
      b.
        (1)
        (2)
    3.
      a.
      b.
        (1)
        (2)
          (a)
          (b)
II. and so on

The Decimal System

1.0
  1.1
    1.1.1
    1.1.2
  1.2
    1.2.1.
    1.2.2.
      1.2.2.1.
      1.2.2.2.
        1.2.2.2.1.
        1.2.2.2.2.
2.0 and so on

- To ensure the correct presentation of outline enumeration, abide by the following rules:

  a. Make at least two parts in each division. This means that if you have a point A, you should have a B. This principle applies to every level of division. The reason is a logical one. Unless a point can be divided, keep the information as one point. If a point can be divided, it has to have at least two parts.

  b. Arrange the notation on the page to show the relation and subordination of parts to other parts. Use capitalization, lettering, numbering, punctuation, indentation, and spacing to show how parts relate to each other and the general outline. Be consistent in use. If you double-space between items noted by capital letters, do so each time; if you capitalize the first letter in each word of items noted by 1., 2., or use all capitals for items noted by Roman numerals, do so each time.

  c. State items under like notations in the same grammatical way. For example, if you make the first statement following a Roman numeral a complete sentence, make all other items following Roman numerals complete sentences. If you make the first item following a small alphabetic letter a phrase that begins with an action verb ("determine"), make all items in that section begin and be structured the same way.

3. Break up the page with short paragraphs, headings, graphic elements, lists, white space, anything to shatter the impact of page after page of solid text.

4. Make spacing consistent. If the report is typed single space, double-space between paragraphs, above and below headings, lists, long quotations, graphics, and other items integrated into the text. If the report is typed double space with indented paragraphs, do not triple-space between paragraphs but triple-space above headings and above and below items integrated into the text; if not indenting, triple-space between paragraphs.

5. Distinguish items in a list by either Arabic numerals (1, 2) or typographical elements such as a + or -- or ● or *. Numerals are often used if there is a sequence or if items in the list may be referred to later. Various other symbols are suitable if the list has no sequence.

6. Use typographical elements to emphasize words, phrases, and sentences. Underlining, full capitals, double-striking, and italics are some useful devices, but be careful not to overdo.

7. Enclose graphics and illustrations in boxes.

8. Select a clear type. Some typewriters and word processing programs allow you to select typeface designs. When choosing type, think about the beauty of its form, its distinct personality, its appropriateness for the document, and its legibility. Whether or not to use serif typefaces is a common question. Serifs are the extenders on the bottoms and tops of letters. See facing page. Some people feel that serifs clutter the line; others believe that the serif leads the reader's eye to the next letter. Whatever style you prefer is fine, but you probably should not mix the two. Think about the weight of the type. Too thin or too thick makes the text hard to read.

serif

sans serif

9. Number pages consistently. Short reports have little prefatory material and use Arabic numbers in one continuous series from the first page to the last. Place these numbers at the upper right-hand corner or centered near the bottom of the page.

One convention for numbering long reports is to count the title page as page i, without numbering it, and number all prefatory pages up to and including the table of contents and abstract with small Roman numerals (i, ii, iii, iv, etc.). Begin using Arabic numbers with the first page of the report and continue in one continuous series to the end. Appendixes may continue with the Arabic numbers or have a distinctive numbering series, such as Appendix A (A1, A2, A3, etc.) or Appendix B (B1, B2, etc.) and so forth. One advantage of this choice is that the reader can quickly separate the different appendixes. The writer can also update or change them without having to renumber the primary text. For material in the appendix that is reproduced from another text and therefore carries its own page number, type the report's page number underneath.

10. Take care of all details. Use 8½ × 11-inch plain, white paper, heavy enough to make a crisp imprint. Do not use onionskin or cheap, thin paper. Use a good typewriter or printer ribbon. If you are going to submit copies, use the best reproduction process available. Do not settle for smudged, uneven, hard-to-read copies.

To Format with a Typewriter

Your main options with a typewriter are capitals, underlining, centering, boldface, and indentation. The typewriter available to you affects the ease of using the options and the degree of creativity. Your object is to create a pleasing and efficient page. The criteria for that are personal. Begin by doing some "roughs"; experiment with page layouts to decide how centering, headings, underlining, capitalization, numbering, and indenting can help present information clearly and also make a good-looking page. Become aware of others' work. What do they do that you like? How can you adapt that to your presentation style?

When working with a typewriter, you primarily try to think of ways to vary the presentation of line after line of typing. Some people choose to paragraph often in order to break up the page; others begin new chapters or sections halfway down the page to let the eye rest; they space between copy and graphics or tables to create openness; they convert any text possible into lists, charts, tables, or graphs. You can overdo these choices until the whole manuscript is filled with white space or looks like a series of lists. Be sensible. Create variety, but retain the look of a serious, substantial report. For example, I could have chosen to list the items in this paragraph. The first sentence could have read the same: "When working with a typewriter you primarily try to think of ways to vary the presentation of line after line of typing." I then could have indented and listed the ideas:

- Some people choose to paragraph . . .
- Others begin new chapters . . .
- They space between copy . . .

I decided not to do this, however, because I had just formatted a long list of "Format Tips" prior to this section.

Depending on your equipment, time, and talent with the typewriter, you can create some special effects:

Change the print wheel from pica type to elite or script for typing material like a quotation, or the identifying information for a graph, table, or illustration.

Double-strike manually a word or phrase for emphasis.

Change ribbons for different colors to vary chapter titles, or headings, even crucial words.

Underline for emphasis.

Tab to indicate subordination. Space right a set number to subordinate an idea, to type information under a heading, to support an outline, or to separate items in a list. (Some typewriters have automatic tab settings that allow you to use indentation easily. If you have such a capability, explore ways to break up space.)

Center for the most emphasis. Some typewriters have automatic centering. What you type remains hidden until you type the correct code. The typewriter then figures the correct spacing and types the line perfectly centered.

To Format with a Word Processor

Everything you do with a typewriter can be done more easily with a word processor, and you can do more. Centering, setting margins, tabbing, changing line spacing, and underlining are automatically accomplished with the right commands. By turning the "justification" off or on, you can have a ragged right margin or a straight one, which gives a typeset appearance. Hanging indentation lets you type any number of lines, indent a certain number of spaces, type using the new indentation, indent again, and continue typing, always moving the left margin to reflect organization, outlining, or subordination.

Word processing allows you to type multiple columns with adjustable gutters (the space between columns). The columns look as if they have been typeset. To such pages, add illustrations, graphics, line and box drawing, shading to highlight text, ruled lines of varying thickness, and you really become a designer as well as a writer. When creating columns, remember to set enough white space between columns to keep the eye from crossing over to the next column when reading. Remember also not to let white space just make holes in the text. Use it to frame graphics, separate topics, or create a visually handsome page.

The following layouts only begin to suggest the number of alternatives you have available as you format text with a good word processing program. You need to know that most programs have a preset or default page format: the line height and paper length and top and bottom margins are determined for an 8½ × 11-inch page, and, unless altered, they will print as preset. Changing the default format is fairly easy to learn. (See following page formats.)

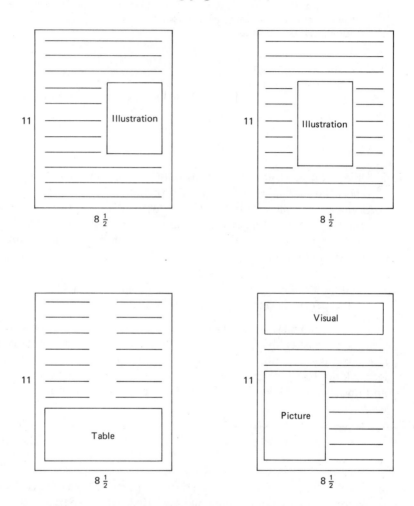

Your printer dramatically affects the preparation of your manuscript. Laser printers are more flexible than daisy-wheel printers. You need to investigate and learn what your printer can and cannot do. Printer capabilities such as the following suggest what is possible now. Other wonders will be available in the future.

1. Boldface type, single and double underlining, and double-striking call attention to altered text.
2. Overprinting lets you correctly accent foreign words (Fabergé) and show deletions ("Printing options ~~really~~ dramatically set apart preparing a text with word processing.") The crossing-out can also be done with slashes ("~~slashes~~").

3. Superscripts, subscripts, and condensed and expanded print ease creating mathematical notations or coefficients of a series.

> In the last sum, $\phi(k)$ occurs once and only once for each positive multiple of k which is less than or equal to n. The lemma follows.
>
> To complete the solution, observe that $S(n)$ is a subset of $\{1, 2, \ldots, 2n\}$. Also, it is a simple matter to show that $[2n/k] - 2[n - k]$ equals 0, if the fractional part of n/k is less than ½, and equals 1, otherwise. Thus,

←condensed print

expanded print   *←regular print*

$$\sum_{k \in S(n)} \phi(k) = \sum_{k=1}^{2n} ([2n/k] - 2[n/k])\phi(k)$$

$$= \sum_{k=1}^{2n} \phi(k)[2n/k] - 2 \sum_{k=1}^{n} \phi(k)[n/k)]$$

$$= \frac{(2n)(2n + 1)}{2} - n(n + 1) = n^2$$

4. Different type sizes allow you to print chapter titles and headings in sizes that reflect the hierarchy of thought and organization.
5. Some printers allow you to stop in order to alter type styles or size. For example, you may want to type the identifying information for a table in italics or in a smaller type size. All is possible with the right printer and commands.
6. A color printer lets you print titles or illustrations or tables in different colors. They stand out from the color used for the primary text.
7. Integrated software lets you insert graphics into your text and have them printed on the page without the old cut-and-paste manual method.

To format with word processing can be both fun and practical. It takes some practice to master the unusual techniques, but they soon become quite simple. Discipline yourself not to be "cute" or too fancy once you are skilled with the technology. Remember always to format so information becomes easier to read and understand. Make the page pleasing to the eye but in a refined, professional way.

Practice Exercises

1. Evaluate the format of one of your past papers. What is good? What could be better, given the equipment you have? Redesign the paper and reprint or retype it. Share your analysis with your teacher or the class.
2. If word processing or a page processing program is available, find out how much it will do. Practice doing it. Apply the capabilities to a paper you are writing. Include a summary explaining your format decisions.
3. Review the points made about headings (p. 100). Take one of your or someone else's papers that used headings and evaluate them. Which are good? poor? why? Rewrite the poor ones. The class may work on the same document. If so, class members can compare their evaluations with others. How and why do you agree or disagree?

4. If you have a good word processing program and a good printer or a sophisticated typewriter, have fun. Decide how boldface type, printer colors, page layouts in columns, whatever, can give your document readability and a professionally printed look.

5. Assume that you are to write a technical paper in one of your courses or select a paper you have already written that does not use outline notation. Outline by either the Roman numeral or decimal system (pp. 101, 102). Decide if the outline clarifies the text, making it easier to refer to and read, or if it clutters and distracts. Share your findings in writing or orally with your group, the class, or the teacher.

6. Use the list of proofreaders' marks on page 108 to mark the mistakes on the copy that follows. Afterward, compare your corrections to the marked copy.

Try your hand (and eye) at this test.
Mark the mistakes and check your corrections with our marked copy

It is impropant to look for certain item when proofing a report , letter, or othr document. Aside from spelling errors, the prooffer should check for deviations in format, consitent use of punctuation, consistent use of capitol letters, undefined acronyms and correctpage numbers listed in the the Table of contents.

After checking a typed draft againts the original manuscript one should also read the draft for aukward phrasing, syntactical errors, and subject/verb agreement and grammatical mistakes. paralell structures should be used im listings headed by bullets or numbers: ie, if one item starts with the phrase "to understand the others should start with to plus a verb.

The final step in proofing involves review of the overall appearance on the document. Are the characrters all printed clearly Are all the pages there? Are the pages free of stray marks ? Is the graphics done? Are bullets filled in? All of the above items effect the appearance of the the document and determine whether the document has the desired effect on the reader.

How did you do?
Check your markup against ours. (We only show corrections in the copy and not the margin notes that most proofreaders typically use.)

It is impropant to look for certain item when proofing a report , letter, or othr

document. Aside from spelling errors, the prooffer should check for deviations in

format, consitent use of punctuation, consistent use of capitol letters, undefined

acronyms and correctpage numbers listed in the the Table of contents.

After checking a typed draft againts the original manuscript one should also read

the draft for aukward phrasing, syntactical errors, and subject/verb agreement and

⌐ Make correction indicated in margin	*lc* Set in lower case (small letters)
stet Retain crossed-out word or letter; let it stand	*sc* Set in small capitals
. . . . Retain words under which dots appear; write "stet" in margin	*caps* Set in capitals
✕ Appears battered; examine	*c+sc* Set in caps and small caps
꞊ Straighten lines	*rom* Change to roman
√√√ Unevenly spaced; correct spacing	*ital* Change to italic
∥ Line up; i.e., make lines even with other matter	≣ Under letter or word means caps
run in Make no break in the reading; no ¶	꞊ Under letter or word, small caps
no ¶ No paragraph; sometimes written "run in"	— Under letter or word, italic
¶ Make a paragraph here	∿ Under letter or word, boldface
tr Transpose words or letters as indicated	⟨⟩ Insert comma
𝒮 Take out matter indicated; delete	⟨;⟩ Insert semicolon
𝒮 Take out character indicated and close up	:/ Insert colon
¢ Line drawn through a cap means lower case	⊙ Insert period
9 Upside down; reverse	/?/ Insert question mark
⌣ Close up; no space	(!) Insert exclamation point
# Insert space here	=/ Insert hyphen
☐ Indent line one em	ⱱ Insert apostrophe
⊏ Move this to the left	⟨⟨ ⟩⟩ Insert quotation marks
⊐ Move this to the right	⟨²⟩ Insert superior letter or figure
sp Spell out	↑ Insert inferior letter or figure
⌐ Raise to proper position	[/] Insert brackets
⌊⌋ Lower to proper position	(/) Insert parentheses
wf Wrong font; change to proper font	⁻ₘ One-em dash
Qu? Is this right?	²⁄ₘ Two-em parallel dash
	bf Boldface type
	⌄ₛ Set s as subscript
	ˢ⌄ Set s as exponent

grammatical mistakes. paralell structures should be used im listings headed by
bullets or numbers; i.e., if one item starts with the phrase "to understand" the others
should start with "to" plus a verb.

The final step in proofing involves review of the overall appearance on the
document. Are the characters all printed clearly; Are all the pages there? Are the
pages free of stray marks? Is the graphics done? Are bullets filled in? All of the
above items effect the appearance of the the document and determine whether the
document has the desired effect on the reader.

Bagin, C. B., and J. Van Doren. April 1986. *Simply Stated* (Document Design Center, American Institutes for Research) 65: 4.

Chapter 7

Technical Illustrations

Graphics Software Replacing Pencil and Paper Tasks

Technical communicators rely on visual images to augment or replace language:

Scientists portray the changing conditions revealed during experiments.

Nurses, medical lab technicians, and doctors illustrate to patients and other professionals changes within and outside the body to explain causes or relationships or possibilities.

Architects draw plans for what they intend to build.

Civil engineers draw land contours, create images of objects to construct, and visualize test results.

Electrical engineers draw circuits.

Mechanical engineers draw parts of machinery.

Computer scientists draw system designs, examples of output, hardware illustrations for user manuals, and charts of the business flow.

Technical secretaries integrate text and graphics to the specifications of the technical person requesting the text.

Your choice of a technical profession requires that you understand the use of graphics and be able to execute them effectively. The times dictate that you acquire an interest and proficiency in computer-assisted graphics. Others educating themselves at the same time as you or coming to the marketplace after you will be trained in creating visually supported information and have the edge.

You also must be good with visuals because your reader or audience expects to be "shown" what you mean—to have page after page or minute after minute of technical explanation broken up with "pictures." Television, advertising, and magazine layouts have educated the public's eye to anticipate visuals—ones well thought out and well presented.

Being "good with visuals" means more than being able to produce them. You must recognize which type is best suited for the information you wish to present, be able to judge whether a graphic prepared by you or someone else is well executed, and develop an eye for placement and design so that text and graphics integrate in a pleasing and functional manner. The more you create graphics and study those of others, the better you will become at making these intuitive decisions.

My colleagues in the School of Engineering have another reason for certain of you to be proficient with graphics. They contend that most engineers think in pictures—that words are often too limited in scope to translate thoughts—that graphics are the engineers' natural language. Computers provide the means for the natural language to be an automatic and easy part of communicating. Before computers, the engineers, while writing, would come to a point in their presentations when a graph or chart or diagram or table would more easily communicate the information. However, the sheer tediousness of manually making the graph deterred the engineers from doing it, and thus they continued to use words. Because of computer-assisted graphics, omitting visuals is no longer acceptable. Engineers who are not interested in mastering the new technology could seem less productive than other engineers and risk being less successful.

My colleagues also believe that computer-assisted graphics will do away with the often expressed criticism that engineers are poor communicators. When they develop the skill to communicate visually without the tedium required to produce graphics manually, the world will discover that engineers have been eloquent all along; they have just not been using their "native" language.

Not every school has the same computer graphics capabilities, but few are void of any application. Most of you will learn both manual and computer-assisted preparation with the percentage of method determined by the availability of hardware and software. The same is true of the companies that hire you. Some will have the latest technology; others will prepare the bulk of work using traditional methods—drawing by hand, giving a draft to the in-house art department, or preparing a draft for an outside company to produce. Whether graphics are prepared by hand or on the computer, their corpus remains the same. It may be that the new technology will produce new images, but so far, graphics software concentrates on making the creation of already familiar graphics easy and fast. This chapter identifies types common to technical work, gives standards for manual preparation, talks about computer-assisted preparation when applicable, and provides exercises for practice.

General Advice about Using Visuals

Use visuals to provide another view of what you have said in words. Do not expect them to replace language completely or to create a report that becomes a picture book alone.

- Let visuals act as a type of main-point outline, to reveal and emphasize the report's main ideas. If used this way, when the reader scans the report, the visuals either introduce or review the report's essence.
- Use visuals to condense information otherwise difficult to read through or to put together diverse data that have relationships difficult to perceive in written form.
- Place visuals next to, above, beneath, or on the opposite page of the text that refers to them. Make the visual and its parts and lettering large enough to be easily read. Whenever possible, spell out words rather than use abbreviations. If abbreviations are necessary, use standard ones and give a key.
- Give complete dimensions of each visual. Specify units of measure or scale.
- Identify every visual as to what it is, what point it makes, how the symbols are read, who created it, and when it was created.
- If you use a visual from another source, give credit to the creator or source. When appropriate, indicate that you are using it with permission (see p. 133, for example). If the label or legend of the visual is also borrowed, let the acknowledgment of the source follow the label or legend.
- Refer to every visual (unless it is included in an appendix and not relevant to the main thrust of the report) in the text. Do so by using either a discussion of the relevance of the visual to the general text (as you can see in Figure 7.2 . . .) or a parenthetical note introduced at the proper place.

Charts/Graphs

The terms chart and graph are often interchanged and belong to a larger group of visuals called figures. This chapter uses four types of charts (bar, line, area, and pie) to illustrate good design and use, but before going to individual types, consider a general checklist of charting standards. The ideas are useful as you both create and evaluate your own or others' work.

Charting/Graphing Checklist

1. Be simple. Keep lines and words to a minimum. Include only information relative to the chart being presented.
2. Number and label each chart. Make the label succinct but specific. Because readers tend to read the label first, make it useful for interpreting the data. The standard is to make the label so clear that the chart can be read and understood independently of accompanying text. Put the number and label in the same place for all charts in your report. A normal place to choose is either below or above the chart and aligned with the left margin, but this is not a rule. You

may decide that another placement is more attractive or effective. That is fine; just be consistent. Wherever you choose, set off the caption from the chart in a way that relates it to the chart and not to the text that follows. For example, you could double-space between the label and chart, then triple- or quadruple-space to divide the chart and all its parts from the text.

A single, consecutive numbering system for all figures in the text or chapter is best. Do not create a separate numbering sequence for charts, one for tables, one for photographs, etc.

3. Strive to make the chart independent if you use a legend (an explanatory caption accompanying a chart) to identify parts. The reader should be able to interpret everything without consulting the explanation. Place the legend where you think best, but do not print it so small that one has difficulty reading it.

4. Letter, whenever possible, so everything can be read from left to right just as words in the text. Do not cause the reader to keep pivoting the chart in order to read lettering going across the page left to right and lettering going up the page from bottom to top.

5. Make the chart easy to read and interpret:

Use different kinds of lines (heavy, thick, dashes, dots) or symbols (*, #) to distinguish variables.

Differentiate variables by color, shading, or pattern.

Make the graph large enough. Often manually prepared charts are reduced when printed, and the symbols, words, or figures become impossible to read.

Maintain order. Move from large to small or vice versa, from past to present or vice versa, chronologically, or anyway that remains consistent.

Make units agree so readers cannot mix time with output or money with gallons. (See Figure 7.1.)

6. Place each chart within a border if the chart's own shape does not create one.

Bar Charts/Graphs

Vertical Bar Chart

Vertical bar charts are simple to create and read and are often used for that reason. They are best used to illustrate comparisons and are probably the clearest means of illustrating quantities at specific times. For example, such a bar chart is good for showing changes in the number of refrigerators produced by assembly lines 1, 2, 3, and 4 in January, February, and March of 1985 (see Figure 7.2).

Figure 7.2 is a vertical bar chart created on a computer, but it could easily have been done by hand. In either case, notice the following:

1. The scale represents quantities clearly and in proper proportions. For example, numbering by units of 100 would be foolish because the scale would become too cluttered or too large for the point it needs to make—something is wrong with the output of line 2; lines 1 and 4 are very consistent; line 3 was down in January but leads February and March.

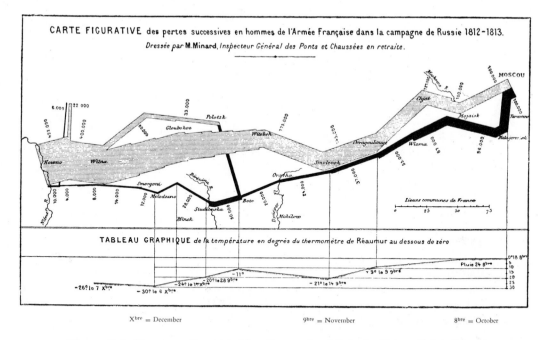

Figure 7.1 The narrative graphic of space and time in Figure 7.1 brilliantly illustrates how more than one dimension can be illustrated in a single graph.

I chose a particular scale to represent increments of 500. Before making this decision, the computer allowed me to try several proportions on the screen to make certain that the proportion did not distort the message. Remember to be honest, for quite possibly use of proportion will cover up unpleasant or self-critical information. For example, you could select a scale and proportion that make a difference of 300 appear very insignificant whereas on another scale the difference would be dramatically apparent. If the difference is unimportant,

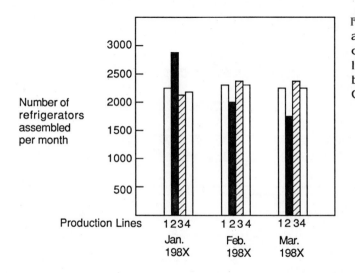

Figure 7.2 Refrigerator assembly line production, 1st quarter, 1985 (production lines 1, 2, 3, and 4). (Prepared by Rick J. Kiegel, Graphics Consultant.)

the first choice is fine, but if the scale deliberately disguises information, then the practice is unacceptable.

2. Pattern is used for emphasis. A more dense pattern is used for line 2 to catch the reader's first interest. A less dense pattern calls attention to line 3. Leaving lines 1 and 4 blank de-emphasizes them. If you create with a computer and use a color printer, you can highlight with brilliant to softer colors or with any type of drawing capability. You can draw an arrow to line 2 and add a question mark—maybe in a brilliant color.
3. Size could emphasize the problem—line 2's output. Bar 2 could be wider than the other three.
4. Each bar is identified.

Horizontal Bar Chart

Some information is better presented by placing the bars horizontally. For example, readers better perceive distances when they are shown horizontally. Also, a greater number of bars are easier to show horizontally. To illustrate a number of data about nontraditional students, I might create a horizontal bar chart such as the one in Figure 7.3. This figure was prepared on a computer, but it could also be prepared by hand. Notice the following:

1. A number of facts are presented in a simple and clear way. This chart makes the point that in the future colleges will depend greatly on nontraditional students for enrollment stability.
2. The horizontal bar chart is best used for comparing similar data at a specific time. For example, it is well suited for an at-a-glance comparison of student population, of monthly sales volume for a number of sales representatives or

Figure 7.3 Growth in college attendance of nontraditional students, 198X–198X. Sources: Bureau of the Census, U.S. Department of Commerce (data by race & age); National Center for Educational Statistics, U.S. Department of Education (all other data). (Prepared July 198X by Rick J. Kiegel, Graphics Consultant.)

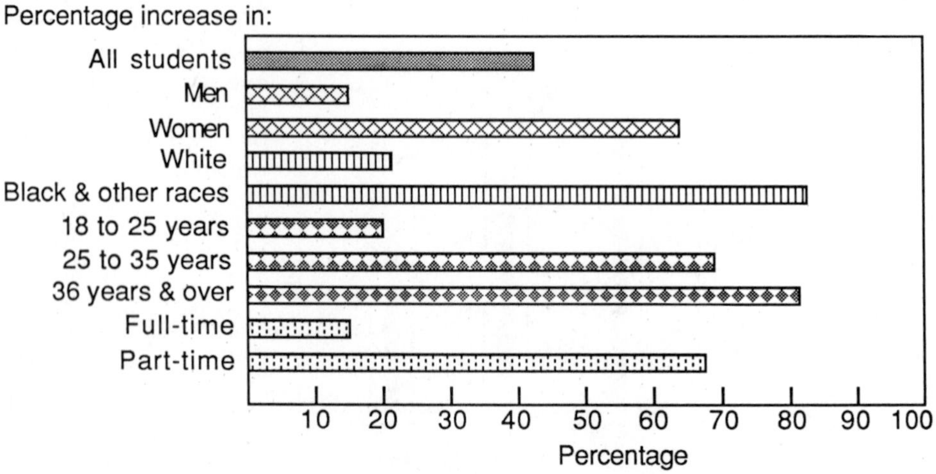

Percentage increase in:

a number of products, of absenteeism by departments or by individuals, of parts requiring repair on a particular engine during a particular time period.

3. This design can accommodate many bars in one graph, as already mentioned. If several bars are used, arrange them in some order but in one that makes the point of the chart clear. For example, an alphabetical arrangement makes finding a particular name or item easier but may make seeing items that should be considered together difficult. On the other hand, a numeric order makes comparing data points easier but locating a specific item difficult. Different or similar patterns or color can relate bars to each other or distinguish them from one another. The wonderful fact about constructing charts on the computer is that you can try different arrangements, save them and compare, choose the one best suited, erase the others, and do all this in a number of minutes.

Stacked Bar Charts

When data are plotted for several items over time, a stacked bar allows the reader to compare the percentage that each contributes to the whole. For example, if a line item in the budget is for materials and supplies and totals $875.00, a stacked bar representing accurate proportions for audio-visual services and supplies ($350.00), computer supplies and services ($250.00), office supplies ($150.00), postage ($75.00), and telephone ($50.00) quickly allows the reader to access the distribution or to question, adjust, or approve the budget. A stacked chart for each line item gives the reader the complete budget picture for both the totals and parts that make up the totals (see Figure 7.4).

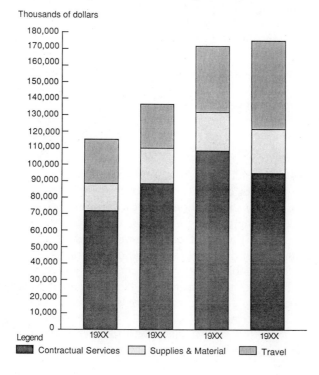

Thousands of dollars

Figure 7.4 Admissions Office operating budget, City University, Collegetown, Iowa. Data supplied by university's accounting office. (Prepared by Rick J. Keigel, Graphics Consultant.)

Pictogram

One variation of the bar chart is to use pictures that represent quantities. Such a chart is called a pictogram, and the pictorial symbol is called an isotype. Properly used, this method can be effective, and it certainly is easier to produce by a computer with paint or draw capabilities than by hand. For example, an isotype representing sales of a certain earth-moving machine may be drawn once and then automatically duplicated as many times as you wish to show an increase in sales.

Beware, however, of creating images that lie or misrepresent statistics. An isotype representing a bag of money, for example, when all dimensions are doubled, represents eight times as much money (not two times as much).

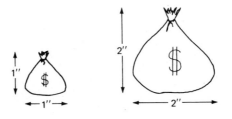

Figure 7.5

Be careful also of terminology. For example, be accurate when using phrases such as "x times as big" or an "increase of x times":

Something that is now	20 units
if it is 4 times as big is	80 units
If there is an increase of 4 times is	100 units.

When you first begin to use computer graphics capabilities, steel yourself not to be "cute" or carried away with possibilities for their own sake. The following are properly prepared pictograms. See Figures 7.6 and 7.7.

Line Charts/Graphs

The line chart is a necessary visual aid for scientists and engineers because it is the best way to plot the behavior or trends of two or more related variables. The independent variable is usually plotted horizontally (the abscissa axis) and the dependent variable vertically (the ordinate axis). Common independent variables include time, distance, voltage, stress, and load; common dependent variables are temperature, money, current, and strain. The dependent variable is affected by changes in the independent variable. Line or curve charts often give another view of data presented in a table. Once you construct the table with charting capabilities using an electronic spreadsheet, you can use a simple command to convert the table into a line chart (or bar or area or pie chart), or break down the data into different categories and select the most suitable chart for each category. You can easily use both the table and whatever other visuals you choose. See Figures 7.11 and 7.12, pages 124–125.

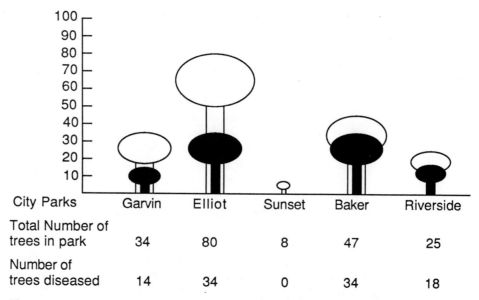

City Parks	Garvin	Elliot	Sunset	Baker	Riverside
Total Number of trees in park	34	80	8	47	25
Number of trees diseased	14	34	0	34	18

Figure 7.6 Number of elm trees with elm disease in Rivercity's city parks. Surveyed by Rivercity Parks Department, Fall 198X. (Prepared by Rick J. Kiegel, Graphics Consultant.)

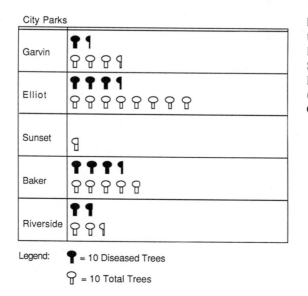

Figure 7.7 Number of elm trees with elm disease in Rivercity's city parks. Surveyed by Rivercity Parks Department, Fall 198X. (Prepared by Rick J. Kiegel, Graphics Consultant.)

Construction Tips for Line Charts

1. Scale is the most important factor.
   a. Full information identifying scale must appear as part of the graph.
   b. The visual impression of the scale must be accurate. Your responsibility is to choose a scale, both vertical and horizontal, that conveys an accurate image. If the visual interpretation misrepresents, then

the scale is poor. The real violation is choosing a scale that deliberately misrepresents or covers up information. Remember when a line goes up or down at a sharp angle or climbs or falls slowly, readers infer that the rapidity or gradualness of the change is significant. It may be, but make certain that the visual impression is honest.

c. No ideal standard exists for scale. You must choose one that best visualizes the parallel between the picture and the information. A wonderful benefit of creating line graphs on the computer with certain graphics packages is that once you select the scale, the computer calculates it for you perfectly. But even without this capability, the computer allows you to try different scales and correct miscalculations easily and neatly.

d. The use of numbers with which people are familiar (multiplies of 10's or 100's, etc.) is the best way to represent the scale. If you use decimals, be consistent when a whole number is used (2.00).

2. Some line charts show more than one line or curve. If so, identify each by a short title on the line itself or use different kinds of lines (heavy, thin, dashes, dots) or different colors for each and provide a legend for identification. If you have color available, choose colors of like value to represent similar trends or those of very different values to emphasize differences.

3. All writing on the graph should appear horizontally except for the identification for the vertical scale function.

4. A line graph can begin at any intersecting point on the coordinate grid. However, when you begin a scale at a point above zero, inform the reader that the zero has been suppressed. One way to do this is simply to state that on both scales. Using the suppress zero makes sense when the values plotted are so high that the lower part of the chart would be left largely empty. (See Figure 7.8).

5. A complete grid is used when absolute accuracy is important.

6. Plot points should normally be omitted. If you use them, make sure they clarify

Figure 7.8

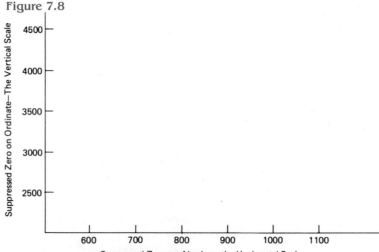

the presentation. When creating by hand, you can use different template data symbols (○, □, ◇). When using a computer, you may choose to show a symbol everywhere a line crosses. Such a function is available to you.

7. The graph should be kept simple. A good rule to follow is not to exceed three different lines or curves.

Examples: Line Charts/Graphs

Exhibit A: The plasticity chart in Figure 7.9 effectively illustrates the previous suggestions.

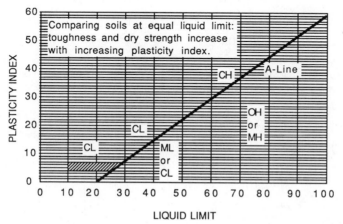

Figure 7.9 **A plasticity chart.**

Exhibit B: This exhibit presents ways to use the computer to plot line charts illustrating vertical and horizontal stress distribution.

EXAMPLES FOR VERTICAL LOADS

PROBLEM 3.5

An oil pipeline weighing 1,500 lbs per foot is placed on the ground surface parallel to an existing house. Plot the vertical stress distribution versus depth below the house wall footing which is 8 feet from the pipe and 4 feet deep. Assume a depth increment of 0.02 feet and a stratum thickness of 42 feet. The given parameters are illustrated in Figure 3.5a.

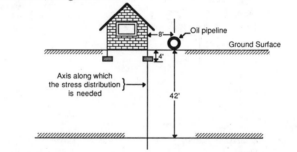

Figure 3.5a Graphical illustration of Problem 3.5.

Solution:

Approximate the pressure on the contact area along the pipe with a line load. Assume that the pipe length is much greater than the soil layer thickness. Load Program 3 from Menu 3; then enter the data, P = 1500, X = 8, Do = 4, Df = 42 and a depth increment of 0.02. Pressing the ENTER key will give:

1. Data Output   2. Graph

YOUR SELECTION = ?

Choose graph option 2, then press the ENTER key. This results in the following prompt:

Graph Option

1. Vertical Stress   2. Horizontal Stress   3. Both

YOUR SELECTION = ?

Now select vertical stress option 2, then press the ENTER key. The desired graphical output will be displayed on the screen. Press the SHIFT and PrtSc keys simultaneously for a hard copy. The resulting distribution is shown in Figure 3.5b.

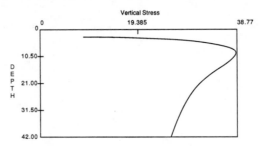

Figure 3.5b Vertical stress distribution for Problem 3.5.

The maximum vertical stress increment beneath the footing occurs at a depth of approximately 13.8 feet with a value of 38.77 lb/ft². Note that the distribution extends from 4 feet down to 42 feet since the initial input depth was 4 feet.

PROBLEM 3.6

Plot the vertical and horizontal stress distribution due to the oil pipeline described in problem 3.5 when it is placed along the backside of a concrete retaining wall 12 feet from the pipe as shown in Figure 3.6a.

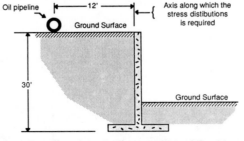

Figure 3.6a Graphical illustration of Problem 3.6.

Solution:

Inputting P = 1,500, Do = 0, Df = 30, and a depth increment of 0.02 ft., then selecting the graph option "Both" gives the distributions shown in Figure 3.6b.

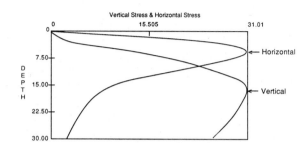

Figure 3.6b Vertical and horizontal stress distributions for Problem 3.6.

Note that the maximum values for both vertical and horizontal stress distributions are equal, but occur at different depths. Additionally, the solution is based on the assumption that the wall is rigid and that no lateral movement is allowed.

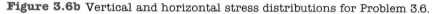

Exhibit C: These line charts are derived from the same table. Each makes a different point. Consider the following discussion when studying Figures 7.10 through 7.14.

If you take seriously the suggestion that charts should be easy to read, the language between the following source table and the derivative charts should match. It does not. The table (Figure 7.10) uses "SALES/FEES," and the line

Figure 7.10 TAC projected operating budget.

CATEGORY	UNIT	YR 1		YR 2		YR 3		YR 4		YR 5		YR 6
		no	am't	no	am't	no	am't	no	am't	no	am't	no	am't
SALES/FEES			$30,948		$216,793		$275,237		$407,676		$612,945		$782,073
CONSULTING	JOB	0	$0	15	$28,488	20	$37,984	26	$49,379	34	$64,193	44	$83,451
TECH ASS'MNT	STUDY	2	$19,948	4	$39,896	6	$59,844	12	$119,688	15	$149,610	20	$199,480
CAD WORKSHOPS	CLASS	1	$6,000	10	$118,800	21	$142,800	30	$204,000	43	$342,000	56	$462,000
CONTRACT R&D	CONTRACT	1	$5,000	1	$5,000	1	$10,000	1	$10,000	1	$20,000	1	$20,000
OTHER INCOME	GIFTS				$24,609		$24,609		$24,609		$37,142		$17,142
DIRECT COST OF SALES			$20,539		$136,595		$116,932		$193,396		$285,195		$385,659
CONSULTING	JOB	0	$0	15	$24,240	20	$32,320	26	$42,016	34	$54,621	44	$71,007
TECH ASS'MNT	STUDY	2	$12,580	4	$25,160	6	$37,740	12	$75,480	15	$94,350	20	$125,800
CAD WORKSHOPS	CLASS	1	$1,416	10	$62,068	21	$43,424	30	$72,452	43	$129,328	56	$181,956
CONTRACT R&D	CONTRACT	1	$3,448	1	$3,448	1	$3,448	1	$3,448	1	$6,896	1	$6,896
OTHER	CONTINGENCY		$3,095		$21,679								
INDIRECT COSTS			$175,235		$281,793		$211,994		$264,314		$334,648		$375,748
TAC OVERHEAD			$168,046		$233,985		$171,068		$196,626		$234,830		$240,767
R&D OVERHEAD (@35%)			$7,189		$47,808		$40,926		$67,689		$99,818		$134,981
CST PAYBACK			$0		$0		$0		$0		$0		$0
TOTAL COSTS			$195,773		$418,388		$328,926		$457,710		$619,843		$761,407
TOTAL INCOME			$30,948		$216,793		$275,237		$407,676		$612,945		$782,073
NET EARNINGS			($164,825)		($201,596)		($53,690)		($50,034)		($6,898)		$20,666

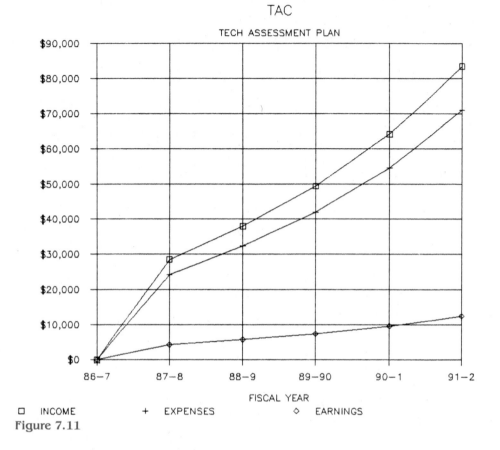

Figure 7.11

chart (Figure 7.11) uses "INCOME"; the table uses "DIRECT COST OF SALES," and the chart uses "EXPENSES." Proofreading for such inconsistences is worthwhile. Editing such inconsistences by hand can be messy and time-consuming; editing by computer takes a minute.

Figures 7.11 and 7.12 also provide a good basis for discussing scale. Theoretically a set of charts derived from the same table should use the same scale, so readers see everything relatively. To follow this standard, the two charts (Figures 7.11 and 7.12) should have the same vertical scale. If the scales are not alike, readers may see distributions between small sums as vast or between large sums as insignificant. However, you must also remember the reader. If you use the same scale for all graphs in this exhibit, the result is hard to read (see Figure 7.13). One criterion may be that if the charts appear on separate pages, the difference in scale is not as important. The reader can adjust to each new page and configuration. However, when several charts appear on the same page and have to do with data derived from a single source, the relativeness of scale is more important. The eye sees several things as part of one. The reference points should be the same.

A source table is presented in Figure 7.10.

A technical assessment plan is shown in Figure 7.11.

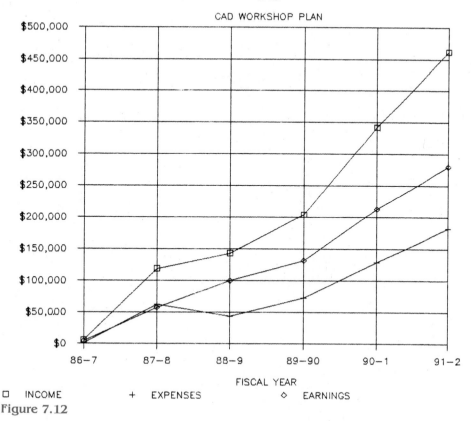

Figure 7.12

A CAD workshop plan is exhibited in Figure 7.12.

The example in Figure 7.13 uses a relative scale, but the scale selected makes the results hard to read and the differences hard to analyze.

The line chart in Figure 7.14 uses minus figures to indicate a deficit. It illustrates the concept that the horizontal scale does not need to begin at zero.

Narrative Graphics of Space and Time

Edward Tufte in his book *The Visual Display of Quantitative Information* comments about graphs showing space and time.

An especially effective device for enhancing the explanatory power of time-series displays is to add spatial dimensions to the design of the graphic, so that the data are moving over space (in two or three dimensions) as well as over time. . . . [An excellent example is] the classic [graph] of Charles Joseph Minard (1781–1870), the French engineer, which shows the terrible fate of Napoleon's army in Russia. . . . this combination of data map and time-series, drawn in 1861, portrays the devastating losses suffered in Napoleon's Russian campaign of 1812. Beginning at

Figure 7.13

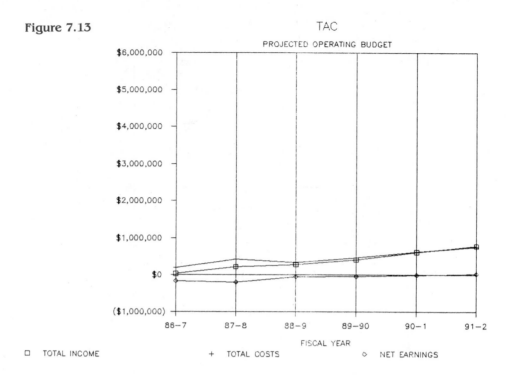

TAC
PROJECTED OPERATING BUDGET

□ TOTAL INCOME   + TOTAL COSTS   ◇ NET EARNINGS

Figure 7.14

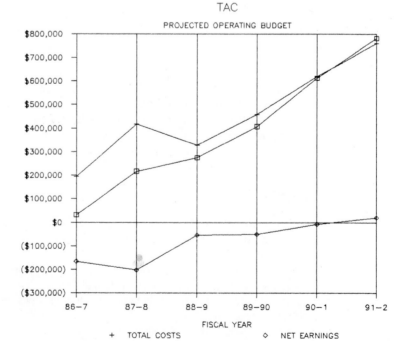

TAC
PROJECTED OPERATING BUDGET

□ TOTAL INCOME   + TOTAL COSTS   ◇ NET EARNINGS

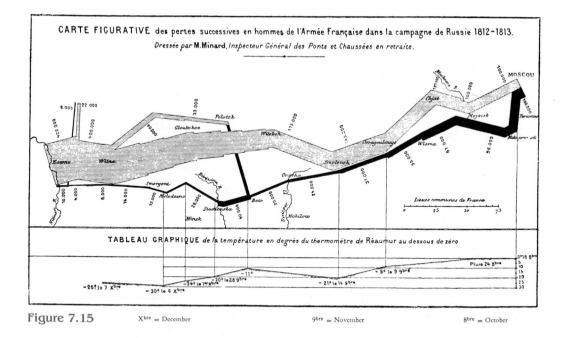

Figure 7.15   X^bre = December   9bre = November   8bre = October

the left on the Polish-Russian border near the Niemen River, the thick band shows the size of the army (422,000 men) as it invaded Russia in June 1812. The width of the band indicates the size of the army at each place on the map. In September, the army reached Moscow, which was by then sacked and deserted, with 100,000 men. The path of Napoleon's retreat from Moscow is depicted by the darker, lower band, which is linked to a temperature scale and dates at the bottom of the chart. It was a bitterly cold winter, and many froze on the march out of Russia. As the graphic shows, the crossing of the Berezina River was a disaster, and the army finally struggled back into Poland with only 10,000 men remaining. Also shown are the movements of auxiliary troops, as they sought to protect the rear and the flank of the advancing army. Minard's graphic tells a rich, coherent story with its multivariate data, far more enlightening than just a single number bouncing along over time. *Six* variables are plotted: the size of the army, its location on a two-dimensional surface, direction of the army's movement, and temperature on various dates during the retreat from Moscow.

It may well be the best statistical graphic ever drawn. (Tufte, E. R., 1983. *The visual display of quantitative information*. Cheshire, Connecticut: Graphics Press, 40–41.)

Combined Bar and Line Charts

Sometimes people place a line chart in front of or behind a bar chart. When you do this by hand, mistakes and erasures make a mess. A computer overlay feature allows you to create this impression easily and neatly. The only caution is not to be carried away by options. Unless the additions make the chart easier to read and understand, resist them.

Area Charts/Graphs

Area charts are best used to show a trend: variations in the value of a measurable item over a period of time. In its simplest form, an area chart looks like a single line chart with the area above the *y*-axis and below the plotted line filled in. When two or more series of data are plotted, the result looks like two or more line graphs with different colored or shaded areas below each. The two or more series of data together show the total, but individual data are also easily seen.

A rule of design is to use the darkest color or pattern on the most stable or significant layer. Place this layer usually on the bottom so it is the easiest for the reader to interpret. The designer of the area chart in Figure 7.16 did not follow this rule. One can speculate that the lecture income was placed at the bottom to emphasize its sudden stop. Remember that design can be altered to serve your point.

Figure 7.16 Combined yearly income from lecturing and consulting.

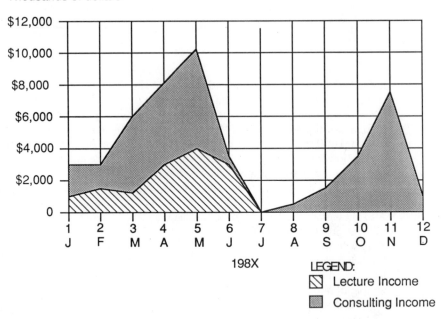

Pie Charts/Graphs

The pie chart looks like its name—a whole pie viewed from above and cut into pieces. Its use is to show approximate divisions of a whole unit. All the pieces must add up to 100 percent.

Traditionally you locate your first radial line at 12 o'clock and move clockwise, in descending order, beginning with the largest segment. The exception to tradition is when more than one pie chart appears on a page as a means of comparison. When this occurs, make the first pie traditional, but order the slices

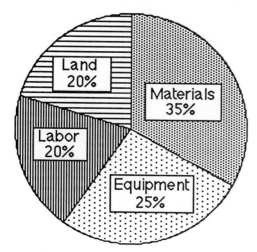 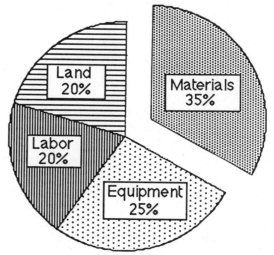

Figure 7.17 Division of house building expenses.

Figure 7.18 One possible variation of the pie chart for interest or emphasis.

of the following pie charts used in the comparison in the same sequence regardless of whether the slices follow the descending order rule.

Label each segment. If the pieces are large enough, place the percentage figures and identifications within the piece. If you place them outside, write so the text is horizontal to the page. If you end up with several tiny pieces, group them into one segment and label it "other." This segment, regardless of size, goes last.

Computer-generated pie charts offer design options that are easy to create: you can draw a thicker border around one segment, color one segment, color or pattern segments using dark or vibrant colors or patterns to emphasize the most important pieces, or draw one piece away from the pie for emphasis. All these options can also be produced by hand, but they take longer.

A nice feature of some computer-generated pie charts is that the computer automatically calculates percentages for you. Your slices of the pie are always mathematically accurate and perfectly proportioned.

Remember that pie charts are thought of as the simplest form of a chart and that exact values of each segment are difficult to interpret. Use them with care for sophisticated, technical readers.

Concluding Comments on Charts/Graphs

Adapt the chart to what you wish to show and to the audience. If the readers are not used to reading charts or graphs, choose simple forms; but for technical audiences, select more informative forms such as multiple line graphs.

Do not place too many charts on one page.

Know when not to use a chart. Sometimes charts make points you do not want or need to emphasize. If it is not necessary to highlight negative information, do not show it in a graph where it cannot be missed.

If you are buying your own computer-graphics package or one for the school or company, you should look for the following features:

1. Choice of line size
2. Choice of colors
3. Floating label and legend (You can move or place the label/legend where you want.)
4. Sizing (You can select different sizes for your graphs.)
5. Font styles (You can select different types for different descriptive items of the graph.)
6. Fill-in capacity (You can choose a number of patterns to fill-in segments of the chart.)
7. A match with your needs (If you need to perform statistical analysis or produce scattergrams on logarithmic scales, be certain the package has such capabilities.)

Tables

A table is best for showing numbers and units of measurement which must be illustrated precisely and without interpretation; the reader is left to provide his or her own understanding. Preparing tables by hand can take considerable time, whereas generating tables by computer takes only minutes. Whenever you realize that the information you are discussing is too dense to be understood without requiring labor and intense concentration, support your text by presenting it in tabular form. If the information you need to present is lengthy, summarize the essentials into a short table and include the remaining data in a table placed in the appendix.

Parts of the Table

Before talking about construction tips or giving an illustration, we should define the table's formal parts:

1. *Titles.* Place the table number and title above the table and number consecutively throughout the report or chapter. Make the title informative.
2. *Stub Column.* Make the first column on the left the stub column. It lists the items described in the horizontal rows to the right. If the column has a heading, it is called the stub head. But if no heading is necessary, the space may be left blank.

     To subdivide line headings without using new columns, indent within the stub column to show subheadings.
3. *Column Heads.* Use column heads. Every column and subcolumn and *every* line or group of lines must have a heading that identifies the data. All headings should be in parallel grammatical form. Because of limited space, choose words carefully to be as descriptive as possible. Standard abbreviations are acceptable.

     Stub and column headings have a vertical reference; line headings have a horizontal reference. Do not ignore this convention.

4. *Rules.* Use rules below the title and column heads and at the bottom of the table. Unless absolutely necessary for clarity, do not rule every line.
5. *Footnotes.* Enter footnotes in lowercase unless you are instructed otherwise. Some designers suggest that you do not number footnotes because the numbers may be mistaken for data. Other ways to distinguish footnotes are to introduce them with a symbol (*, †). Use footnotes to explain or clarify individual data.

Illustration

Table number: Title

Stub Heading	Column Heading	Column Heading*	
		Subheading†	Subheading

Line heading
  Subheading
  Subheading
Line heading
	Individual blocks for tabulated data		

Footnote*
Footnote†

Construction Tips for Tables

1. Include all factors that affect the data in the table.
2. Introduce the table in the text and prepare the reader to understand it. Place the table after discussing it.
3. Set the table off from the text by spacing.
4. Do not have the table extend into the margins of the text.
5. If you must turn the table sideways, place the top of the table against the inside binding.
6. If the table is too large to fit on one page, write "continued" on the first page and begin the second page by repeating the same headings at the top of each column as they appear on the first page of the table. If totals are included at the bottom of columns, the subtotals should be at the bottom of the first page and at the top of the second page. Write "Forward" at the left side of the subtotals to indicate that the figures are not final totals.
7. Indicate the source of the table even if you make your own table from borrowed data. Starting at the left margin, list sources below the table.
8. Place the column and line headings in some logical order, such as geographical, quantitative, temporal, alphabetical.
9. For easy and accurate reading, place columns to be compared next to each other; also align decimals in a column, round numbers if possible, and use standard symbols and units of measure.

The table in Figure 7.19 illustrates the tips presented in the preceding discussion.

Table I

Number of apples produced in Stuart's backyard orchard

YEAR	Total number of bearing trees	Type of apple trees	
		Macintosh	Golden Delicious
198X	6	4	2
198X	6	5	1
198X	5	5	0

Figure 7.19 Table of apple production. (Prepared by Rick J. Kiegel, Graphics Consultant.)

Photographs

In technical reporting, photographs are among the best means to illustrate the truth of assertions. If someone claims or reports that materials are breaking up, expanding, shrinking; that ground is sinking, sliding, eroding; that dramatic changes are occurring in leaf forms following an insecticide spraying of the particular land area, the best visible proof other than a site visit is a photograph.

Problems exist for using photographs effectively. They show only the surface. They often include extraneous information. The quality diminishes with reproduction. To achieve the best results use a high-quality original, and if in-house capabilities are not sufficient and the photograph is an important exhibit, have it profes-

Figure 7.20 Actual photograph—shows a break in pavement, water retention, and erosion of subsoil.

sionally printed. You may choose to use originals and hand-attach them to the text.

Computers allow you other options. For example, you can print a photograph with optical scanning equipment. The definition will not be the quality of the actual photograph, but for an illustration to appear in multiple copies of a report, it may be just what you need.

Figures 7.21, 7.22, and 7.23 present an actual photograph and two different computer-generated reproductions of the same photograph.

Figure 7.21 Photograph printed with permission of Carmen Lynch Herrenbruch, model. See computer-generated reproduction of same photograph (Figures 7.22 and 7.23).

Figure 7.22 Photo scanned by ComputerLand/Evansville using the ThunderScan™ digitizer on a Macintosh™ Plus computer and printed on the Apple Imagewriter II™ printer. ThunderScan is a trademark of Thunderware, Inc. Apple, Imagewriter, and Macintosh are trademarks of Apple Computer, Inc. Image produced by dot matrix printer.

Technical Drawing

The job of creating fully dimensional and annotated drawings is demanding but essential work to many technical professions. Traditionally this work is created by hand, and for some professionals, the manner and care of creation become a

Figure 7.23 Image produced by laser printer.

personal trademark and a physical image of pride in workmanship. For others, even those who are very good at technical drawing, it is always a tedious, time-consuming task.

The work of engineers in particular cannot go forward without good technical drawings. Electrical wiring plans; schematic diagrams illustrating how certain equipment operates; drawings depicting actual appearance, relative location of objects, and the way in which equipment functions are examples of information well shown by technical illustrations. Technical drawings have the advantage of being able to picture the interior rather than just the surface of an object. They allow the designer to omit what is unnecessary and to highlight what is essential.

The subject of teaching drawing is beyond the scope of this book. What is within its sight is a discussion of how computer-assisted drawing is affecting traditional methods and how you can take advantage of the new technology.

Computer-Assisted Drawing (CAD)

 The availability of computer-assisted drawing (CAD) is important to both the draftsperson and whoever needs to communicate with that person about preparing the technical drawing. In engineering, for example, the engineer often conceives the design, analyzes the problems, and makes a sketch that he or she gives to the draftsperson along with written or oral specifications. CAD has not yet changed this order, but it may. More professional engineers are doing their own drawing now that it can be produced efficiently and with less tedium.

In word processing, the program does not write for you; in computer-assisted drawing, it does not draw for you. If you need to produce a single drawing, you may do it by hand just as efficiently. The difference comes when a drawing uses multiple or often produced images or you require multiple drawings. Some uses of CAD follow:

- *Ability to Plot Many Copies.* Once the original is completed, the plotter can plot as many copies as you need.
- *Ability to Repeat Images.* If you are drawing the blueprint of a house with four bathrooms and you finish a drawing of the washbasin in the first bathroom, you can ask the computer to repeat that image in the other three.
- *Ability to Complete Other Half.* You may draw one-half of an architectural blueprint or a piece of machinery that is exactly the same on the other half. If the computer package has mirroring capabilities, you can ask it to complete the other half.
- *Ability to Store Images.* You can store images used over and over and call them up to insert into the drawing you are presently doing.

Your personality as a draftsperson is not entirely sacrificed. Depending on the software, a wide array of choices is available that allows you to "personalize" the drawing. You can choose the type or width of line, select type fonts for lettering, decide whether or not to align text, place lettering wherever it pleases you, frame the drawing, select proportions for the drawing, layer a particular part of the base drawing with a color or a pattern to highlight, create a pleasing appearance by adjusting the size of the drawing to the size of the paper on which it will be produced. Just as in drawing by hand, the person who pays attention to detail, cares about placement and proportion, and thinks of ways to make the drawing more effective produces the better drawing and gains recognition for his or her work.

If the advantages to the individual are not enough to guarantee the long life and improvement of CAD programs, the benefits to business are. The personal computer has made it possible for small companies as well as noncomputer professionals to have and use CAD systems on their desktops. A few years ago, such programs were available exclusively through a mainframe. The person wanting a drawing had to interface with the professional computer staff who alone were able to work with the technology. The mainframe equipment had to be housed in special atmospheric conditions. All that is changed. In addition, productivity studies show that producing the original drawing by the CAD method versus by hand is 4:6 times faster; to edit an existing drawing is 20:1 times quicker. The savings in labor alone assure the continued use of computerized drawing.

If careful drafting is relevant to your major, experiment with a CAD program. If your school does not have one, find a business or someone in business or industry who will show you how to use it. The technology is in place; you cannot afford to be uninformed. It is better if you are practiced. The drawings you produce will be neat, uniform, of high quality, and drawn without the anguish associated with errors, adjustments, and changes.

CAD Tips

Know your whole system. Investigate functions and facilities. Some CAD functions make drawing easy, but if users do not understand their system, they tend to fall back on manual procedures even when working on the computer.

Build your experience. You cannot learn how to use CAD by watching someone else or by reading the manual. You also cannot learn to do everything the first week. Start with simple commands, expand, and enjoy.

The exhibits in Figures 7.24 and 7.25 are examples of CAD.

Figure 7.24 Example of object that might be duplicated, stored, and used again and again.

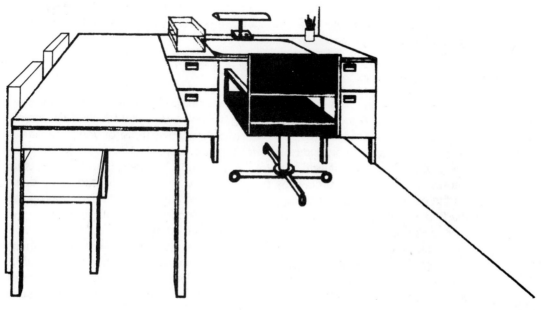

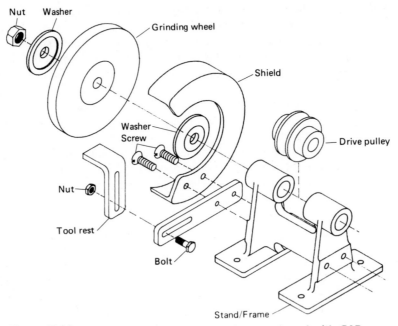

Figure 7.25 Example of a detailed drawing produced with CAD software.

Labeling Technical Drawings

The type of drawing in Figure 7.26 often has the parts labeled. The technical term for doing so is "callout." The callout can be written directly onto the drawing itself, or if that is too complicated or too hard to read, the parts can be assigned numbers and labeled in a separate index or legend. It is customary to begin item numbers at 11 o'clock and proceed clockwise.

Technical Drawing via Computers

Digitizer tablets and "paint or draw" software programs allow you to draw freehand, integrate into your freehand drawing symbols available through the program, and even copy existing drawings. This capability allows more of you in technical fields to make use of computer-assisted drawings. Consider, for example, the situation where you are noting a biological experiment. You set up and format your "notebook" on a word processing program; using a mouse or lightpen, you draw on the computer whatever changes occur to the matter being studied; you merge the two when you print the notebook so that the pure data are illustrated.

Take the need for civil engineers to test the strength of a steel beam. You draw the beam, enter the calculations for adding stress, tell the computer where to apply the stress, and the computer "shows" you what will happen (Figure 7.27). It is possible, of course, to obtain the same results using numbers, but numbers are more difficult to interpret. If you can actually "see" the curve or what emerges

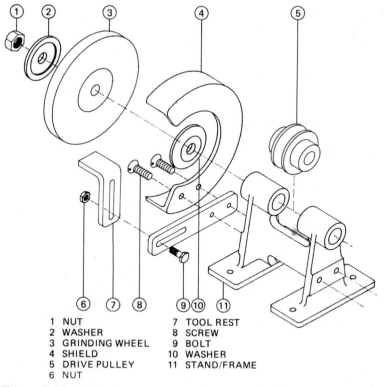

1 NUT
2 WASHER
3 GRINDING WHEEL
4 SHIELD
5 DRIVE PULLEY
6 NUT

7 TOOL REST
8 SCREW
9 BOLT
10 WASHER
11 STAND/FRAME

Figure 7.26 Labeled technical drawing.

Figure 7.27 An example of a technical drawing produced with a "paint" program.

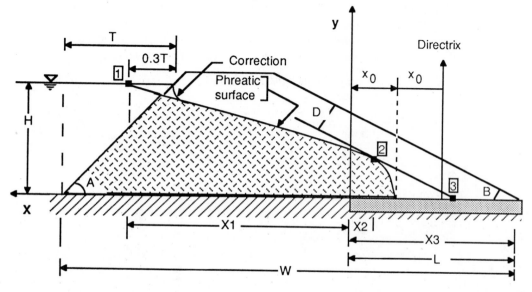

after plotting the numbers, you can understand more quickly and sometimes more accurately. Also, you can do this over and over again in a matter of minutes and have a printout of each stress application and the results.

A Closing Word

Computer graphics are fun! Try drawing by computers, and I bet you will like it. Learn to use as many applications as the equipment available to you allows. At my school, different departments own different types of hardware and software. Some students know everything available and someone who has access to the equipment, and they share and experiment. If functions are not available that you would like to know about, think of people who do have them. Most people respond to those who are interested.

Practice Exercises

1. Select from a technical journal or magazine in your discipline an example of a table, bar chart, pie chart, line chart, and drawing. Write a brief paragraph evaluating each. Choose one you think is particularly good or bad and report why it is to the class. If bad, what suggestions would improve it?

2. Determine a set of data in your discipline that can be presented in a formal table, a formal pie chart, a formal multiple bar chart, a stacked chart, a line chart, and an area chart. This exercise can be accomplished by either a group or individuals. Create the graphs and use the computer to create as many of the types as possible. Turn in the data separately. Choose the graph you or the group judges the best. Show it to the rest of the class and explain the choice.

3. Read again the information on scale (pp. 114–116, No. 1; 119–120, No. 1). Illustrate by both a good and bad scale how information can appear different from how it really is.

    Use the computer to experiment with a scale if one is available to you.

4. If you have available a CAD program, prepare the following drawing.

Req'd: Lay out the goggle lens illustrated below.

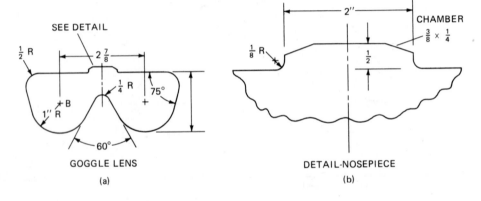

GOGGLE LENS
(a)

DETAIL-NOSEPIECE
(b)

Notes
1. All dimensions are in inches.
2. Establish a point for reference at the center of each lens.
3. Save the drawing on floppy disk to use later in a dimensioning exercise.

5. If you have available a CAD program and have practiced, select one of the two following problems and draw it. Experiment to personalize the drawing. What functions can you use to make it both easy to read and pleasing in appearance?

Req'd: Option—Select one of the following problems.

1. Film reel
2. Floor plan

Special Note   The final drawing is to be plotted in two colors, that is, one color for object and a different color for text/dimensions.

CAD Problem 1

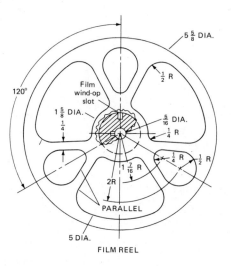

FILM REEL

Notes
1. Utilize ARRAY and MIRROR commands where appropriate.
2. Establish a centerline layer with a different color and create appropriate centerlines.

CAD Problem 2

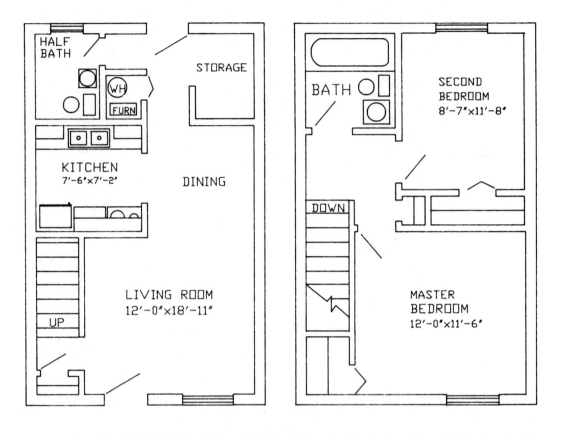

Notes
1. Use 5″ interior walls and 9″ exterior walls, and assume typical dimensions for those not given to create the 1st and 2nd floor size to be equal.
2. Develop layers for:

   a. 1st floor walls   d. 2nd floor walls

   b. 1st floor fixtures   e. 2nd floor fixtures

   c. 1st floor dimensions/text   f. 2nd floor dimensions/text

---

6. Choose from another class some work that needs documenting and illustrating. If you are not doing anything suitable, make up your own assignment—the progress of tulips from the first time the leaves break ground to the actual bloom; the change in anything due to weather, temperature, and the like; the growth of something. Design a format for recording the data in an organized way. (Use word processing if possible.) Illustrate by using freehand drawing. (Use a graphics paint or draw program if available.)
7. Create a series of graphs that illustrates how certain data are best presented by

certain graphs. Choose data that are best or appropriately presented by a/an

bar chart
pie chart
line graph
table
pictogram
area chart

Write a summary paragraph for each graph explaining why the data are best or appropriately presented in this graphic way.

Part 3

Specific Types of Technical and Scientific Writing

Part 3 defines writing common to technical work.

Chapter 8: Memoranda, Letters, and Résumés
- identifies common types of correspondence
- talks about memoranda standards and format
- gives examples of effective memoranda
- discusses business letter formats
- considers letter writing style and content
- gives examples of effective letters
- covers application letters and résumés
- provides practice exercises

Chapter 9: Proposals and Feasibility Reports
- discusses proper content and form for these reports
- gives examples of both types of reports
- provides practice exercises

Chapter 10: Formal Reports
- defines the formal report
- identifies its individual parts

- includes examples
- provides practice exercises

Chapter 11: Working Reports
- gives guidelines for good report writing
- discusses particular reports:
    giving technical information
    reporting about work performed
    reporting about people and things
- provides practice exercises

Chapter 12: User Documentation
- identifies types of user documentation
- lists content expected in user documentation
- offers tips for writing software documentation—particularly manuals
- gives a professional's view of user documentation
- provides practice exercises

Overview

Industrial prophets foresee paperless factories, plants, and companies. All in-house and out-of-house written communication will be recorded on electronic devices, and information will be either stored or transmitted electronically in a readable form. For this dream of the future to become a reality, a lot of uniformity and conversion must occur.

The part of the vision important to you is that regardless of how information is captured and stored, the need to write, the amount of writing, and the types of writing are not prophesied to change. People in business and industry will continue to produce and use documents having to do with selling, production, delivery, labor, equipment, maintenance, facilities, management, clients, experimentation, and testing.

The more you practice preparing and evaluating writing common to the technical professions, the better you will perform your responsibilities. Part 3 of this book defines writing pertaining to technical work, gives suggestions for writing and formatting, and provides exercises for practice.

Chapter 8

Memoranda, Letters, and Résumés

Word Processing Offers Convenience

Much of what you say or think in business ends up in writing. Memoranda and letters become records of ideas, performance, commitments, expectations, requests, and understandings. They are important to both the writer and the company, for they document and establish a permanent record. They provide a reference for answering questions and comprehending what was actually said, agreed to, or accomplished.

A common condition among people in business and industry is to be mired in paperwork. You should expect to write a lot when you are in the workplace. You can cut through this work, stay on schedule, and gain the respect of others if you discipline yourself to answer in writing promptly. When you do write, express yourself clearly, accurately, and briefly. This chapter gives guidelines for format and content of common types of correspondence. It closes with a discussion of the résumé.

Memoranda

A memorandum (often called memo) is a short report written to someone in-house. The subject is often familiar to the recipient. Therefore, you can be direct in writing about the subject and purpose but not so blunt as to be rude. Remember that people who work in the same company with you receive your memos. Would you like to receive what you have written? Be careful not to let your directness appear curt nor your briefness hamper understanding.

The form has a bad name because too many people write too many memoranda, but it is a very useful form if used prudently.

Memoranda Format

Memoranda have a specific format. The format can be set by the company, printed, and distributed for use. If memoranda forms are not furnished, the following standard format is one you can use or adapt to your purpose.

```
                        MEMORANDUM
     TO:                              DISTRIBUTION:
     FROM:                            (optional)
     SUBJECT:
     DATE:


           (message written in this space)
```

Because the memo is an informal communication, you may sometimes write the message in longhand. Whether you handwrite or type, the form does not require a salutation or signature. You will, however, see a memorandum with initials written by the name on the "From" line; they signify that the memo was read and approved after it was prepared. You may wish to do the same.

The following are suggestions for writing effective memoranda:

Write a memorandum only when necessary.
Use a standard form.
Keep to one page if possible.
Organize material so it is easy to see and read: use lists, headings, an outline, and
    white space.

Type whenever possible; single or double space; be consistent.

Use block or indented style to show paragraphs; be consistent.

Use headings against the left margin. Type them in full caps, in a different type font, underline them, or distinguish them in some other way.

Make headings precise and meaningful.

Identify subsequent pages by subject, date, and page number.

Omit a complimentary close.

Sign only if you wish; you may initial the memorandum next to your name at the top.

Develop a clean, to-the-point writing style.

Write well. Present yourself as a logical, no-nonsense, relevant thinker.

Memoranda Examples

The three examples on pages 149, 150, and 151 illustrate the different kinds of information that can be shared through the memorandum, the range of audience, and a good, clear writing style.

Letters

Most of us write few letters in our domestic lives. Instead, we call people on the phone or get into our cars and visit those with whom we want to talk. Just three generations ago such conveniences were unavailable, and people relied upon letters to communicate both personal and business matters.

If you are fortunate enough to have any of your grandparents' or great-grandparents' correspondence, look through it sometime for the way people took time to describe and for the amount of technical information they sent to one another—weather conditions, crop yields, new construction, medical news. My maternal grandfather was the principal carpenter in a small Kentucky town of around 700 at the turn of the century. My mother has a box of his letters detailing information of his craft: the price and availability of materials, the number of men employed and cost of labor, delivery dates or problems with transporting materials (mainly lumber) over dirt roads by horse and wagon in bad weather, contracts presented and closed, construction progress on particular houses being built around town. People like my grandfather understood the need to write letters, and many became known for and took pride in their individual writing styles.

Our fast-paced lives today make us impatient with writing details. Many of you may not yet have written enough letters to develop a signature style. Your letter writing activity will increase dramatically after you begin working.

Business Letter Formats

In personal correspondence it matters little where you place the date, salutation, inside address, or close, or whether you include all these formal parts of the letter.

Example 1

MEMORANDUM

TO: Administration
     Department Heads
     Directors of Nursing
     Coordinators
     Head Nurses

FROM: Linda Prater, R.N.
       Director of Surgery/Emergency Nursing

DATE: June 3, 19XX

Susan Kern, R.N., is now Head Nurse over Emergency and FlightHelp.

Janet Sims, R.N., has been appointed as Chief Flight Nurse (Assistant Head Nurse) of FlightHelp and will report to Susan.

Please join with me in congratulating Susan and Janet in their new positions.

LP:fkm

Example 2

MEMORANDUM

TO: All Nursing Units

FROM: Sally McKenzie, Housekeeping Manager

RE: Night Discharges

DATE: October 13, 19XX

Many of you already know that the Housekeeping Department maintains two housekeepers on staff until 9:00 p.m. to complete evening discharges. Of late, the two housekeepers are not being notified of discharge rooms. This situation leaves rooms uncleaned and creates problems for Admitting because rooms aren't being readied after evening discharges.

Kindly notify our housekeepers as soon as possible of a discharge so they can ready the room that day.

Your assistance is appreciated. The housekeepers can be reached by the beeper system. Their beeper number is 140.

Copies: Sue Smith, Director of Maintenance
         Ruth Nobel, Director of Admitting

Example 3

MEMORANDUM

TO: All Hospital Physicians

FROM: Carol Blalock, Transcription Supervisor

SUBJECT: Dictation over telephone lines

DATE: January 23, 19XX

Misusing the dictation system can delay the delivery of your report to the patient record.

When you dictate using the telephone lines (426-6845 or 426-3479), remember first to enter your physician ID code (888) plus the report code (2 for H&P, 3 for consult, 4 for op note, and 5 for discharge). If you do not enter the above 4 digits, the first 10 seconds or so of your dictation do not record. Therefore, the transcriptionists miss the patient's name and identification information and often the first sentence or two of your dictation.

We appreciate your cooperation and want to continue to provide you with the best possible service.

In business writing, it matters. Several options are available. No one option is better than the other, but when you choose, you must stay with that form and not pick and choose among the options. The company you work for may have its own letter standard and expect you to use it; therefore, if such information is not included in your job orientation, inquire.

The three models on pages 153, 154, and 155 assume you are not using letterhead stationery and therefore indicate where to type your address. Most likely the company you work for will have its own printed paper, which will eliminate the need to type this item. When using letterhead, type the date underneath wherever the heading appears (left margin, center, right margin). Afterward, proceed with one of the letter formats.

Explanation of the Letter's Formal Parts

1. *Heading and Date.* The heading gives your correct address but not your name. The date is part of the heading. When giving the address, write out words like "street," "avenue," "road," "circle," "east," or "west." (The exception is in situations where the compass direction follows the street, "5400 Treeline Drive S.W."). Be complete. If the address includes a specific department, postal drop, or building's name, state it. Do not abbreviate the name of the city, but you may use the postal service's two-letter abbreviation for the state, territory, or district; no other abbreviation is acceptable. (See list on page 156.) The date may be written either September 25, 19XX, or 25 September 19XX. Do not put "th" or "rd" after the day (25, not 25th).

2. *Inside Address.* Companies, like individuals, are particular about their names. Write the inside address exactly as the person or company refers to him- or herself or itself. If the company abbreviates Company as Co., do the same thing; if the person signs her name Professor Sarah Smith, address her the same way. Do not be redundant and address someone as Dr. ——— and follow the name with M.D. or Ph.D. Abbreviate "Mr.," "Mrs.," and "Dr." used before names, but fully write out people's titles. It is a courtesy to include titles. If a person's title is one word like "Supervisor" or "Manager," type it after the name (Dr. Sarah Smith, Director). If the title is longer, type it on the next line by itself:

   Mr. George L. Tooley
   Senior Appraiser/Analyst

3. *Subject Line.* Modern usage often prefers a subject line, but it is not required. Inquire of your teacher or company if it is preferred. The main benefit of the line is to allow people to file or locate letters easily. It also eliminates the awkward beginning, "With reference to your phone call of Tuesday, October 25, 19XX, ..."

One-Page Letter Formats

1. *Block Letter*

6333 8th Avenue North	Heading
Evansville, IN 47715	
November 23, 19XX	Date
Mr. Charles P. Sims	Inside Address
Executive Vice President	
Medical Products Co.	
1234 Woodlawn Road	
St. Petersburg, FL 33710	
Subject: Requested price for product #329	Subject Line
Dear Mr. Sims:	Salutation

Opening of the letter---. ----------------------
--. --------
---.

Body of the letter requiring as many paragraphs as needed----------
--------------------. ---------------------------------. -----------------------------
---. -------------
---.

Close of the letter---. ------------------------
---.

Sincerely,	Complimentary Close
	Space for Signature
(Mrs.) Laura H. Hatchett	Typed Signature
LHH:ld	Identification
Enclosures (2)	Enclosure
c: Mr. John Smith	Copy Line
Ms. Jane Adams	

2. Semiblock Letter

Heading   7200 Greenwood Drive
Atlanta, GA 30301

Date   10 December 19XX

Mr. Lee L. Billingsly   Inside Address
Chief Executive Officer
Acme Tooling Company
534 Winding Street
St. Louis, MO 63121

Dear Mr. Billingsly: Salutation

Opening of letter--

Body of letter requiring as many paragraphs as needed---.

Close of letter--.

Complimentary Close   **Cordially,**

Space for Signature

Typed Signature   **Lee O. Campbell**
Executive Vice President

LOC:bw   Identification

Enclosure   Enclosure

c: Dr. L. Watson   Copy Line

3. *Alternative Block Letter*

January 5, 19XX   Date

Dr. Virginia R. Grimm   Inside Address
Senior Chemist
Clayton Biological Laboratory
15 Westbury Road
New Orleans, LA 70123

Subject: Your letter of December 21, 19XX   Subject Line

Dear Virginia:

Opening of letter--
---.

Body of letter--
---.

Close of letter---
---.

Sincerely yours,   Complimentary Close

                                                     Space for Signature

Jack T. Riley   Signature
8345 Redwing Drive   Address
Frankfort, KY 40601

Enclosures (3)   Enclosure

c: Dr. Kay Carson   Copy Line

POSTAL SERVICES'S OFFICIAL STATE ABBREVIATIONS

Alabama	AL	Montana	MT
Alaska	AK	Nebraska	NE
Arizona	AZ	Nevada	NV
Arkansas	AR	New Hampshire	NH
California	CA	New Jersey	NJ
Colorado	CO	New Mexico	NM
Connecticut	CT	New York	NY
Delaware	DE	North Carolina	NC
District of Columbia	DC	North Dakota	ND
Florida	FL	Ohio	OH
Georgia	GA	Oklahoma	OK
Guam	GU	Oregon	OR
Hawaii	HI	Pennsylvania	PA
Idaho	ID	Puerto Rico	PR
Illinois	IL	Rhode Island	RI
Indiana	IN	South Carolina	SC
Iowa	IA	South Dakota	SD
Kansas	KS	Tennessee	TN
Kentucky	KY	Texas	TX
Louisiana	LA	Utah	UT
Maine	ME	Vermont	VT
Maryland	MD	Virginia	VA
Massachusetts	MA	Virgin Islands	VI
Michigan	MI	Washington	WA
Minnesota	MN	West Virginia	WV
Mississippi	MS	Wisconsin	WI
Missouri	MO	Wyoming	WY

Begin subject lines with either "Subject:" or "Re:" and be specific in reference.

Re: Order problems   (The reference is too broad and not useful.)

Re: Gear breakage in Order #879; Shipped 3/18/XX
          (The reference is specific and useful.)

4. *Salutation.* A formality that remains in our casual world is to address the person you are writing to as "Dear Mrs. Shepherd:" or "Dear Professor Pickett:." Given today's informality, you may at first feel strange writing this, but do so. It is expected, and you will appear blunt and rude if you omit it. Follow the salutation with a colon (:).

The emphasis on nonsexist language has created a dilemma when you do not know the name of the person to address. The traditional salutations of the past—"Gentlemen" or "Dear Sir"—are frowned upon. No single solution has been accepted as tradition. You may want to experiment. Some address the department, "Dear Auditing Department:" or simply "Auditing Department:"; others give up and omit the salutation altogether. Do whatever you are comfortable writing, unless the letter is very important to you. If it is, find out a name even if you must make a phone call.

5. *Body.* For very short letters, add space before the heading so the letter does not appear top-heavy with too much white space at the bottom. For a discussion of letter content and style, see pages 159–162.

Not all letters can fit onto one page. Remember to note correctly the continued pages. Before you use two pages, look to see if you can reduce the letter by editing. As you edit, check to see that you do not split a date or a person's name between two lines. In formal letters, it is also better not to split words between lines.

6. *Complimentary Close.* Be reserved. Choose standard closes, such as "Sincerely," "Sincerely yours," "Cordially," or "Very truly yours." Capitalize only the first letter of the first word, and place a comma (,) after the close.

7. *Signature.* Type your name four lines beneath the complimentary close. Do not precede the name with a title such as "Dr." or "Senator." You may, however, follow the name with professional initials such as M.D. or P.E. If you wish to include a title, type it beneath your name. A married woman should use her own first name, not her husband's.

Sign above your typed name. Write naturally but clearly. Avoid colored ink, flair pens, and fancy handwriting. Read the letter before you sign it. Your signature indicates approval. Do not sign letters that have errors or look messy. The letter you send reflects the care you take in your work.

To help recipients of correspondence avoid awkward situations, women can indicate in parentheses before their names how they want to be addressed, for example, (Mrs.), (Miss), (Ms.) Jane M. Scott. Placing the title in parentheses keeps the writer from violating the custom of not placing a title before the signature.

8. *Identification.* When someone other than yourself prepares the letter, an identification line is used. The writer's initials appear first in capitals; the typist's follow in small case (WAS:jmc).

9. *Enclosure.* In technical correspondence, people like to know they received all that was sent. If you enclose two pieces of separate information along with the letter, you may want to use an enclosure line. Formats vary for identifying enclosures. Some possibilities follow:

Enclosure	(The number and subject of the enclosure are not identified.)
Enclosures (2)	(The reader knows to expect two enclosures.)

Enclosures: Woolrey Abstract Drilling Permit #19876	(The reader expects two enclosures and knows specifically what they are.)

10. *Copy Line.* No one wants to be surprised to learn that someone else received a copy of a letter sent to him or her. Always list those people to whom you sent copies of the letter.

Additional Page Formats

Letters that continue for more than one page need to be identified on each page so that if individual pages become separated, they can easily be inserted in the right order and into the right letter. Identification also tells the receiver whether he or she has received all the pages written (see Additional Page Example). Such accounting is particularly desirable in letters of agreement or other legal matters.

Use letterhead stationery only for the first page. Use a plain paper of the same quality for additional pages. To identify subsequent pages, type (beginning at the left margin) the name of the person receiving the letter, the page number, and the date.

Additional Page Example

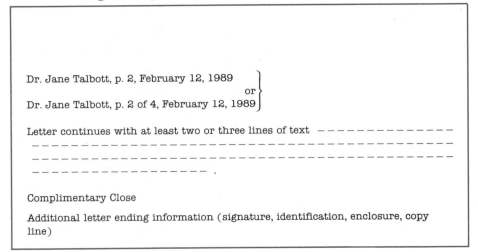

Dr. Jane Talbott, p. 2, February 12, 1989

or

Dr. Jane Talbott, p. 2 of 4, February 12, 1989

Letter continues with at least two or three lines of text – – – – – – – – – – – – –
– –
– –
– – – – – – – – – – – – – – – – – – – .

Complimentary Close

Additional letter ending information (signature, identification, enclosure, copy line)

Envelope Format

The envelope makes the first impression on the reader. Type it correctly or see that it is done correctly. Space attractively. It is not presumptious for a secretary or co-worker to open business mail, so if your letter contains confidential or personal information, type "PERSONAL" or "CONFIDENTIAL" on the envelope directly below the address. (See Envelope Example, facing page.)

Letter Formats and Word Processing

If you type many letters using the same format, a word processing program with a preset format is a nice convenience. You can call up the program and begin writing without having to think about spacing. Some programs have default settings so that information like the date automatically appears as the current date. The heading, complimentary close, and signature appear typed. To change the information, you merely type over the default settings.

Envelope Example

Mr. William R. Martin
Sportsman Archery Inc.
5384 Willow Road
Sacramento, CA 95813

Mr. Raymond P. Rawley
Production Manager
Laminated Products Inc.
145 Eighteenth Street
San Antonio, TX 78291
CONFIDENTIAL

Letter Stationery, Margins, and Equipment

If you are buying your own paper and not using the company's, buy a good quality, white or off-white, unruled, standard sized (8 1/2″ × 11″), bond paper. It will take the imprint well and make a good impression for you.

Leave at least an inch for all four margins: top, bottom, both sides.

Prepare your letter on the best equipment available. Do not settle for type-writers with dirty keys that make o's look like ●'s or e's look like *e*'s. If you use word processing, be certain the printer is letter quality. Some dot matrix printers are now near letter quality. Ribbons should be fresh and make a crisp imprint.

Letter Writing Style and Content

Rules have exceptions, including the rules set forth in the following guidelines; however, for general use, observe tradition. You will have better success doing so than creating your own style and organization. After you write with assurance, you will recognize times when an out-of-the-ordinary style, format, or organization is an advantage.

General Guidelines

- Think out all letters beforehand and write with the reader in mind. What role or relation does the receiver have to you, the writer? What exactly is it that you need to say?
- Follow the established organization:

    Introduction. Open with a short paragraph. If possible, begin in a gracious way—thank the person for the inquiry, request, order, opportunity, a recent lunch, or conversation. Remark positively about a subject related to the letter being written. State forthrightly the subject or purpose of the correspondence.

Body. Develop the subject or purpose. Write only related information. Delete the extraneous, the aside. Begin each paragraph with a clear purpose sentence. Write to-the-point paragraphs. Use simple but accurate language and direct, uncomplicated sentences. State clearly what you expect from the reader. Technical terms relating to any discipline should be avoided or explained when writing to the nonspecialist in the field. Be complete when giving instructions, asking for information, stating a complaint, specifying an order or responsibility. Present information logically, chronologically, or in some other way that makes understanding complete and easy. If a reply is required, give a phone number and include the area code. Also, give the address and include the zip code.

It is acceptable to type the letter so as to make it easy to read. For example, you can list information and distinguish it by numbers or another mark like a bullet (●) or asterisk (∗). You can introduce paragraphs with headings. However, do not use such methods unless they truly aid clarity. For the most part, proper paragraphing will do. Place everything about the same topic or idea in the same paragraph. Introduce the paragraph with a direct sentence telling its purpose.

Conclusion. Thank the receiver again or offer assistance in some way. When appropriate, foster future relations. Tell of another service or product the receiver may be interested in acquiring or learning about.

An application of the preceding discussion on letter organization follows:

Skeletal Outline for Letter That Gives Bad News

Introduction:
A letter that gives someone bad news should open by stating why the news is being given, how the decision about the news was decided, and what the reason(s) for the decision was.

Body:
The body of the letter needs to be written carefully because future relationships with the receiver can be affected by the tone and style of your writing. When someone can correct a situation, he or she should be told how; when the company or you can assist, an offer should be made. In any case requiring specific action, the receiver should be told clearly what to do. The objective is to correct the situation, if possible, without embarrassing or insulting the receiver.

Conclusion:
The closing, depending on the circumstances, may express regret or offer assistance.

- Very often letters should focus on a "you" concept rather than "we" or "I." Remember, the receiver is more interested in how the information affects, benefits, relates to his or her work or life than what it means to your company or to

Example That Generally Uses the Bad News Outline

Re: Check No. _____ dated April 24, 19XX
    On City Bank
    Account No. _____ for $367.90

Dear _____ :

On April 26, 19XX, you cashed the above listed check at our Fairlawn Branch at 2380 Waterworks Road.

The first time this check was presented for payment at City Bank it was returned due to "Insufficient Funds." We sent it through the second time, and the check was returned "Account Closed." We spoke with you on the phone about this problem on May 18; you said you would send payment, but you have not.

I must receive payment of this check from you by June 8. If payment is not received by this date, I will have no choice but to turn your account over to the Credit Bureau of Smithtown, Inc., for collection.

Should you have any questions, please come in or call me at (xxx) 479-xxxx. Thank you.

                Sincerely,

you. If you emphasize the relation to the receiver, you increase the potential for results.

- Write grammatically correct sentences. Avoid trite remarks and wordy phrases like "I am writing to ask if . . . ." For the most part, use active rather than passive verbs ("write" rather than "was written"). Spell and punctuate correctly. If you appear unlearned about language, the reader can wonder what else you do not know.

- Proofread. Do not send letters with errors. Consider the tone. Are you going to be comfortable about having sent this letter two days from now? If you have been sarcastic, insulting, or cute, you may dream of ways to break into the post office to recover the letter before it is delivered. Avoid the need for such agony by waiting to send letters about which you are unsure or in which you are too emotional. Words are powerful weapons; once said or written, they cannot be retracted. They remain in people's memories regardless of whether people say they will forget what was said. Use language carefully, and remember that manners in the business world are essential. If you have not cared before about being polished, care now.

Letters for Different Occasions

The number of reasons for writing letters is too large to be covered completely in this text. Texts devoted entirely to letter writing are available to you through the library or bookstore. They will offer far more examples. The intention here is to discuss several common types and illustrate good organization and style.

Inquiry Letters

Normal inquiries ask a person to do something for you: give information, send equipment, perform a service, or let you do something. You are the one making the request, so remember to ask, not tell, someone to do something. Inquiry letters usually include the following elements. They may be written in another order, and the individual situation will determine how much detail you need to write about each point:

1. Identify yourself.

2. State clearly and completely the information, opportunity, or materials you want and the reason/need for the request.

3. Identify what you plan to do with the information or materials or how they will be used.

4. Offer confidentiality, if appropriate.

5. Tell the reader why you specifically are making the request of him or her.

6. Close with a gracious thank you.

Example 1. A Bank Asks a Customer for Information

Dear _____ :

It seems like a very short time, but the first year of your Opportunity Account has passed, and it is time for us to update your annual financial statement. A form to complete and a postage-paid return envelope are enclosed for your convenience.

We are happy to have served you this past year with this unique financial service. We look forward to serving you and all your financial needs in the future. Remember that we offer full service banking, including loans, investments, and checking.

Please call us if you have any question or if we can help in any banking service (507) 378 XXXX.

Sincerely,

Example 2. Student Inquires about Summer Work

3210 Elm Street
Evansville, IN 47715
February 7, 19XX

Ms. Susan Cronk
Art Director
WVIS Television 9
P.O. Box 1764
Memphis, TN 38101

Dear Ms. Cronk:

Summer is quickly approaching, and I am looking forward to my internship
with you, particularly since this internship will be strictly in computer
graphics. As you know, I am working toward a degree in Computer Science
with emphasis in computer graphics at the University of Evansville. As a
requirement toward the degree, each student must complete a senior project,
a practical application in one's area of study. Each student must also find a
company or faculty member to sponsor his or her project. Is there a graphics application to your systems that would benefit the station and also help
me fulfill my graduation requirement?

The Computer Science Department is very flexible about the definition of the
project. I prefer to begin work this summer, but realize that the project
could not interrupt the station's daily business or replace the work expected
of me as a summer intern. However, I am willing to work in addition to my
regular work time. Depending on the size and complexity of the project, I
would need some technical information and advice from your staff, but I
would work primarily on my own.

I hope you will consider sponsoring me. I am very anxious to graduate, and
completing this project will bring me a step closer to fulfilling this goal. Already I have learned a great deal from working with you, and I appreciate
your help. I will call the week of February 10 to learn your decision. Thank
you.

Sincerely,

Jeanne Marie Groene

Jeanne Marie Groene

Comments on the Student Letter

Jeanne Marie uses a very nice tone. She is clear in explaining her request; remembers to ask, not tell; and assures the art director that the project will be worked out with little bother to the station and on the student's own time. Most people like to help others, so her closing remarks about having "learned from" the director and being "anxious to graduate" are appealing. It is good to stay in control as much as possible. Jeanne Marie tries to do so by saying she will call the director. If she had said, "Please call me sometime next week. . ." and the director did not, Jeanne Marie is in an awkward position. It is embarrassing to call and say, "I haven't heard from you, so I thought I would call." It is equally unsettling to sit by the phone waiting for the call that may never come.

Good News—Bad News Letters

Answers to inquiries, responses about job opportunities, personnel evaluations, news about contracts are but a few of the types of letters carrying good or bad news for the receiver.

Everyone enjoys writing the good news; it is important, however, to learn to write bad news—to say "no." Do not hedge. If the loan cannot be made, the job cannot be offered, the order cannot be filled or given, the delivery cannot be made by such a date, say so. Do not offer false hope or mislead. Your reputation will be enhanced if you can be relied upon to give straight information. Always be humane.

A common outline for response letters is as follows:

Good News	*Bad News*
Refer to the request or subject.	Refer to the request or subject.
State the good news.	Give reasons for the bad news.
Explain completely all that is needed to satisfy the request or make happen the good news.	State clearly that the request is denied—that the decision is no.
Does the recipient need to complete papers, sign anything, or is everything needed enclosed in the letter?	Suggest alternatives.
Give additional suggestions if applicable.	Thank the person for the request or whatever. If appropriate, compliment the person for his or her initiative. When can the person inquire again and perhaps be successful?
Close in a courteous way.	Close in a courteous and sincere manner.

A Note about Form Letters

Efficiency demands that certain letters, like the two following, be developed and used over and over again. No one can dispute the business sense of this idea. The abuse occurs when people or companies use form letters even though they do not exactly fit the situation or when the form is poorly reproduced. For example, as a result of being copied, the form may appear crooked on the page, or some forms are reproduced with lines drawn in for the writer to fill in particular infor-

Example 1. Termination of Part-Time Employee

Dear _____ :

Part-time employees are a valuable asset to the work force at Smith County Bank. However, we find it necessary periodically to review our files and terminate those who, for various reasons, have not worked recently. We regret that your name falls in that category.

After reading the enclosed termination papers, please sign and return one copy to us in the envelope provided; the second copy is for your records.

We request that you close your employee checking account and hope that you will open a regular checking account at the branch of your choice. This action will allow the 200 series to remain employee accounts.

Please call me at (112) 574 **XXXX** if you have any questions.

                                        Sincerely,

Example 2. Notification of Account Approval

Dear _____ :

We are pleased to inform you that your Smith Bank's Gold Checking application has been approved. Personalized checks—both the Gold Checks and Choice Checks for your VISA or MasterCard—have been ordered for you. Your new VISA or MasterCard and Automatic Teller cards with a daily withdrawal limit of $400. are also being processed.

Your Gold Checking package will be available approximately seven to ten banking days from the date of this letter. At that time, a customer service representative will call you to schedule a convenient time to present the Gold Checking package to you.

Thank you for selecting Smith Bank. We are pleased to include you in a special group of customers and are committed to being responsive to your financial needs.

Sincerely,

mation. The person receiving this form is insulted that he or she deserves so little attention. When you use a form letter, be certain that it totally applies; if it does only partially, use the form letter as a basis and construct a letter that is more appropriate. Memory typewriters, word processors, good copy machines, and letter quality printers allow the creation of professionally appearing form letters. Do not settle for less.

Cover/Application Letters

Cover letters accompany formal reports, proposals, and other formal documents. The type most relevant to your needs probably is an application letter to accompany your résumé. Apply the guidelines for letter writing style and format (pp. 152–160) and consider the following advice.

The application letter is an opportunity to reveal your ability to communicate and a bit of your personality. Focus on "you" rather than "I"—how your interest or experience or education can serve the company rather than what the company can do for you. For those jobs that you most want, find out about the company and demonstrate that knowledge and interest. The reference librarian will direct you to the library's sources on companies. Read about the product line, number of employees, locations, annual income, organizational structure. Use what you learn to write why you want to be part of the organization or why you want to be involved in the production of the company's product. Companies also publish their own annual reports and other publicity pieces. Write for and use such to demonstrate in your letter and interview that you have done your homework and have real reasons for making this application.

Organize the letter carefully and write about specifics. Most application letters should consist of one page, omit a subject line, and address a specific person. The following suggestions provide a guide:

Introduction. Tell how you learned of the opening, specifically apply for a position, and make some kind of statement about how you can contribute to the firm. (In other words, demonstrate that you know something about the company.) Set a tone for the letter that is neither too subservient nor too assertive. Be confident but comfortable with your attitude.

Body. Write strong topic sentences. Include specific detail instead of general facts ("I graduated from . . ." "I worked for . . ."). Think about what you did in school and work that is applicable to the position you want. Say that. Show the reader you have thought about yourself, this position, and the company.

Conclusion. Be gracious, but keep whatever control you can. If the company is local, say you will call. Remember that the whole purpose of this letter is to acquire an interview. Move toward that goal in the close. Explain when you are available. Tell when you can travel.

Example 1: Student's Application Letter

Notice the tone, organization, and relating of her experience to the company's needs.

Student's Application Letter

300 S. Frederick Street
Evansville, Indiana 47714
February 4, 19XX

Mr. David R. Estes, Manager
College Relations
McDonnell Douglas Corp.
P.O. Box 516
Dept. 062-CPA
St. Louis, MO 63166

Dear Mr. Estes:

This August, following my graduation from the University of Evansville, I plan to pursue a career in mechanical engineering. In the CPC ANNUAL I noted your need for design engineers. My senior design project and my academic achievements in machine analysis and design, mechanical vibrations, experimental methods, environmental systems, and fluid mechanics, in addition to courses in basic thermal and design areas, qualify me for a position in aircraft design and flight simulation with McDonnell Douglas Corporation.

My senior design project, the design of an on-ship testing system for the ram air turbine of the EA-6B aircraft, with the Naval Weapons Support Center at Crane, Indiana, is providing practical work experience. I am working with another student, a faculty adviser, and two engineers from the Naval Weapons Support Center on this project, which, along with my other qualifications, is outlined on the enclosed résumé.

I would like to meet with you or another representative of McDonnell Aircraft Company to discuss your organization and what I might expect as an entry level design engineer. I can be contacted by mail at the above address. If you are interested in my qualifications, I would appreciate hearing from you. Thank you for your consideration.

Sincerely,

Cathi Crabtree

Cathi Crabtree

Enclosure

Example 2: Student's Application Letter: Drafts 1 and 2

Notice the editorial remarks on the draft on page 171 and compare this letter with the student's effective second draft on page 172. The first writing illustrates our tendency sometimes to use informal language for formal situations. Remember to adjust language and tone to suit appropriately each writing situation.

Example 3: Student's Letter Confirming an Interview Appointment

The letter on page 173 shows initiative. Not every student takes the time or makes the effort to confirm campus interviews. Alan does. In so doing, he introduces himself and tells why he is particularly interested in and suited for the position. His letter is articulate and courteous. Very likely, the company will be favorably impressed and anticipate the opportunity to interview him. You can do the same thing.

Résumés

The task is to present whatever experience you have in the best manner in order to obtain an interview. Most students will design a one-page résumé because their experience is not extensive. Senior applicants are generally on equal footing. Everyone has a degree; everyone has taken a similar core of courses; most have had some part-time work; everyone can write about something accomplished in college—such as student government work, sports, social organizations, or independent projects. Your job is to make the most out of your schoolwork and experience.

Format

- Base your organization on logic. No single pattern is best. What do you most want to highlight? Place it first.
- Arrange information attractively on the page. Be consistent in presenting information within a unit like "Experience." Capitalize and punctuate alike.
- Use phrases and dependent clauses rather than complete sentences to present information. Make every piece of information active and persuasive.
- Type the résumé perfectly and reproduce it in a manner that looks professional. Select a clear type and a good paper in a conservative color.

See page 173 and 174 for a sample format.

First Draft of Student's Application Letter

1264 Washington Street, Apt. A
City, State Zip Code
November 6, 19XX

Mr. John Burdette
Personnel Superintendent
SHW Industries Inc., Midwest Division
Denver, CO 80201

Dear Mr. Burdette:

Thank you for interviewing ~~with~~ me at Southwestern University on
Repetitious structure. Too much emphasis on "I".
Tuesday, November 4. I enjoyed talking with you and watching the SHW

video presentation. I am impressed with the company and would like to see
Watch tone. You are not judging the
one of the plants or the corporate headquarters. *Company as much as they are*
judging you.

During the interview, I mentioned that R&D at corporate would be my
Will everyone understand that this means Research & Development?
initial preference. However, I am very flexible and I wanted to add that the
weak sentence structure *wordy*
small plant setting sounds appealing as well. This is because I enjoy devel-
best word? ~~Do not use contractions in~~ *formal writing.*
oping good working relationships with plant people. I've found I can gain
poor language
the respect of these folks because I care about their opinions and will listen
spelling error) Poor language. Do not use slang. This language
to their ideas verses just blowing them off because they don't have a "for- *could seem to*
be street language.
"mal" education. *avoid* *Be careful.*
contractions
sounds pompous and elitist
In any case, SHW sounds like a company that works with its people so

they are both productive and happy. So I'm confident that if and when I

have an opportunity to be employed by SHW, the initial job direction will not

make or break my career. *Suggests poor attitude*

Thanks again for coming to Southwestern and I hope to see you again.
Sounds as if you were the
host, and invited them. Sincerely,
Watch pompous tone.

Student's Name

Second Draft of Student's Application Letter

1264 Washington Street, Apt. A
City, State Zip Code
November 6, 19XX

Mr. John Burdette
Personnel Superintendent
SHW Industries Inc., Midwest Division
Denver, CO 80201

Dear Mr. Burdette:

Thank you for interviewing me at Southwestern University on Tuesday, November 4. I enjoyed talking with you and was impressed by the SHW video presentation.

During the interview, I mentioned that Research and Development at corporate headquarters would be my initial preference. However, I am very flexible and want to add that the small plant setting sounds appealing as well because I enjoy developing good working relationships with plant people. I have found through my co-op experience that because I care about their opinions and will listen to their ideas, I gain their respect.

In any case, SHW sounds like a company that works with its people so they are both productive and happy. I am confident that if and when employed by SHW, whether placed in a headquarters or plant setting, I will learn and be a productive, useful employee.

Thank you for interviewing me at the university. I hope to see you again.

Sincerely,

Student's Name

Student's Letter Confirming Interview

Sender's Address

_____

Date

Inside Address

_____

_____

Dear Sirs:

According to Kurt Black, the personnel director at Southwestern University, you have openings for electrical engineers. In May 1989, I will graduate with a degree in Electrical Engineering and am interested in McDonnell Douglas as a potential employer.

As a pilot and co-op engineering student, I feel that my background and interests in many ways match the needs of several groups within McAir. Those that I am best trained for and most interested in are Flight Test and Operation, Avionics, and Weapons Systems. Given my flying experience and my practical electrical engineering training and experience, I believe I would be able to integrate smoothly and quickly into the McDonnell Douglas Corporation and be productive sooner than average graduates.

On October 21 at 8:30 a.m., I am scheduled to interview with campus recruiters from your company. I look forward to that time.

Sincerely,

Alan Wolfinger

Alan Wolfinger

enc. résumé

Sample Format for Résumé

RÉSUMÉ
Name
Street Address
City, State Zip Code
Telephone Number(s) including area code

CAREER OBJECTIVE

This item is not necessary to include. If you do, make it specific and thoughtful. In general, avoid saying that you seek a position that will lead to management. Your work experience and career are too young to talk about you as a manager. Instead mention topics relevant to the work you are applying for and topics that make you an attractive candidate: your ability to be flexible, your desire for responsibility and advancement, your interest in continued learning, your wish to put into practice your communication skills.

PERSONAL INFORMATION

Today, with Affirmative Action, such information is less important than it used to be. If you want to include this data, place it first or last before "References." I suggest last. This is not information that will get you the job.

Height: Health:
Weight: Marital Status:
Hobbies & Interests:

EDUCATION

_____

_____

_____

List schools beginning with the present. Give the name of the school, its location, dates attended. Other items to include are relevant courses and grade point average. (You may as well include it even if it is not outstanding. If you omit it, people can assume it is worse than it is. Try giving the average only in your major if that is better.) Tell scholarships or honors. Specify the qualifications for receiving the scholarship or honor and the date you received it. List languages you speak other than English.

EXPERIENCE

_____

_____

List places and positions beginning with the most recent one. Identify the position and specifically note responsibilities. Refer to work or experience that prepares you for the position for which you are applying.

COLLEGE ACTIVITIES

_____

_____

_____

In addition to listing college activities, list offices or duties you performed. If an organization or activity is not easily familiar to others, identify it. Give dates of participation.

REFERENCES

_____

_____

If you give names and addresses, ask the people first if you may list their names. You may want to have each of your references write a general letter and have it filed in the college placement office. If so, say that your letters of reference are available upon request from the office and give the address.

Example 1: Student's Résumé

The first and second drafts of this résumé illustrate how the student revised her résumé to present her qualifications in a more specific and relevant way. The first draft misses opportunities that could help the applicant.

Student's First Draft

RÉSUMÉ

CATHI ANN CRABTREE

300 S. Frederick Street
Evansville, Indiana 47714
Phone: (812) 477-5941

Objective	Mechanical engineering design position, preferably with a variety of projects.
Education 1982–1986	UNIVERSITY OF EVANSVILLE EVANSVILLE, INDIANA Bachelor of Science in Mechanical Engineering in May 1986. GPA of 3.14 on 4.0 scale. President's Scholarship recipient.
Employment 1982–Present	FINE & HATFIELD EVANSVILLE, INDIANA Word Processor Operator
1978–1980	REIS MOBILE CATERING SERVICE EVANSVILLE, INDIANA Waitress Earned 75% of college expenses.
College Activities	Four-year member of Society of Automotive Engineers. Secretary sophomore year. Four-year member of American Society of Mechanical Engineers. Participant in Society of Automotive Engineers' Mini Baja competition in sophomore and senior years.
References	Personal references available upon request.

Student's revised résumé:

RÉSUMÉ

CATHI ANN CRABTREE

4400 Schmitt Road
Wadesville, Indiana 47638
Phone: (812) 963-6430

Objective   Working as a mechanical engineer.

Education   University of Evansville   Evansville, Indiana
1982–1986
Bachelor of Science in Mechanical Engineering in May 1986.

Senior design project with Naval Weapons Support Center, Crane, Indiana: design of a ram air turbine on-ship testing system for the EA-6B aircraft; worked with another student and two engineers at NWSC; included research in air ejectors, nozzles and compressors; nominated for Most Outstanding 1986 Mechanical Engineering Senior Design Project Award.

Received Certification for Engineer-In-Training.
President's Scholarship recipient.
The National Dean's List, 1985–86.

GPA of 3.14 on 4.0 scale.

Earned 75% of college expenses.

Employment
1982–Present   Fine & Hatfield, Attorneys   Evansville, Indiana
Word Processor Operator: Lanier One-Step Word Processor; handled confidential information; assisted in training new word processor operators; trusted with securing of entire office building on a weekly basis (consists of possession of keys to main entrance and security alarm system).

1978–1980   Reis Mobile Catering Service   Evansville, Indiana
Waitress: gained experience in dealing well with the public.

College   Mini Baja competition participant (Society of Automotive
Activities   Engineers) in sophomore and senior years, Project Coordinator senior year.

Society of Automotive Engineers, four-year member, Secretary sophomore year.

American Society of Mechanical Engineers, four-year member.

References   Personal references available upon request.
Contact: Cathi Ann Crabtree at above address.

Example 2: Student's Résumé: Promotes the Student's Work Experience

ALAN WOLFINGER

School Address:
1631 Franklin, Apt. A
Evansville, IN 47711
812-423-1837

Home Address:
R.R. 2
Haubstadt, IN 47639
812-867-2804

CAREER OBJECTIVE:
An **electrical engineering** position in which I can advance through accomplishments to a management position in Manufacturing, Product, or R&D Engineering.

EDUCATION:
Bachelor of Science in Electrical Engineering, May 1987 University of Evansville, Evansville, Indiana

GPA: 3.67/4.0 scale, Dean's List 6/8 times, Eta Kappa Nu (electrical engineering honor fraternity), Phi Beta Chi (science honor fraternity).

Major Subjects
Advanced Microprocessors: Completed design and construction of a basic microprocessor-controlled robot. Optical Electronics, Control Systems, Lasers.

Degree requirements place emphasis on electronic design.

Financial
80% self-supporting after freshman year.

EXPERIENCE:
Whirlpool Corporation, Evansville, IN Co-op May 1983 to August 1986

Designed and built a computerized chemical mixing control system which went on-line in production ahead of schedule. Resulted in increased productivity by allowing technicians to do other tasks while the computer controlled mixing. Project involved software and hardware design as well as custom design and construction of the computer chassis, cabinet, and control panel.

Conducted a competitive product analysis on room air conditioner products, studying the effect of product design on noise level. Successfully adapted competitive evaporator fan assembly design to a current Whirlpool model air conditioner achieving increased air flow rate and reduced noise level at original fan motor speed. Recommended engineering investigate redesign of that aspect of product.

Conducted sound frequency spectrum analyses on refrigerator and freezer products to correlate product design and noise level/frequency. Performed aural evaluations and special tests and investigations as needed for test fixture design and development.

Designed and supervised construction of specialized laboratory equipment requiring good mechanical comprehension.

Conducted performance tests on dehumidifiers and sound tests on room air conditioners and dehumidifiers while working in Product Engineering as a product tester.

Initiated work orders and expedited completion of work. Prepared project layouts, wiring plans, parts lists, and machine tool drawing modifications. Self-taught Pascal prior to using it to develop test programs.

Radio Technician. Milan, Italy June 1985.
Worked one month in a radio station in Milan, Italy. Modified the station's sound mixing equipment to allow for remote control of recording equipment.

Keypunch Operator. Emge Packing Co., Ft. Branch, IN, August 1980 to June 1982.
Took distributor orders over phone, entered order data, operated IBM System 34 computer for data processing.

Familiar Equipment and Software:
CAD drafting (AutoCAD system), Audio Spectrum Analyzer, TI990/101 single board computer and support boards, Allen-Bradley Programmable Controller, Wordstar, Dbase3, Lotus123, MacWrite.

ACTIVITIES: President, Inter-Varsity Christian Fellowship
Lead the 4 member executive committee in program planning, goal setting, and evaluations.

Attended month-long "School of Leadership Training" camp offered through Inter-Varsity.

IEEE, Mortar Board, Kappa Mu Epsilon, Blue Key.

Private Pilot-Airplane Single Engine Land. Current in Cessna 152 and 172.

REFERENCES: Available upon request.

Example 3: Student's Résumé: Promotes the Student's Academic Experience

RÉSUMÉ

Ronald E. McRae Jr.
2010 Lincoln Avenue, Apt. 10
Evansville, IN 47714
(812) 473-7160
(812) 324-2908

CAREER OBJECTIVE

Design/Test Engineer in aerospace or automotive industry.

EDUCATION

B.S. in Mechanical Engineering; emphasis on design; University of Evansville, Evansville, Indiana: Will graduate with honors in May 1987. Current G.P.A. 3.87 overall, 4.0 Engineering on 4.0 scale.

Senior Design
Currently writing a computer program that will monitor a boiler feed pump at Sigeco Power Station in Warrick County, Indiana.

Educational Financing
Financed 100 percent of education through summer employment and scholarships, including President's Scholarship awarded for academic achievement, Pott Foundation Scholarship awarded for science achievement.

Student Activities
Phi Beta Chi (honorary fraternity)
Phi Kappa Phi (honorary fraternity)
Sigma Phi Epsilon (social fraternity)
American Society of Automotive Engineers (student section)
Society of Automotive Engineers (student section)
Secretary-Treasurer of Society of Automotive Engineers

Miscellaneous
Attended Harlaxton College in Grantham, England, for one semester. Member of University of Evansville Mini-baja team that competed in 1986 SAE Midwest baja competition.

WORK EXPERIENCE

Service Department, Memering Buick, Vincennes, Indiana, summers of 1984, 1985, and 1986.
Job function: Mechanical maintenance including service, body work, and major clean-up of cars.

REFERENCES

Available upon request.

Example: Student's Computerized Form Letter

> 1631 Franklin, Apt. A
> Evansville, IN 47711
> &DATE&
>
> &TITL/O&&FN/O& &LN/O&
> &POS/O&
> &DEPT/O&
> &ADDR1/O&
> &NAME1&
> &NAME2/O&
> &ADDR2/O&
> &ADDR3/O&
> &CITY&, &STATE& &ZIP&
>
> Dear &TITL/O&&LN/O&&SIRS/O&:
>
> I am a prospective Electrical Engineering graduate (May 1987) of the University of Evansville in Evansville, Indiana, and am very interested in &INFNAM& as a potential employer. My résumé is enclosed for your review.
>
> The high commitment of &INFNAM& to &AREA1& &AREA2& &AREA3& is what interests me the most about the company. Having completed the co-op program with Whirlpool Corporation, Evansville Division, I have gained practical engineering experience in project management, design, analysis, and testing.
>
> I believe my education, experience, and interests match the needs of several groups within &INFNAM& and would like to schedule an interview to that end.
>
> Sincerely,
>
> *Alan Wolfinger*
>
> Alan Wolfinger
>
> aw
>
> enclosure

Word Processing Conveniences

Writing résumés and application letters is made easier by word processing because you can call up the basic letter, copy it to another file, edit it to fit the particular position, print and send it, and still have the basic letter available. This process saves time and allows you easily to personalize the correspondence. Word processing also lets you update or edit the résumé as experience and situations change. The editing is so simple with word processing and so fast. Information can be deleted and inserted and pages reformed in a matter of minutes.

Example: Application Form Letter with Variable Information to Be Inserted by a WORDSTAR's Merge Program

With WORDSTAR, the writer types an ampersand (&), the name of the variable, and another "&" each place in the letter that a piece of variable information is to be inserted. By entering correct commands, the writer can designate the length of the insertion and/or skip an insertion. The program will also let you create abbreviations to use as variables. For example, in line 3 of this letter, &INFNAM& means informal name. To learn the WORDSTAR commands or ones applicable to the program available to you, study what your user's manual has to say about merge programs. You need to study the particular word processing program available to you.

Practice Exercises

1. Write a letter of inquiry. Answer the inquiry. Format and organize well.
2. Collect a sample of form letters sent by companies or individuals. Evaluate whether they are personalized to fit the situations and whether they make a good impression. Explain your evaluation either orally to the class or in writing to the teacher.
3. Look through the newspapers or professional journals in your field. Find an ad for a job you would like to have upon graduation. Write a cover letter to the company and design a résumé.
4. Your teacher will distribute a package of memoranda. Decide which are good and say why, which are poor and why, and which never needed to be written. The class can discuss their impressions.
5. Write a letter of bad news. In a group, exchange letters and have others in the group tell how they felt upon reading the letter and what they do or do not understand.
6. Use word processing to write as many of these assignments as possible.

Chapter 9

Proposals and Feasibility Reports

A company needs work to stay in business, and the proposal is one way work is acquired. It suggests a solution to a specific problem and requests permission to develop the solution. Proposals also seek permission to investigate subjects and/or sell services or products. The proposal can be made informally in a conversation. An oral agreement can be reached at the time and a work schedule or delivery time set. Proposals can also be presented formally in writing. We are concerned with those in writing.

Most entry-level positions do not involve writing formal proposals, but you will advance. When you do, you will need both to write and to use this type of document. This chapter tells about content and form in order to prepare you both to write and evaluate effective proposals. It does the same for the feasibility report.

Proposals

Solicited and Unsolicited

Solicited proposals occur when a company or individual recognizes a need and asks either an individual or company to submit a proposal. If others also are invited, your proposal must compete not only for the reader's attention and approval but also for a better solution, product, service, and price. The advantage of solicited proposals is that clients recognize the need, so the writer does not have to sell the idea. Unsolicited proposals occur when someone sees a need and, without being asked, writes a proposal. The difficulty is that the writer must convince the reader of a need as well as of the value of the proposed idea. The advantage is that the proposal most likely is not competing against other proposals offering alternate solutions or products. Your reputation will in part be made by the number of real problems or needs you recognize and solve. You must be successful not only in perceiving ideas but also in effectively communicating your understandings.

Audience

Begin the prewriting study with an audience analysis (see pp. 29–31). The reader is not interested in how great you think the idea is or how wonderful you believe it would be for the company to buy this new equipment or change a procedure. The reader wants to know how the idea saves the company time and money or causes work to be more effective. Put yourself in the reader's position. Anticipate what the reader must know to be persuaded and to give approval.

Find out how many people will read the proposal and who they are. If you cannot find out names, find out positions. Is the group diverse? Does it include people from different areas: finance, personnel, maintenance, product engineering, and marketing? If so, you should use language that everyone can understand or place technically complicated discussions in appendixes for those who seek detailed and quantified answers. The makeup of the group also defines the range of information to be covered: budget, work loads and work duties, sales advantages, and the like. If you know who will be reading, you know their interests. You can anticipate and answer their questions.

Proposals are often written to others in-house. The data processing department may suggest automating an in-house procedure. Personnel may suggest a different organization of people and duties. Maintenance may suggest a new procedure for an in-house production line. Even if the person who will approve the proposal is a friend or acquaintance with whom you work and are on a first name basis, or someone with whom you play golf on Saturdays, or attend the same church on Sundays, the business world expects you to know when and when not to be formal. In addressing anyone in the organization about a formal matter, you should use for the presentation a tone and quality that is businesslike and without assumptions. Using the "old buddy" tone or assuming the reader can ask for specifics later can cause you embarrassment when the proposal is returned marked incomplete or is refused. Remember that people who approve projects must justify their decisions. If you want your proposal approved, write clearly and accurately so the reader can make an informed decision. You will not always succeed, but you will gain a reputation for doing your homework and being well prepared.

Persuasion and Ethics

Good persuasion involves logical argument to convince the reader to accept the writer's viewpoint. You should not use your skill as a writer to handle information in such a way that the reader accepts it because of the skillful manipulation of facts, not because of the clear, fair presentation of fact. Rather, you have a moral obligation to be fair and forthright. Do not omit negative information about your plan or product or omit favorable information about a competitive plan or product you discuss as an alternative. Any good reader is going to research the alternatives and discover your omissions. Trust the reader. Develop the most logical and best-suited solution and present it clearly. Then allow the reader to make his or her own decision. If your proposal is accepted, you fairly competed. If it is rejected, your reputation is untarnished.

Nothing in the previous paragraph means you must tout the competition or belabor negative and objectionable points of your proposal. Good sense dictates that you accent the positive. Just remember to be ethical. Your own sense of right will tell you when you are not telling everything that needs to be known. Follow your conscience.

Evaluation

Before starting to write, find out, if possible, how and by whom the proposal will be evaluated. Some agencies or businesses have well-worked-out schemes for evaluation; others have none. It is not impertinent to inquire about the evaluation procedure. Some companies are very open with the information, and it can help you prepare. For example, often evaluation is by a point system—so many points for problem definition, for solution, for implementation plan, and so forth. You then know what the reader considers most important, and you can weigh the proposal in the same way. You can also organize so that information most important to the reader is presented first. Ordering in this manner can give you a psychological advantage. If the evaluator gives the first items high points, an affirmative attitude is developed. The reader is likely to judge other items in the proposal positively.

It is useful also to know that some agencies or companies will send, upon request, the evaluations of proposals that failed once the award or awards have been made. The reviewers' comments are often an excellent learning source. They may bruise the ego, but in order to improve, you need to know how your writing is perceived by others and learn by your mistakes rather than keep writing in the same ineffective style, using the same ineffective methods.

Common faults of proposals include the failure to state the problem clearly, failure to persuade, and failure to organize well. Do not let these factors cost you approval.

Writing Plan

Proposals can be detailed and reasoned documents. Allow time to analyze the subject and audience, gather information, and outline and decide what information should make up the content (see pp. 187–188). After you have studied the material, write, rewrite, and proofread. Even if you let the proposal sit only overnight, you return to it with a fresh eye—with a critical sense. Correct errors. Add where the writing does not make sense. Change the order of information or sections of the proposal so ideas flow logically and persuasively. Do not leave the writing until the last moment. The logic, command of language, appearance, format, and neatness all contribute to the sense of competence the proposal makes on the reader. Sloppy work rarely wins the award.

Content

Many proposals written for the government, foundations, and large businesses are a reply to a Request for Proposal (RFP). The RFP specifies both the content and form. Failure to comply results in your proposal's not even being read. When writing in this situation, acquire the specifications and follow them to the letter. (See Exercise No. 6, p. 214, to gain practical experience.) If there are no "specs" or you are writing a student proposal, the following is a standard list to consider. Only the most formal proposal will include all items. The subject and audience will help you decide what is needed. For example, an in-house proposal will not require résumés of in-house project personnel.

Front Material

1. *Transmittal Letter.* The transmittal letter is a courtesy. It introduces or reminds the reader of the subject, sometimes gives major points, expresses interest in doing the work, and thanks the person or company for the opportunity to submit the proposal. Sometimes a reference is made to how the opportunity came about: through a published RFP or a conversation, meeting, or letter that granted permission to submit the proposal.

   If no date is set for approval, you should keep the process moving. For example, say that you will call in a week to answer questions or arrange a meeting for discussion, but be careful. If you push too hard, you may lose the opportunity.
2. *Title Page.* If the RFP does not lay out the title page, consider including the following:

- title of the proposal
- name, formal title, and address of the person(s) or organization receiving the proposal
- name, formal title, and address of the person(s) or organization presenting the proposal
- signature and date lines for presenters to sign their approval
- identifying number of the proposal (if there is one) that ties the proposal to an RFP
- date of submission
- total budget sum
- abstract—summarize the total offering; state if specifications were met or if exceptions occur; be brief. (Sometimes the abstract appears on a separate page following the title page or table of contents.)

Title Page Format

```
                              TITLE
                           A Proposal

                               for
                     Company or Person's Name
                             Address

                               by
                     Writer or Company's Name
                             Address

                             Date

     Abstract: _____

     _____

     _____ .

     Approved By                        Date

     _____           _____

     _____           _____
```

3. *Table of Contents.* Use a table of contents for proposals longer than five pages. List internal chapter information so the table can be used for reference. Headings and subheadings are good indicators for internal listings. Use Roman numerals in small case for page numbers before the actual text.

Table of Contents Format

Contents

1. *Introduction.* State what is proposed and why. Catch the reader's attention by showing the value and relevance of the work to the reader's business. Recognize that the proposal's purpose is to persuade. Business must be sought. Others respect those who acquire business. Learn to write so that you gain such respect. In your enthusiasm to sell the proposal, remember to present information truthfully. Do not omit negative items; admit and deal with them. Do not inaccurately color facts to favor the proposed idea.

2. *Problem Statement.* Explain the need for the proposed idea. Why is the service or product needed—why does the procedure need to be examined? Show the reader that you clearly understand and know why the subject is being proposed. Tell how the problem or need relates to business functions other than the obvious ones and what ramifications will occur if the subject is ignored.

    Use your capabilities with language. You may want to shock, overwhelm, scare, bowl over with accurate but persuasive information. The approach is yours to choose. But remember that if you overshock or overscare, the reader may just hide the proposal away and not deal with it. Be careful of exaggeration. Also be wary of humor. To be clever, depending on the situation, is all right; to be cute is not.

3. *Solution.* If you reveal a need or problem, you obviously must offer a solution. Explain if your solution builds upon prior work. Discuss previous solutions, their shortcomings and progress. Talk about the suitability of your proposal and state that it can be practically accomplished.

    Decide if you need to cite recent literature on the subject. Some readers want to know that you are an expert in the field and are aware of and understand the latest information.

4. *Scope.* Define what you will do and what is expected from other personnel or the company. This section is important for future relations. You do not want an agreement based on assumptions. Perhaps you are planning to stop after a certain stage, spend certain monies, and use certain space; the reader may expect you to complete different work, deliver a different product, have another budget in mind, or plan differently for the space. Set the limits at the beginning, so everyone has the same understanding.

5. *Methodology.* Your proposal depends on delivery. Prove that you can produce the solution, service, or product. What methods will you use? Do you need to explain them or justify why they were chosen over others? Are they innovative? If so, why or what guarantee can you give that they will work?

   Show a schedule of work and tasks. Who will do what? The schedule helps convince the reader that you have thought carefully about the project.

   You may want to make a statement of the likelihood of success. In today's world, people sue at the "drop-of-a-hat" and juries award record judgments. It is terrible to think that you must guard against litigation in everything you do, but it is best to protect your reputation and financial security. Money, time, politics, economy—things outside your vision—can influence the outcome of a proposal. Be wise and estimate the success and/or qualify the project.

6. *Facilities.* Justify overhead costs. The equipment and facilities should be reserved or determined as possible. Unusual conditions of the facility, such as being static-free, sterile, or air-conditioned to a certain degree, need to be specified. Are they available? If not, can they be reasonably provided? If part of the equipment and facilities belong to the company, will they be available to you? If you provide them, what must you purchase? For equipment and facilities you already own, what part of their cost or upkeep do you plan to charge to the project? Who will service the equipment and pay for the servicing?

7. *Personnel.* List the people who will be doing the work. You may wish to include their résumés or at least those of key personnel. Can you attest that these people are free to take on the responsibility of the project? If some will be working only part-time, indicate the percentage of time and identify their other commitments. (Readers may see, for example, a conflict of interest.) If the personnel are yet to be hired, set forth the qualifications and criteria for hiring. Is training necessary? If so, who will develop, offer, and pay for it?

8. *Reports.* Identify which reports you plan to provide, when they will be delivered, and who is responsible for preparing them.

9. *Budget/Costs.* Itemize costs under appropriate headings: equipment, salaries, overhead, and so forth. Some items will need to be estimated, but do so with care. Rarely does the person or company allow you to charge for additional or unconsidered time or items. You usually end up living with the budget, which could mean working for less an hour if costs are incomplete or inaccurate.

Format

Unless specified in the Request for Proposals, no single format is best. Include what you need, in the order you decide most effective, and arrange information on the page so it is easily read and understood. Regardless of arrangement, consider the following:

- Use white space meaningfully to aid the reader's understanding. (Do not create holes on the page just to have white space.) Break up the page with headings, short paragraphs, visuals, columns, lists, or anything to pique the reader's interest and not cause him or her to dread reading a whole page of dense content. Whenever information compares or contrasts or relates in another way, consider side-by-side columns.
- Use a visual to communicate information whenever appropriate and possible.
- Follow correct outline notation (see pp. 100–103.). Step down titles, headings, and subheadings by some logical typographical system: for titles, use full caps; for headings, capitalize the first letter in each word; for subheadings, use small case. You also can differentiate among titles, headings, and subheadings by selecting different typefaces. Be consistent once you choose a system.
- Proofread the proposal to eliminate all types of errors.
- Use the best equipment available to prepare and copy the proposal.
- Use a good quality paper and binder. Choose a binder that will lie back. It is irritating to read a document where the cover keeps closing and the reader must hold the document open. Plan so that the left side of your text is not hidden in the spine of the binder.
- Consider how the proposal is delivered. Its impression begins whenever it arrives. If the proposal is mailed, pack it neatly so that it will arrive in excellent condition, not wrinkled or bent. If it is hand-delivered, the binder is probably sufficient. In either case, be certain the proposal is received before or on time.

Proposals and Word Processing

Word processing is a convenience for any document that progresses through several drafts or is written in bits and pieces. The proposal is one such document. With word processing, you can write whatever section you are ready to write and later reform and renumber to fit it correctly into the whole work. You can alter information as experiments or research changes data. Language and style can be reworked, deletions and additions can be made, and multiple formats can be tried.

If you write proposals regularly, many sections can be written, formatted, and saved to use in other proposals. Facilities, personnel, and budget formats are some possibilities.

Student Example: Proposal

As a student you normally will not write formal proposals with all the information identified in the "Content" (pp. 187–188). Most likely you will write something like the example that follows. A student was given a problem that he needed to solve, so the task of "selling" or seeking approval was actually eliminated. The student was expected to demonstrate the ability (1) to communicate his understanding of the problem and proposed solution, (2) to organize and write well, and (3) to present an effective format and well-presented report. He fulfills this expectation.

Engineering 495 Proposal

Photoplethysmographic Feedback

Prepared by

Stephen McRoberts

December 11, 198X

Table of Contents

List of Figures

iii

Abstract

Controlling hypertension using current biofeedback techniques has met with limited success. Non-medicinal techniques, such as temperature related biofeedback, have been in use for several years but have not been nearly as effective as medicine. Because medicine has serious side effects, researchers continue to look for other methods of treatment.

Some research has been conducted using photoplethysmography as a form of biofeedback. A plethysmograph has been created using a commercially available infrared LED (Light Emitting Diode) and a phototransistor in a single package. With emerging technology in infrared photosensor techniques, quicker response time can be gained, yielding more reliable feedback to the hypertensive subject.

Dr. John Lakey in the Department of Psychology at the University of Evansville has requested a dedicated system to continue his research in photoplethysmographic feedback. This project will design and implement a microprocessor controlled feedback unit to be used by the Psychology Department.

The system will consist of the photo-emitter/detector to detect changes in venous pressure and microprocessor system. The microprocessor system will process the information, provide audible feedback through a controlled function generator and amplifier, and communicate with a microcomputer. The system will be designed to be used as a stand alone unit or as a microcomputer intelligent peripheral with a serial interface using the IEEE RS-232 standard.

Cost requirements should be no more than $150.00 for the basic unit. Some additional costs may be incurred in the microcomputer interface if a serial input is not available.

1

Introduction

Dr. John Lakey in the Department of Psychology at the University of Evansville is conducting research on the treatment of hypertension. Traditional methods of treatment have produced dissenting results. Hypertension medications are usually successful but have many potential serious side effects. Non-medicinal techniques employing biofeedback have been in use for several years. These techniques yield mixed results because they rely upon changes in temperature to detect a difference in vasoconstriction related to blood pressure. Other techniques such as electromyography (EMG) are being used, although many patients find having electrodes attached to their skin to be uncomfortable and nonconducive to relaxation. Dr. Lakey's research has been using photoplethysmography as a means of providing feedback to control hypertension.

Photoplethysmography is a sophisticated method of using reflected light to measure the varying blood density in periperhal tissue. Typically, the more blood volume, the greater the amount of reflected light. Photoplethysmography is sophisticated because it requires complicated electronics to interpret the very small percentage of reflected light. Currently Dr. Lakey requires an expensive plethysmograph to interpret the input which is sent to an Apple //e computer to provide audible feedback for the subject. The equipment requirements are cumbersome, and the Psychology Department does not have additional personal computers consistently available for this research.

Dr. Lakey would like a dedicated system for three reasons. One, Dr. Lakey does not always have an Apple //e available when it is needed for research. The Apple is on loan from the CIS and must be shared with other services. In addition, using an Apple //e simply to drive an external speaker does not justify such a large expenditure for full time service. Second, more attention is required with the many pieces of hardware involved, and reliability is reduced by the complexity. Lastly, Dr. Lakey feels there is a definite commercial need for such a dedicated product.

I was consulted by Dr. Lakey to determine the feasibility of building an inexpensive stand-alone system so he may continue his research. The proposed system will consist of an infrared emitter-sensor combination in a single housing to produce a waveform representing blood volume pulse. The waveform will be amplified and shaped, converted to digital representation,

2

an audio signal generator for audible feedback. In addition, the microprocessor interface provides a standard serial interface so a more powerful microcomputer can do historical recording, display graphics, and print a permanent copy of the results. This capability is built into the current design, but software drivers must be written before serial communication may be employed.

The Existing System

The existing system used by Dr. Lakey and the Psychology Department is shown in Figure 1. The Narco plethysmograph supplies output voltage to the proprietary infrared sensor/emitter. The output from the emitter is amplified, then fed as an input into the plethysmograph. The plethysmograph supplies an output signal to an A/D convertor, which converts the analog signal to an eight bit digital representation. The current Apple //e software is an assembly language program[1] designed to sample the digital data and output a tonal representation using the Apple's hardware to drive an external speaker.

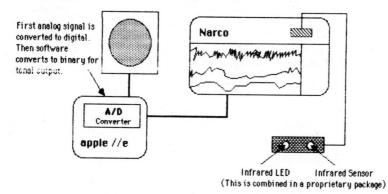

First analog signal is converted to digital. Then software converts to binary for tonal output.

A/D Converter

apple //e

Narco

Infrared LED   Infrared Sensor
(This is combined in a proprietary package)

Figure 1
The existing system is cumbersome since it requires many different pieces of hardware to perform the desired function.

---

[1] The assembly language program was written by Dr. Keith Matheson of the Department of Medical Education of the University of Evansville.

3

Specifications for the New System

The proposed photoplethysmographic feedback system will be designed to meet the following criteria:

1. Emulate the current functions now being provided by the Narco/Apple combination.

2. Provide simple high-level software example for an Apple //e and IBM-PC to record, display graphics, and print results of research session. The new system package will include documented software designed for easy modification and user's manual written for operators with minimal computer experience.

3. Be economical, reliable, and flexible in design.

These criteria were established through talks with Dr. Lakey. Most important is duplicating the current functions provided by the existing system. The new system must accurately be able to record blood volume pulses and provide a discrete output. The output will be audible and should provide some means of adjusting sensitivity and pitch preference, either in software or hardware. Ideally these adjustments should be included in the software, so that an automatic means of adjusting sensitivity could be provided.

Since there will be fewer parts and therefore less complexity, the new system should be easier to use than the current system. Hookup should be minimal since this is a dedicated system. All that should be required is attaching the sensing unit to the phalanx of the finger and adjusting pitch/volume to personal preference.

The second criterion will be instituted last and will depend mostly upon time restraints. Currently, a microcomputer with a serial interface is not available and this option will be written mostly for future expansion.

The system should be designed to be safe, reliable, and inexpensive. Safety is important since the input device may be attached to many research subjects and exposed to wear and physical abuse. Therefore, the unit will be electrically isolated from the subject with double insulation. Since the voltage to the emittor/sensor is 5 volts and the amperage typically in the

4

microamp/nanoamp range, respectively, electrical conduction does not pose much of a problem. The human subject interface should be protected against short circuit to prevent higher current levels from coming into contact with the subject.

Proposed Design

A block diagram of the proposed design is shown in Figure 2. The detailed proposed design is divided into the following main sections: microprocessor based hardware, interface specifications, the personal computer interface, and the software. These topics are numbered in Roman numerals, and each topic may also include additional subtopics.

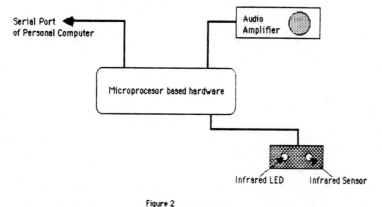

Figure 2
Diagram of Proposed Design

I. Microprocessor Based Hardware

This hardware is composed of a microprocessor, A/D (Analog to Digital) convertor, and USART. See Figure 3.   The USART is described under Interface Specifications following this section.

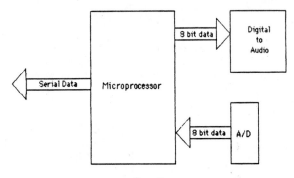

Figure 3
Block Diagram of Microprocessor Hardware

Microprocessor Specifications

The microprocessor selected for processing the digital signals must meet the following requirements: be an I/O (input/output) oriented design; be programmable in a higher-order development language to permit quick and easy modification of the controlling software; be arithmetically oriented; and be easily adapted to a standard serial interface for communication to other computers. The microprocessor will not have to support large amounts of data memory but may require several thousand (K) of program memory, depending upon how much numerical manipulation is required.

The Intel 8031 is an appropriate choice because it meets all of the above criteria and has drastically fallen in price. The Intel 8031 is readily

6

available in the University of Evansville stockroom and therefore is easily programmed with the engineering department's development systems.

II. Interface Specifications

Three different types of interfaces are required: the input interface, the audio output, and the optional serial interface. Each type of interface is described in detail in the following text:

Input Interface

The analog input device will be the most challenging part of the design because discovering the best optical sensing device will mostly be based upon trial and error. Typically, the type of sensor needed is designed for bar-code reading. I have spent considerable time searching for articles documenting its use in photoplethysmography without helpful results. However, I have learned the emittor/sensor package should have an infrared wavelength emittor since this type of light has proven most reliable. In addition, it should be light weight and require minimal operating current.

I have decided to develop the emittor/sensor interface in the final phase of the project because of the possibly long development time. It will be easy to interface the current Narco proprietary sensor package to my microprocessor design, and this will provide the Psychology Department with a working system more quickly.

Audio Output

The audio output is determined as described in the following: First, a variable number of sample amplitudes are examined. Next, the samples are averaged, and this value represents a tonal output. Finally, a variable number of samples are discarded, and new samples are added to provide a new trailing average.

7

I have two design solutions possible. One, a completely analog circuit could be employed as follows: amplify the voltage output by the emittor/sensor and feed the amplified signal through some "enveloping device" then to a voltage-to-frequency convertor. This method has a relatively low design cost. However, compensating for different amplitudes could be very difficult and time consuming. Since time is more important now than cost, a second approach could be to convert the emittor/sensor signal to a digital representation with an A/D convertor. The digital number can then be manipulated under software control to determine the weighted average. The average would then be reconstituted into an analog waveform which would be converted to an audible frequency. The advantages of this method are greater control over the sample voltages (represented by digits) and a much easier method of changing parameters by simply changing the software. Of course, the disadvantage is a higher cost than the completely analog counterpart.

Serial Interface

This optional interface will depend upon the type of microprocessor used in the design. Since this is an optional item, it will not influence the type of microprocessor. In order that a standard serial interface may be maintained, the serial output will require a programmable UART (Universal Asynchronous Receiver/Transmitter). Baud rates will need to be determined in hardware or software. This preferably should be done in software to keep costs down since baud rate generators are somewhat expensive. (The Intel 8031 provides a built-in UART with a baud rate generator at about the same price as a single baud rate generator.)

III. Personal Computer Interface

Interfacing to a personal computer will be accomplished through a standard RS-232 serial port. I will write some sample software programs in Pascal to simulate graphically the graphs produced by the Narco plethysmograph. Routines will be written so that a research session may be saved to disk for later recall or sent to the printer for a printed copy of the results. This interface will be completed on a time/cost availability basis.

8

IV. Software

The software for the microprocessor will be designed to alleviate as much hardware as possible. The software for the 8031 microprocessor will be written in PLM 51. This software will permit easy modification for future enhancements. All development will be done on an iPDS development system available in the University of Evansville Microcomputer Lab.

Expected Results

Since this project is very much experimental in nature, desired results may not be obtainable within the time and framework alloted. I will make every effort to develop a working system enabling Dr. Lakey to continue his research. However, at the very minimum, I should be able to deliver a working system using the emitter/sensor equipped on the Narco plethysmograph while avoiding the Apple //e requirement for audible feedback.

Capabilities

I am well prepared to design the digital logic system and write the software. I have been programming computers for several years and have completed various projects on as many different types of microprocessors. I am currently attending a digital design class (EE-455) which is expanding my knowledge even further, and I feel competent in the digital design work. My experience in analog interfaces is not as well developed, but I have many resources available to me at the University of Evansville in both faculty advise and test equipment. Dr. Lakey has also gained considerable insight into the type of electronics needed for this project and has made himself available for any help he can provide.

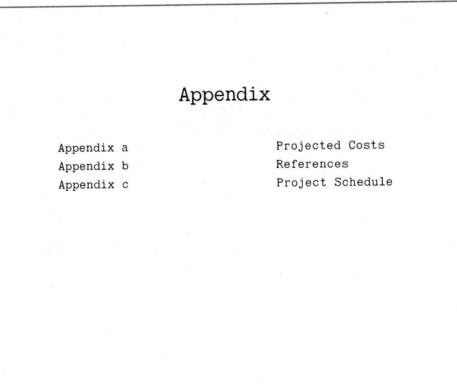

Appendix

Appendix a	Projected Costs
Appendix b	References
Appendix c	Project Schedule

Appendix a

Projected Costs

8031 Microprocessor	10.00
8212 Latch	5.00
2732 EPROM (200 nS)	6.00
74LS138	2.00
Line Drivers/Receivers	5.00
Buffers/Inverters	2.00
6264 (16K RAM)	11.00
ADC0809 (A/D converter)	4.00
DAC0831 (D/A converter)	6.00
LM380 (amplifier)	2.00
Discrete Components (Including custom 11.059 MHz crystal)	20.00
Jameco Function Generator	20.00
Power Supply components	15.00
Miscellaneous (connectors, knobs, case, etc.)	25.00
Total	$ 133.00

Appendix b

References

[1]Lee, Tahmoush, Jennings. An LED—Transistor Photoplethysmograph. *IEEE Transactions on Biomedical Engineering*, May 1979, 248—250.

[2]Tahmoush, Jennings, Lee, Camp, and Weber. Characteristics of Light Emitting Diode—Transistor Photoplethysmograph. *Psychophysiology*, 1976, 357—362.

[3]_____. Schematic for Using an Infrared Emitter/ Collector as a Pulse Rate Monitor. *Radio—Electronics*, September 1982, 47.

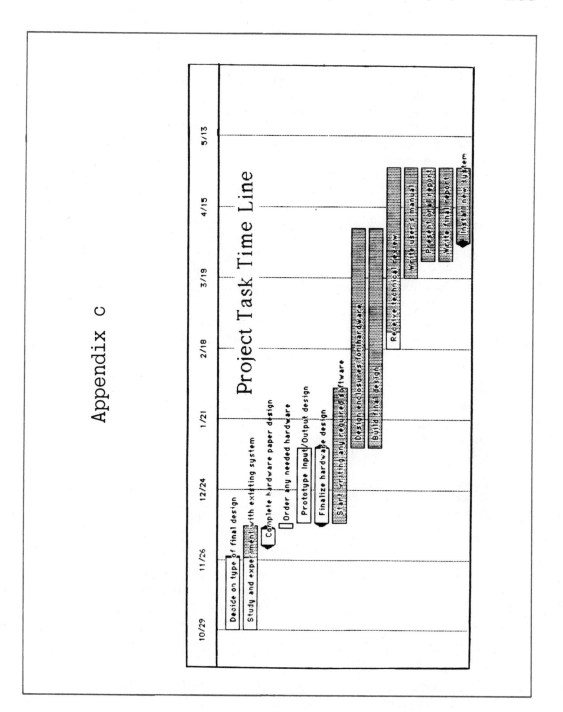

Appendix c

Project Task Time Line

Feasibility Reports

The feasibility report presents the findings of a study and makes a number of recommendations. It is related to the proposal in that it suggests work, change, or a purchase, but unlike the proposal, it is not selling or asking for approval. The feasibility report simply makes recommendations using the same criteria for evaluation. This difference is important because it changes the writer's focus, the study of audience, and the emphasis on persuasive language. What remains the same is the need to do a careful study and to organize and write the report well.

The feasibility study involves a choice among options. The writer must clearly see the options, gather information about each option, and analyze the facts about each one using the same criteria. The writer may or may not reach a conclusion and make a recommendation. If the writer does recommend one choice, the report must be written in language and in a style that helps readers understand the logic and validity of the writer's choice and helps them make their own decisions among the options. No single pattern exists for style and content, but the following are some of the items commonly included.

Content

Cover letter
Title page
Abstract
Table of contents   If needed
List of illustrations
Introduction
Discussion
Criteria
Possible solutions
Conclusion/Recommendations
Appendix   If needed

Format

The report should be organized and presented as any other good technical report, but one factor deserves special consideration: the need to study the options and their comparisons. Present options so that readers can easily and validly do this. For example, use comparison or contrast, a table, or a chart.

Student Example: Feasibility Report

The example belongs to a computing science student who investigated the feasibility of converting certain office functions of her church. Notice that information is clearly partitioned. Technical language is avoided for the most part. The benefits and alternatives are organized so they are easy to compare. She omits some suggested content and even adds her own ("Benefits"), yet the report illustrates attention to style, format, and serving her audience.

Cover letter

1207 Parrett Street
Richmond, VA 23201
February 19, 19xx

Mr. William Philpot, Minister
Third Avenue Church
821 Third Avenue
Richmond, VA 23201

Dear Mr. Philpot:

Enclosed is the study we discussed for computerizing certain of the church's office procedures. My recommendation is included.

I will call on Monday to answer questions or arrange a meeting to discuss anything in the report.

Thank you for the opportunity to evaluate the need for a computerized system. It helped me in my schoolwork. I hope it helps you and your committee decide how to make certain office functions easier and more efficient for the staff.

Sincerely,

Phyllis Rabb

Phyllis Rabb

Title page

STUDY TO COMPUTERIZE OFFICE PROCEDURES

PRESENTED TO

THIRD AVENUE CHURCH

821 THIRD AVENUE

RICHMOND, VA 23201

SUBMITTED BY

PHYLLIS RABB

COMPUTER SCIENCE SENIOR

UNIVERSITY'S NAME

Street Address

City, State Zip Code

February 19, 19■■

STUDY: TO DECIDE IF THIRD AVENUE CHURCH SHOULD COMPUTERIZE CERTAIN OFFICE OPERATIONS

INTRODUCTION

Third Avenue Church has experienced rapid growth in the past few years; consequently, there are more people to keep track of and more incoming and outgoing information to process. The expansion continues, so the church can expect to process more information. At present, the office staff types individual correspondence and prints mailing labels on a labeling machine. For each additional church member or a member's change of address, someone must prepare a new mailing-label plate. Each week the staff writes on a printed form the weekly contribution of each member's household. Quarterly and year-to-year totals are calculated and entered by hand for semiannual mailings to members.

DISCUSSION

The typing of church correspondence, updating of membership files, and recording of membership contributions can all be automated and made more efficient. The changeover will require the purchase of three software programs and the lease or purchase of certain hardware.

A. Correspondence: A Word Processing Program

Word processing is like typing, except that documents can be kept in the computer's internal memory, so they can be reprinted, changed, and printed at will. The Word Processing program will allow the secretary to type, make changes, and keep standard documents ready for printing. Form letters can be personalized. It will eliminate duplicate work. A merge facility will let the computer personally address the correspondence.

B. Membership Files: A File Maintenance Program

The File Maintenance program requires that all members' names and addresses be typed initially into the computer. Thereafter, changes, deletions, and additions can be easily made. Listings of total or partial membership can be printed. The lists can be compiled alphabetically by last name or compiled by state, city, and zip code, or by custom criteria. Mailing labels can also be printed using special commands and forms.

C. Membership Contributions: An Accounts Receivable Program

The Accounts Receivable package requires a one-time entry of all contributions for each member from the beginning of the calendar year until the time the package is installed. Afterward, weekly entries will be made, and quarterly, semiannual, and annual reports will be compiled. An "update" function allows the secretary to correct membership or money information, so the file can be corrected and made current. The secretary will be able to make weekly entries, produce reports, and make corrections easily and quickly.

D. Software and Hardware Requirements
1   personal computer with a hard disk
1   letter-quality printer
3   software packages: word processing, file maintenance, and accounts receivable.

BENEFITS

ITEM OF COMPARISON	MANUAL	COMPUTERIZED
A. Word Processor: Time Savings	Type new document; if mistakes appear or changes are needed, type an updated document; make carbon copy or make multiple copies on copier.	Type document; enter changes; save selected documents; print as many as needed.
B. File Maintenance: Mailing Savings	Prepare new label plate for each membership and address change; have volunteers prepare mass mailings at a location away from church.	Make membership and address changes on the computer (changes are effective as soon as the computer runs an update); use the computer to prepare mailing labels; use volunteers to prepare mailings at the church.
Membership Changes	Make handwritten changes to membership list; retype entire list to reflect corrections; make carbons or copy new list.	Use File Maintenance options to change membership list (changes are effective after the computer runs an update); use the computer to print a new list anytime.
Membership Lists	Make manual determinations as to how to organize list; search manually the list; type list.	Select whether the computer will print lists alphabetically by names, by city, state, and zip code, or by other criteria; have the computer print the desired lists.
Arrange Groups	Search lists for members meeting given criteria; type the list.	Select criteria and ask the computer to search lists for members; have the computer print list.

Availability of Information	Search list(s) for information.	Select function and have the computer search; read information on the screen.
C. Accounts Receivable: Weekly Contributions	Search manually alphabetized contribution sheets for member's name and hand enter amount.	Enter family account number into the computer and amount of contribution or enter name and amount; have the computer automatically add the amount to quarterly and year-to-date totals.
Semiannual Mailing	Calculate manually the quarterly and year-to-date totals; write totals on each member's contribution sheet; hand write a report; hand address or make labels; assemble and mail.	Have the computer calculate totals; print individual member's reports; have the printer prepare labels; have volunteers assemble items and mail.
Availability of Information	Look manually for information.	Let the computer search for information; read information on the screen.

ALTERNATIVES

A. PURCHASE ONLY THE WORD PROCESSING PACKAGE:

Advantages:
1. Eliminates the one-time purchase price of both the File Maintenance and Accounts Receivable packages.
2. Lowers the amount of memory needed on the personal computer, which lowers the cost of the computer. The cost of the Maintenance Agreement on the computer will be slightly lower.

Disadvantages:
1. Leaves most office procedures as they are. Either another secretary or more volunteers must be found in order to keep up with manual editing of membership lists and manual entering of weekly contributions.
2. Requires a continued time interval between when information is requested or needed and when the secretary or volunteers can search, locate, and provide it.

Summary:
Purchasing the Word Processing package alone requires the more expensive letter-quality printer, so the small savings in buying a computer

with less memory and not buying the two other packages is minimal. In addition, the File Maintenance and Accounts Receivable packages together provide the information needed to eliminate much of the manual sorting of papers and searching of lists. They free the secretary and others to do different tasks and increase the accuracy and timeliness of information provided.

B. PURCHASE ONLY THE FILE MAINTENANCE AND ACCOUNTS RECEIVABLE PACKAGES:

Advantages:
1. Eliminates the one-time purchase price of the Word Processing package.
2. Eliminates the expense of a letter-quality printer as a dot-matrix printer will be adequate. The Maintenance Agreement will be slightly less.

Disadvantages:
1. Leaves the ineffective correspondence procedures unchanged.
2. Necessitates hiring an additional secretary (an ongoing payroll expense) because of membership growth.
3. Requires an additional typewriter for the additional secretary. The typewriter must be purchased or leased and another Maintenance Agreement added to ongoing expenses.

Summary:
The File Maintenance and Accounts Receivable packages will eliminate much of the searching of lists for information, retyping lists to update information, and sorting papers to enter weekly contributions by hand. However, the cost of the Word Processing package and the letter-quality printer will also make the secretary's work more efficient, and the cost seems too small to justify eliminating the word processing operation.

C. DO NOTHING. KEEP THE PRESENT SYSTEM AS IS:

Advantages:
1. Requires no additional purchases or expenses.
2. Means no one must learn to do anything differently.

Disadvantages:
1. Increases cost to the church. Even with the assistance of volunteers, church growth will require hiring an additional secretary and purchasing additional equipment.
2. Offers no challenge or progress to the staff.

Summary:
Doing nothing is not in line with the stated goals of the Third Avenue Church. The changes, if implemented in their entirety, will allow all operations to be performed in the church office, by the secretary or with volunteers, and permit additional operations—which now are either not possible or possible only by laborious searches or by relying on memory—to be quickly and easily accomplished.

RECOMMENDATION

I recommend that the church move to computerize its office procedures. The hardware can either be leased or purchased. A budget follows suggesting costs.

BUDGET/COSTS:

The following equipment is needed for implementation of the computerized system.

A. Initial Costs:

Personal computer with hard disk (if purchased outright)	$3,000.
Letter-quality printer	2,000.
Diskettes for permanent records	75.
Total Initial Costs	$5,075.

B. Monthly Costs:

Personal computer with hard disk (if leased)	$200.	
Letter-quality printer (if leased)	125.	
Maintenance Agreement on personal computer	26.	
Maintenance Agreement on printer	10.	
Monthly total equipment costs		$361.
Additional diskettes for backups	$ 3.	
Printer ribbons	17.	
Printer paper	30.	
Monthly total supply costs		50.
Total monthly costs		$411.

C. Savings:

Lease on typewriter (includes Maintenance Agreement)	$ 80.	
Ribbons for typewriter	3.	
Labeling plate costs	20.	
Travel time and expense to labeler	5.	
Payroll expense of additional secretary to handle increased work load manually	700.	
Purchase/lease of additional typewriter	70.	
Maintenance Agreement on second typewriter	10.	
Total savings per month		$888.

Saving	$888.
Costs	−411.
PROFIT (excluding initial costs)	$477.

Author's Comment: The budget format needs work. For example, "lease" costs are shown in "Monthly Costs", but they would not appear if the personal computer and printer were purchased ("Initial Costs"). The same distortion appears in "Savings". The two options — lease or purchase — need to be separated and the format needs to be redesigned so information is easily and accurately read.

Practice Exercises

1. Write a proposal that is persuasive in both fact and tone. Your instructor will decide if the writing is to be a group project or an individual one. Propose something practical that you can learn or know well enough to be persuasive. Pay attention to format and appearance as well as to content.

2. Make an oral presentation (see Chapter 13) of the proposal to the class. Prepare visuals and information to persuade. Entertain questions from the audience after the presentation. (You may want to distribute beforehand copies of your proposal so the audience is prepared to listen and respond.)

3. Present your proposal to another individual in the class or another group. Have the person(s) read, accept or reject, and write comments for the decision.

4. Prepare and write a feasibility report.

5. The instructor will bring to class a number of proposals. In a group or by yourself evaluate the one given to you. Use the information given in this chapter to write your opinion of the proposal's strength and weakness.

6. Your instructor will divide the class into writing groups and ask the school librarian to direct you to finding sources for grant proposals (the *Annual Register of Grant Supports,* the *Foundation Directory,* the *Grantsmanship Center News,* the *Federal Register*). Have your group select a grant possibility suitable to your school's department or college. Analyze, prepare, and write a proposal. If your group along with your instructor decides the proposal is valid and competitive, send it off! If it is funded, you will acquire a résumé item because you helped write a successful proposal and the school will receive whatever was proposed.

Chapter 10

Formal Reports

Everyone respects the formal report. It is long, looks important, has many parts, and obviously represents much effort. Both the reader and writer acknowledge its importance. Most people pale at the thought of beginning a report, which is understandable if they think of the whole project and all that is required. My suggestion is to set short goals: a section, a series of tables, the introduction, or abstract. You feel a sense of accomplishment after finishing each unit, which gives an incentive to continue. The challenge with writing in sections is to keep the whole in mind. All parts need to relate, and transitions need to combine parts in logical ways. Be careful not to write a disjointed report. This chapter identifies the report, its individual parts, and includes an example.

Definition and Parts of the Formal Report

Definition and Function

The formal report combines formal research with interpretation and recommendation. The function of the formal report is not unique. Other reports perform parts of the same purpose (feasibility report = recommendation, process report = how something works), but the formal report is set apart by its magnitude or thoroughness. The subject examined—whether it is a problem and recommended solution, original research, or current literature—is considered in depth and presented formally. The report can have many parts and cover much detail.

The purpose of the report is analysis. We analyze to answer a question or solve a problem. The report writer follows the question or problem to its source to discover and examine root principles. From this factual base, the writer reconstructs the subject, checking every stage of construction to see if the building of theory or practice is truthfully grounded on the root principles or whether the subject deviates from the foundation. Any deviation is analyzed. Results are recorded. The end report makes sense of the history, development, and present state of the problem, research, or information printed about a subject. The reader knows the origin of the subject, its path of growth, its present state, the influence of the present on the future. As the writer, you may forecast development, find a solution to a problem, or make recommendations based on your analysis.

To fulfill the report's function, you need to prepare mentally for the search and discovery. Know what you are looking for before you begin. Spend whatever time is required to define clearly the problem or question. Divorce yourself from any prejudice or assumptions you have about the subject. Determine if the information you analyze is accurate. Do not accept information as accurate just because it is printed or available or given to you. When you add to the history of this subject with your own information or analysis of existing facts, be certain to state it accurately. When the time comes in the report to interpret, do so. Do not merely list what you have found and leave the work of interpretation to the reader; you have a responsibility to your audience. Explain what you see and what you suspect. Be direct and clear. Your value as an analyst and your effectiveness as a communicator are put to the test when you present your conclusions and interpretations.

Audience

People with different backgrounds and needs read and use formal reports, so the identification of audience is crucial. A plan is required for serving the identified readers. You may want to write a management summary or set aside a section for personnel requirements. You may need to write a very technical discussion for scientists and engineers. Information may have to be repeated in different parts, with the difference being the amount of detail and depth given in the discussion. Whatever the plan, produce a report in which readers can find what they need without having to page through the whole work. Specific chapter titles and accurate headings within sections help. An accurate and complete table of contents is essential.

Review the information on audience (pp. 29–33). It will remind you of ways to consider audience and ways to distinguish among different groups of readers.

Preparing to Write

The topics discussed in Chapters 3 and 4 are directly relevant to the formal report. The task is too large and too detailed just to begin writing. Allow time to think about subject and audience; to consider different ways to order information; to gather material; to outline; and to rewrite, rewrite, and proofread. Do not let time get away from you. As soon as you are given a major report to write, begin working. The day when it is due comes too soon.

Preliminary Decisions Concerning Format

You will save time by making certain editorial decisions at the beginning. For example, decide upon heading styles (size and type of print, capitalization, under-lining, boldface), how to make notations, and how to use spacing and margins throughout. In general, allow a 1-inch margin on all sides. You may want to make the left margin wider if a binder will be used. Double-space the text. Single-space long quotations (more than four lines), information in notations, individual entries in the bibliography, the abstract, and usually material in the appendix. Double-space between footnotes and between bibliography entries. Triple-space below center headings and above and below quotations and formal listings.

Parts of the Formal Report

The size or complexity of the formal report is revealed by the number of standard items to include. The following are common entries. To decide what to include, study your audience, subject, and purpose. For example, if every reader is some-one intimately familiar with the problem or question, a glossary is not needed; a synopsis of background literature is probably superfluous. As a rule, include only what is needed to understand the analysis, but remember all the readers and guard against making assumptions.

Front Matter

1. Cover
2. Transmittal letter or preface
3. Title page
4. Table of contents
5. List of figures
6. List of tables
7. List of symbols (or in end matter)

8. Glossary (or in end matter)
9. Abstract

Body

1. Opening
2. Literature search of information related to problem
3. Methodology, approach, and materials
4. Alternatives
5. Results
6. Analysis and discussion
7. Interpretation
8. Conclusion
9. Budget
10. Recommendation
11. Close

End Matter

1. Appendixes
2. Footnotes

Definition of Formal Parts

Front Matter

The front matter introduces the document and you to the reader. If your prefatory work is haphazard, messy, incomplete, hard to use, the reader is prejudiced against your work before beginning to read the body.

1. *Cover.* Covers should be substantial and attractive. Companies often have their own prepared covers. If not, purchase one. Type a gummed label, or in the window space, type the title (capitalized and underlined), the report number, and the date.
2. *Transmittal Letter or Preface.* Both serve the same purpose; they differ only in format and audience. A letter is written to an individual or single group. It appears immediately after the title page or just inside the cover or stapled onto the outside of the cover or sent separately through the mail. Do what is customary for the company, or if there is no custom, do what seems most appropriate or what your teacher assigns. A preface is written for a general audience. For example, authors of books write prefaces because they have no particular audience to address.

    Both the letter and preface should indicate the following:

    a. The subject and purpose
    b. How the report was authorized or requested
    c. Significant features or findings

d. A thank-you to those who helped and for the opportunity to prepare the document

Items that may be included are:
a. A summary
b. Total budget sums
c. Conclusions and recommendations
d. An offer to be of future service

3. *Title Page.* The title page is a first-impression item. It actually has no report content. It is similar to a speaker's walking to the podium and the audience's making a judgment on his or her effectiveness based entirely on surface impressions. For this reason, create an effective title page. Format to make a good appearance. Do not clutter the page. Type the most important items in bold print or full capital letters. Items to include are the following:
   a. Name of company, person (include title), or student preparing report
   b. Name of company or teacher for whom the report was prepared
   c. Title of report
   d. Date of submission
   e. Contract number of report
   f. Name and signature of the person authorized by the company to present the report
   g. Proprietary and security comments
   h. Abstract or synopsis
   i. Reproduction restrictions
   j. Distribution list (If the letter of transmittal did not list copies, the title page should.)

If you choose to include most of these items, you may need two pages. See the example following on pages 220, 221.

4. *Table of Contents.* The contents page shows the contents of the report and serves as a means of reference for the reader. Decide to what level of subordination you want to list and stay consistent. You rarely need to go beyond the third level of subordination (I., A., 1.).

Opinions vary on the best way to format a table of contents page. Some people include the outline notations (I., A., 1.); others type only the Roman numerals to separate main divisions; still others use a decimal system (1, 1.1, 1.2). Some people type a line of dots from the item to the page number; others think this clutters the page. Decide what you like and be consistent. The following are some guidelines:
   a. Type "Table of Contents" at the top of the page. Center and underline it. You may want to capitalize all the letters.
   b. Triple-space between the table of contents and the text. Double-space between major items. Single-space between subtopics.
   c. Begin major headings flush with the left margin. If a Roman numeral is used, place it against the margin. Indent second-order headings

MULTITERM TECHNOLOGY FOR TEACHING AND LEARNING:

EXPERIMENTING WITH COMPUTER INTERACTIVE

CLASSROOM INSTRUCTION

A PROPOSAL

PRESENTED TO

THE INDIANA CONSORTIUM FOR COMPUTER
AND HIGH TECHNOLOGY EDUCATION

APPLICANT: UNIVERSITY OF EVANSVILLE
1800 Lincoln Avenue, Evansville, IN 47714
Contact Person: Dr. Ann Stuart
Phone: (812) 476-6393; 479-2977

IN CONJUNCTION WITH: BALL COMMUNICATIONS, INC.
1101 N. Fulton Avenue, Evansville, IN 47710
AND
EVANSVILLE VANDERBURGH SCHOOL
CORPORATION
1 Southeast Ninth Street, Evansville, IN 47708

JANUARY 1, 1986

MULTITERM TECHNOLOGY FOR TEACHING AND LEARNING: EXPERIMENTING WITH COMPUTER INTERACTIVE CLASSROOM INSTRUCTION

Project Synopsis: The University of Evansville and the Evansville Vanderburgh School Corporation propose to use GenTech's computerized MultiTerm Group Response System in classrooms to explore and assess its effects on teaching and learning. Ball Communications, of which General Technical Corporation is a subsidiary, will work with the University and School Corporation to implement this educational experiment with their high-tech computer-video product initially designed and marketed for business communication and industrial training. Elementary, middle, and high school teachers, in conjunction with University faculty, will design, implement, and evaluate the use of this computerized response system in three Evansville Schools.

Project Period: March 1986–June 1987

Expected Participants: 12–15 school teachers; 4–6 subject area supervisors; 3 principals; 4–6 University faculty; and several hundred schoolchildren.

Total Support Requested: $83,828. (Basic)

SIGNATURES OF APPLICANTS' AUTHORIZING OFFICIALS

University of Evansville   Ball Communications, Inc.

_____   _____

Dr. Malcolm H. Forbes   Mr. Kenneth Quakkelaar
Vice President   Executive Vice President
for Academic Affairs

_____

Dr. Robert Garnett
Vice President   Evansville Vanderburgh
for Administration   School Corporation

_____   _____

Dr. Ann Stuart   Dr. Victor L. Fisher, Jr.
Project Director   Superintendent

five spaces and third-order headings ten spaces. You rarely go beyond the third step in the table of contents.

d. The appendix is the last entry. Type it against the left margin. Indent the individual appendix items five spaces. The bibliography comes first. The different appendixes are usually lettered "Appendix A, Appendix B," and so on. If the bibliography is the only entry, eliminate the word "Appendix" from the contents page and type "Bibliography" as the last entry.

e. Type "Page" once at the top of the page and next to the right column. This saves typing the word over and over.

TABLE OF CONTENTS

5. *Lists of Figures, Tables, Symbols.* If the report contains more than four figures or four tables or four symbols, they are customarily listed separately. They can be listed on a separate page or under a centered title as a continuation of the table of contents. No single way is best for compiling the lists, but the following tips are useful:

a. Center the title at the top of the page or wherever it occurs on the page, and follow the format rules you have selected. If you underlined "Table of Content" and typed it in full capitals, do the same with this title.

b. Triple-space between the title and the list. Double-space between entries; single-space entries of more than one line.

c. List items in the order they appear in the text.

d. Label figures and tables so they are self-explanatory (i.e., "Battery Charger"). Omit the word "figure" or "table" from the list entry.

e. Capitalize the first letter of each major word in the label of figures or tables.

f. Type "Figure" (as you did "Page"; see letter e in the previous list) at the top of the list to avoid having to type the word each time.

A list of symbols and abbreviations is necessary if the readers are not schooled in the topic of the report. People inside a technical area sometimes assume that everyone outside the area understands as they do. This assumption can be incorrect and block understanding. To address the issue, list and define common symbols and abbreviations used in the report.

6. *Glossary.* A glossary is compiled for the same reason as a list of symbols—to be certain readers understand key words in the report. Create a format that is neat and easily read. One choice is to type the word against the left margin. Find out the length of the longest word. Use that length to decide the margin to begin definitions. Leave white space between the longest word and the definitions:

Demultiplexer   Definition -
Nonmaskable Interrupt   Definition -

Definitions do not need to be written in complete sentences, but the definition form should be parallel. If the first definition is a sentence, all should be; if it is a phrase, all should be.

7. *Abstract.* The abstract says in a few words the essence of the entire report. Some people consider it the most important writing of the whole report because it is read by top decision makers. The president of a firm or chief chemist of a research laboratory may not read the details of the report, but he or she will most certainly read the abstract.

One type of abstract is the descriptive abstract; it merely describes the report. It describes what the report covers, but not what it says about any subject. Its value is to inform readers whether they should or need to read the document. The second type is the informative abstract, sometimes called a summary or synopsis. It is the report in miniature. Findings, recommendations, and other pertinent information are given. Such an abstract is a challenge to write because most of us find it difficult to condense and summarize. Nevertheless, you should accept the challenge. Learning to say only what is essential and being able to see and report main points is a valuable communication skill in the technical professions.

To prepare for writing the abstract, you must reread the report well and be a good reader. You need the ability to take in large amounts of information, see relationships among ideas, and see clearly the essential points of the information. Those salient points are what you should include in the abstract. It goes without saying that you write the abstract after you have written the report.

Adopt the same tone as that used in the report and avoid the pronoun "I." Limit your writing to 200 or 400 words. (Some informative abstracts use the measure of 5 percent of the total report to determine length.) Type the abstract single-spaced. See the example on page 224. Even though you want to be brief, do not write short, choppy sentences. Write as you would within the report: in clear, interesting, and correctly constructed sentences.

If you have no experience with abstracting, go to the library and ask the reference librarian to help you find reference books that contain abstracts or look in the professional journals of your area. Many writers begin an article with an informational abstract. The journal path is a good one to pursue because you can read the article and compare it to the abstract. You can also analyze what the writer includes and how it is written.

Abstract example: The following article was given to a group of students. Each wrote an informative abstract. Three examples follow. They differ in style and effectiveness, but each intends to condense and present the essence of the Asteroff article. Compare them with the article. Decide what topics are covered and left out. Are the omissions appropriate? What is effective or ineffective about each? Use what is effective as models for your own writing.

3

On Technical Writing and Technical Reading

Janet F. Asteroff

Many members of the university community are beginning to take advantage of mainframe and microcomputer systems for a variety of services such as online library catalogs, electronic mail, word processing, programming, and textual and statistical analysis. One aspect of support is documentation, long the stepchild of computing. To understand the position of printed documentation in computing is to observe the form on several different levels of experience. As print, a manual represents a five-hundred-year-old technology. It exists side-by-side with computing, a technology barely forty years old. The complaint seems to be, however, that in both form and content even this old medium fails the user. Its mere presence not only is not reassuring, but is often cause for trepidation. But documentation is not as bad as many think. Nor, when one considers the many factors that make a system usable, including hardware and software design as well as user attitudes, should documentation be identified as the only problem.

INTRODUCTION

Computer documentation is receiving its share of criticism these days. A recent popular magazine article with the subtitle "No Matter What Happens, Do Not Look at the Manual" explained the concept of "wall-stare": after people read a computer manual, they put it down and stare at the wall.[1] In academia, these wall-starers most often are social science and humanities students and faculty, who in ever-increasing numbers are the newest computer users in the university. They have joined those in the hard sciences who for twenty years were the overwhelming majority of users of university computing facilities. Many members of the university community are beginning to take advantage of mainframe[2] and microcomputer systems for a variety of services such as online library catalogs, electronic mail, word processing, programming, and textual and statistical analysis.

As this heterogeneous community develops, those who administer computing resources are raising anew questions about accessibility, functionality, and support. They recognize that it is difficult for most users, regardless of their discipline, to find their way into computing, and once having done so to make profitable use of the resources, whether in the library or in the computer center.

For all users, training and ongoing support are critical for success. One aspect of support is documentation, long the step-child of computing. Manuals and other forms of assistance now are receiving more attention as humanists and social scientists, who need different kinds of support than

Janet F. Asteroff writes documentation for the academic systems of the Columbia University Center for Computing Activities in both printed and online form. She is a doctoral candidate in communication in the Department of Communication, Computing and Technology in Education, Teachers College, Columbia University.

those in the hard sciences, become involved with computing. The types of manuals that may have worked for technicians and those in the hard sciences are insufficient for those in the humanities and social sciences, as well as librarians using computers to assist them. For users at all levels and in many capacities, printed documentation is crucial when consultants are not available to provide personal attention.

To understand the position of printed documentation in computing is to observe the form on several different levels of experience. As print, a manual represents a five-hundred-year-old technology. It exists side-by-side with computing, a technology barely forty years old. Although the need for documentation varies with expertise, users at all levels always need some printed instruction to use the computer. This situation, in part a "paradoxical combination . . . of seeming continuity with radical change," is similar to one identified by Elizabeth Eisenstein in *The Printing Press as an Agent of Change*, which describes the incunabula period when, during the shift from script to print in the latter part of the fifteenth century, early printers duplicated scribal manuscripts, but through a totally new mode of production, the printing press.[3] At least for the moment, computing still is learned mainly by reading printed materials, since most users are not fortunate enough to have ongoing personal support and instruction. Trends in online documentation and system design, however, will in the future decrease the reliance on printed forms as the entire experience becomes more completely electronic.

On a more conscious level, whether new users are faced with a terminal connected to an invisible mainframe system or with a microcomputer with a system unit, monitor, and disk drives, only two components of the computing experience initially appear recognizable: the keyboard and the printed documentation. New users soon discover that there are several keys that make a computer keyboard substantially different from a typewriter's, which has not changed much since 1873. This leaves the printed manual as the most familiar technology, in many cases the sole lifeline

to a system they have never seen before and which offers an almost totally new environment for thinking and learning. The complaint seems to be, however, that in both form and content even this old medium fails the user. Its mere presence not only is *not* reassuring, but is often cause for trepidation.

DEFINING THE REAL PROBLEMS

Does reading computer manuals really bring about catatonia? Certainly they do provoke a wide range of emotions and, for the most part, criticisms of technical manuals are valid. But documentation is not as bad as many think. Nor, when one considers the many factors that make a system usable, including hardware and software design as well as user attitudes, should documentation be identified as the only problem.

Among the valid criticisms of computer manuals are that they are poorly written and printed; the index is incomplete, esoteric, or nonexistent; the table of contents is too detailed or too sparse; there is no cross-referencing in the text; there are no usage examples or diagrams; they are too elementary or too advanced; and finally, they are condescending in tone. These criticisms are true of many manuals, and significantly hinder those learning how to use a system.

These criticisms are not applicable to all manuals, however. Technical documentation is getting better, in part because of the widespread use of personal computers and, therefore, the vendor's responsibility to make products usable. Many technical writers and editors now are reaching out to their readers with clear prose narratives, good usage examples and diagrams, and more than a little humor.

The most important criticism that can be made about computer manuals is one that users rarely think of. The manual fails to *teach* users how to apply information and concepts to different situations. The best computer manual not only explains what users need to know to perform a specific task, but teaches them how to apply this knowledge in a variety of ways. Such explanations are not always presented in prose, but often through usage examples and diagrams that illustrate a variety of procedures in one situation applicable to many others, e.g., how to create, modify, and save a text file in a typical session, not only how to create a file.[4]

Most manuals fail to teach users for three reasons. First, technical writers often think of themselves rather narrowly as communicators of information, not as teachers of computing in the larger sense. Second, it is always difficult to write effective instructional material without access to potential users, without knowing the audience. To teach only through writing, or with the complete absence of verbal and nonverbal communication, may never really be teaching in its purest sense, but only imparting information. Third, the computer system or software application may be too complex to explain clearly in writing.

To be fair to the art of technical writing and to hard-working users, there are systems even the best writer cannot explain, and the most skilled programmer or analyst cannot understand very well. These hardware- and software-related problems remain obscure because users do not know enough to evaluate system design from a functional or technical point of view. They do not ask of a system "Why does it make me do it this way when the other way is easier?" Poor documentation is not the only failing of computer systems, even if it is the most identifiable one, and it certainly is not the problem if it is good.

Users also share a great deal of responsibility for their success or failure. It is clear that systems are not perfectly designed, manuals are not perfectly written, and users do not take time necessary to learn how to use either well. Even in the best possible circumstances, no technical manual, particularly in computing, can be all things to all people. Some make very profitable use of a manual, while others are confused by it and only use bits and pieces. Generally, if most users applied to learning computers only a fraction of the time they spent learning to use another technology, such as the alphabet, they all would be technical wizards. Like any new and complex technology or tool, learning to use computers requires a great deal of time and patience.

THE DISCERNING READER

Many users are unaware that documentation has always been a significantly weak point in system development and application even for those inside the computer industry at all levels. Poor documentation is not a wrongdoing perpetuated only on new or unsuspecting users. The reasons for this traditional failing could fill a book, but is traceable to a lack of skilled technical writers. Most often documentation was left (and in some cases still is) in the hands of programmers, analysts, and other technicians who did and do not communicate well orally or in writing, particularly to those at a lower level of technical expertise than themselves. More attention to the profession of technical writing, including master's degree programs at such schools as Carnegie-Mellon University and Rensselaer Polytechnic Institute, as well as professional programs leading to certificates in technical writing, is beginning to rectify this situation.

Still, computer documentation follows in a long line of technical literature that was never adequate, including instructions for assembling a child's toy or hooking up the latest stereo component. This comparison does not imply that bad computer documentation is excusable, but only that bad technical literature is not limited to computing.

Further, perhaps we should pay more attention to the amount of bad literature we tolerate with minimal complaint. Of course our lives still go on rather well, even if journals, newspapers, and magazines contain only a few worthwhile articles. This is not the case with computer manuals because of their utilitarian function. And no matter what the content, the form should not be ignored. Ultimately the impact is the same: the literature is poorly written, confusing, and not worth reading. Bad computer manuals have lots of company.

Harper's editor Lewis Lapham, who *does not* contribute to bad literature, speaks directly to these issues in his essay, "On Reading." "On first opening a book,"

6 *Information Technology and Libraries* / March 1985

he writes, "I listen for the sound of the human voice. By this device I am absolved from reading much of what is published in a given year."[5] Lapham argues that the institutional codes used by writers in academic, political, and technical fields make these kinds of literature unworthy of his attention, unless they are absolutely necessary for professional reasons. They have no human voice, just the "messages already deteriorating into the half-life of yesterday's news."[6]

Regardless of the genre, the sound of the human voice should be listened for in all *good* writing, and surprisingly it may be heard when least expected. It may never be heard in Heathkit manuals, which do their jobs very well without it, but it can be heard in some computer manuals.

FORM AND CONTENT

When users cannot get their work done, they place the responsibility on someone, or something, other than themselves. It is easiest but least fulfilling to be angry with—or at—a book or manual that does not do its job. In *Orality and Literacy*, media theorist Walter Ong observes that what is stated in a book goes on forever. The writer cannot be refuted, and the book or manual still survives, no matter what the reader thinks about it.[7] Print confers many things, among them permanence and legitimacy, even to thoughts we do not like.

This is why when writers and editors, technical or otherwise, emerge from behind the prose and meet their audience, they sometimes find a fair amount of hostility waiting for them. The reader finally attaches a person to those instructions or ideas that did not work, and the writer is going to hear about it. It is almost as though readers expect that writers and editors start with the worst of intentions. Yet this is rarely the case. Most writers, editors, consultants, programmers, and other technical support staff do their best; sometimes their best is not good enough, in part because users' problems are very individual. Writers and consultants can just as easily meet people who found their work to be helpful, and the gratification is enormous, but those in any service capacity usually hear only the complaints, rarely the praise.

TRENDS IN SYSTEM DESIGN

Ironically, just when printed documentation seems to be getting better, or users have adjusted to its being terrible, there will be less of it. More documentation now exists solely online and not in printed form, and some systems are easy enough to use without reading volumes in print or on the screen.

Online documentation is hardly new, but it is getting more attention by designers and writers. These electronic print[8] documents, including "help messages" and other forms, provide assistance at the terminal, and are not duplicated in print. Context-sensitive help and error messages are particularly important, since they provide assistance geared to the user's current situation, unlike standard messages, which are the same in all situations. (OCLC users will recognize "Message not clear" as an example.) Personal computing software usually has more context-sensitive online documentation than do mainframe applications. For the most part, standard help and error messages appear much more frequently than the context-sensitive type, and this now should be considered a serious design defect.

Recent developments in system design indicate that computers need not be the cryptic machine some specialists would like it to continue to be. This is particularly true of Apple's Macintosh, which because of its icon interface[9] and other design features not only requires less printed documentation than most systems, but uses audio tapes linked to tutorial/guided tour computer disks as an effective alternative to print for getting started with the system.[10] However, most personal computers, and certainly most mainframes, are not designed to be easily understood. While some quite correctly argue that computing is complex and cannot be summarized in a few simple sentences, Apple demonstrates that this need not always be the case, although Macintosh users cannot make full use of the system without reading the manuals. Most manufacturers and designers try but fail to understand where the threshold actually is—

where they must meet their potential users—and so they do not make a system reasonably easy for people to use.

Good system design does not automatically lead to good documentation, nor is the converse true. A good case in point is MCI Mail and Western Union's EasyLink, two popular electronic mail services. MCI's printed documentation is inadequate and confusing, even if it is printed in several colors (which really does make it easier to follow; it's not all for aesthetics). And yet, the MCI mail system is designed in such a way that even a novice user can send and receive messages without making too many mistakes.[11] The EasyLink documentation comes in an expensive binder, complete with good, clear examples and explanations, but the actual system is esoteric and does not follow the thought patterns of rational individuals. You need the documentation to use EasyLink, which is probably (and fortunately) why it is so thorough. It is not always the case that good documentation means an otherwise difficult system, yet this is something to consider when evaluating computer systems.

Even with better system design, it will be some time, if ever, before printed documentation is completely replaced by the supremely easy-to-use computer or alternative forms of assistance. Printed documentation, or books of any kind, will not be totally displaced, at least not until disks or their successors can be read easily and inexpensively on a park bench or at 30,000 feet. Furthermore there is no reason to believe that the perfect system will emerge soon, one that does not even need online documentation. Predictions not too long ago about how computers will create a paperless society now appear frivolous, since current indicators show that the paper industry, unlike most others, is operating at full capacity. The trend, however, seems to be that various kinds of online assistance, including electronic print as well as audio and video technology, will emerge as effective alternatives to printed forms.

CONCLUSION

There is no shopping list of what to look for in documentation, how to separate the good from the bad, easily. Most times this is not clear until it is used. But some features that may indicate a good manual are:

- clear prose narratives
- usage examples and diagrams
- sample sessions
- cross-referencing in the text
- a complete index with logical entries and *see* and *see also* references
- a specific and comprehensive (but not overly detailed) table of contents
- a clearly defined level of instruction
- clear printing and overall spacious design and layout

Computer manuals are books, not scribal manuscripts. Features that differentiated these two media in the early sixteenth century, such as indexes, tables of contents, cross-referencing, and portability, and thus made the former easier to use than the latter, should not disappear in the age of electronic print. Pagination seems safe on all fronts, however.

Three guiding principles should be followed when considering the use or purchase of a computer system:

1. Choose a *total* system, which consists of three components: hardware, software, and documentation.

2. Evaluate the documentation with the features above in mind. Like any book or publication, it has to have qualities that make it worth reading or buying.

3. When using the computer, do not try to read the manual cover to cover in one sitting, which will always produce extreme cases of wall-stare. Technical manuals are not bedtime reading, no matter how well written, how pretty the pictures, or how funny they may be. Like testing the water before swimming, proceed cautiously at first, then dive in, but know when to come up for air. Often it works best to first read for comprehension away from the terminal, and later, at the terminal during actual use. Reading for reference is almost always done as needed while using the system.

The computing experience can be profitable and enlightening, and perhaps even fun. As in all learning, a willingness to think, experiment, and work hard are always the fundamental ingredients for success.

8   *Information Technology and Libraries*   /   March 1985

REFERENCES

1. "How Does This #%¢@! Thing Work?" *Time* 123:64 (June 18, 1984).
2. A mainframe system, which may also be a minicomputer, is a large computer that accommodates several users at once through a time-sharing environment.
3. Elizabeth Eisenstein, *The Printing Press as an Agent of Change: Communications and Cultural Transformations in Early Modern Europe* (Cambridge Univ. Pr., 1979, 1980), p.51.
4. Ideas on these points have benefited from electronic mail "discussions" with Purvis Jackson (PMJ@CM-CS-CAD), Writer and Lecturer in Technical Writing, The Robotics Institute and Carnegie Institute of Technology, Carnegie-Mellon University.
5. Lewis H. Lapham, "On Reading," *Harper's* 268:6 (May, 1984).
6. Ibid.
7. Walter Ong, *Orality and Literacy: The Technologizing of the Word* (New York: 1982), p.79.
8. Electronic text/print is text that is displayed on a CRT or TV screen. It is interactive in the sense that users may modify their own textual product, and because the system responds to user commands that are entered in textual symbols. This would include computer systems and videotex applications displayed on TV sets, but not electronic text presented in silent or sound films.
9. The Macintosh interface is primarily composed of icons, or small pictures representing various system components, e.g., a file is represented by a small picture of a file folder, with the name of the file in text on it. Files are deleted by "throwing them away" in the "trash" which is a picture of a trash can.
10. *A Guided Tour of Macintosh.* (Cupertino, Calif.: Apple Computer, 1983).
11. MCI Mail is a completely menu-driven system, which does not accommodate a direct command structure to bypass the menu options. This slows down users who already have some expertise, as well as new users as they gain such expertise.   ∎∎

Abstract 1: Michael Bobek, student

With the increased use of computers by humanists and social scientists, a new problem arises: the inability of computer manuals to communicate information to nonscientific people. For users at all levels, printed documentation (computer manuals) is crucial when consultants are not available.

The most important criticism made about computer manuals is that they fail to teach the user how to apply information and concepts to different situations. Most manuals fail to teach the user for three reasons. First, technical writers often think of themselves "as communicators of information—not as teachers." Second, "it is always difficult to write effective instructional material . . . without knowing the audience." Third, "the computer system of software applications may be too complex to explain clearly in writing."

Some steps taken to alleviate the problem of poor documentation are icon interfaces (small pictures on the screen that represent system components and functions) and better online documentation. This better online documentation includes audio cues, help messages, and error messages.

The following features are characteristics of good documentation: clear prose narratives, usage examples and diagrams, sample sessions, cross-referencing, a complete index, a comprehensive table of contents, and a clearly defined level of instruction.

Abstract 2: Student work

Many computer user guides and manuals are not easy to follow. In fact, many of these manuals cause frustration more than they answer questions. This communication failure occurs primarily for three reasons: (1) technical writers often serve only to inform others, not to teach others to use the system, (2) technical writers fail to know their audience, and (3) computers and software are difficult to explain clearly. Even though online help programs, audio tapes, and other methods are used to aid computer documentation, they will not replace printed manuals. When purchasing a computer, choose a total system. Check the documentation for features such as clear narratives, examples, sample sessions, a good table of contents, index, and an easy-to-follow format with pictures and diagrams.

Abstract 3: Ron McRae, student

Technical manuals encounter many problems conveying their intended ideas. One specific type of manual facing this problem is computer documentation. Computer use has increased significantly in recent years. The majority of the new users come from nontechnical fields such as the social sciences and humanities. The difficulty occurs when the reader does not have the background to comprehend what is written. The writer most often makes the mistake of not writing to the level of the reader.

The computer manual is difficult to read or write at best. The problems with writing include having to explain a complex computer system or obscure software applications. The problems with reading include a mismatch of intended reader to actual reader and the failure of technical writers as teachers. Luckily, good manuals do exist. When looking for a good manual, the reader must choose one that will match his or her technical background. Other factors include examples and diagrams, cross-referencing in the text, and a complete index. The manual must also match the system.

So the purchaser of a system or of system time should choose a three-part system: hardware, software, and quality documentation. With this complete system, patience, and a little luck, a successful bond between the person and computer will form.

Body

No one can tell you the best way to write the body of a major report. Each report differs too much in purpose and subject matter. One of the best ways to acquire an understanding of reports is to read some. If you have a part-time job where formal reports are written and not classified, ask to read several on your own time. If your parents receive annual reports on companies in which they own stock or have some other interest, ask them to save or send you the reports. Read them. Also, go to the library and ask if the library has any formal reports from the government or other sources; if so, look them over. You will quickly gain a feel for the style, format, and task of writing a formal report. Gaining the ability to write an effective report requires practice.

The body of most reports has three divisions—the opening, development, and close. Each of these sections is discussed generally in the following paragraphs.

A speaker does not just stand and begin a formal address. A formal report does not just begin. Both need to be introduced. In the opening tell the subject of the report; the purpose of the study; the limits of the study; and the method of study, research, or development. Summarize and make recommendations. The opening should give decision makers all they need to understand and act upon the findings of the report. No need exists to be coy. Write clearly. If your writing style is just developing, simplicity, clarity, and accuracy will win you points. To write, "The purpose of this report is . . . ." is fine. As you polish your own style, you will find ways to add eloquence.

The midsection adds technical details. In this section you explain criteria, analysis, and interpretation of experiments or facts. Use patterns of organization to make information clear—cause and effect, chronology, problem and solution, comparison and contrast, space. Format with headings, subheadings, indentations, and white space. Work to make the report easy to read and understand. Do not overwhelm with pages of densely presented information. The midsection often finishes with detailed conclusions. The writer's job is to write the results or make conclusions based on the evidence presented. Readers should not have to correlate information, draw together information in the report, and make their own conclusions. Some readers will not. They simply will return the report to you: tell you to finish it, tell you they are unhappy with your work, or tell you nothing, but remember you unfavorably.

A formal report needs a close. It should be graceful and courteous as any formal leaving should be. You may thank the appropriate person(s) for the opportunity to do the study. You may say something about the future of the project and its significance. You may summarize.

End Matter

If a bibliography is included, it should open the end matter. For examples of form, see pages 53–55.

Supplemental material that interrupts the continuity of the text or is not applicable to the majority of readers can be presented in appendixes. Be certain that you show in the table of contents the subject of the appendixes and you note when writing about a subject that more information is available in the appendix. You can do so by inserting in brackets: [See Appendix D, p. 218]. Do not expect readers to look ahead or examine a set of appendixes to see if there is information they should read. Tell them it exists.

Index

A complicated or long report sometimes includes an index so that a person can selectively read topics particularly interesting to him or her. An index also helps a reader quickly know if certain information is included in a report and quickly helps the person locate it.

You can prepare an index manually or with indexing software. Most people who manually create an index use 3×5 cards, write one term per card, and record on the card the page number on which the term appears. After all terms are noted, the indexer makes a group of all cards recording the same term, arranges the groups alphabetically, then compiles a list of alphabetized terms. All pages on which the term appears are recorded sequentially following the term.

Indexing software lets you enter a term and its page reference. Afterward, the program will sort and gather together all page references to the same term, arrange the page references sequentially, and later alphabetize the list of terms. Printing options allow you to format effectively.

The newsletter *Simply Stated*, a publication of the Document Design Center, American Institutes for Research, carried an article on preparing an index. The following tips are derived from that piece (No. 67, July–August 1986, p. 3).

- Include nontechnical terms that appear in the report as well as technical terms or jargon that specialists may use. Cross-reference the technical terms or jargon to the nontechnical reference.
- Use "See" or "See also" to refer the reader to an entry that has more information. Do not use this convention when references have exactly the same page references.
- Include several words that a reader might use to find the same information.
- Select references that make a significant comment. Do not index a reference to a term when it is only mentioned.
- Use separate entries for a term that has more than one definition. Gather together all page references using one definition, all references using a second definition, and so on.
- Divide or subordinate information if a term has more than four or five page references. Look for different ways the term is used and let these form the basis

of the subordination. Use subheadings to tell readers how the term is used on different pages or how the subordinate terms relate to the primary term.

- Format or print the index to show the importance of a term or idea in the report. Important terms can be set against a left margin and subordinate terms set-in a number of spaces to the right. Important terms can also be printed in boldface or in another outstanding typeface.
- Proofread for accuracy. Be certain page references are correct.

Final Format

Before the final reading, decide certain format options and make decisions about the paper and printer. When deciding upon a format, remember that the reader needs to be able to refer easily to different parts of the report. A formal report often is read in sections; some people read only certain parts. A report can be discussed in meetings and attendants asked to turn to certain sections or pages. People often return to a formal report and reread sections. All this activity requires you to design the report so that information is easy to access. You can do this several ways—by preparing a detailed and accurate table of contents, using specific headings within sections, placing headings on the page so they are easily seen.

The report should be typed or printed on a heavy bond, white paper.

Paging should be consistent. Different writers have different preferences. Some like to page at the top, others at the bottom. You decide and then do the same throughout. Some standards for paging follow:

- Use Arabic numbers except for front pages. Use no punctuation after the number.
- Number in the upper right-hand corner. Align with the right-hand margin, two lines above the first line of the text.
- Omit the page number for the first page of text. Begin numbering on page 2 with the number 2.
- Center and type page numbers at the bottom on pages that begin main sections of the report.
- Number front pages in lowercase Roman numerals centered at the bottom of the page, about ¾ inch from the bottom of the page.
- Omit page numbers from the title page and the cover letter but count these pages; consequently, begin the table of contents or whatever is the third entry with Roman numeral iii.
- Number pages of the appendix as a continuation of the text, in the upper right-hand corner.

Word Processing and Formal Reports

 The very nature of the formal report makes it suitable to word processing.

- A long document often is not written from start to finish, so to be able to write sections when the information is available and later to reformat and renumber pages to fit correctly into the larger document is a wonderful convenience.

- Often a report is begun, but information changes during the project; editing functions make change no problem.
- It is difficult to see a long document as a whole. With word processing, a draft can be printed and any inconsistencies changed and a corrected document printed with little trouble.
- Outlining programs can be helpful in effectively organizing a large writing project and be a means of reminding or keeping the writer on track.
- Graphic programs and the correct interface allow the writer to add illustrations directly into the text.
- Format possibilities let the writer create a quality printed document with many features previously available only through typesetting.
- Finally, word processing lets the typist produce a document that appears error-free. No dots of white-out are visible. No odd spacings reveal letters squeezed together.

Student Example 1: Engineering Report

The following report is the result of a year-long project conducted by two senior engineering students at the University of Evansville. All graduating engineering seniors complete a similar project and report as part of their graduation requirements. The report varies somewhat according to the instructor who oversees the project, but all the reports attempt to imitate the type of writing students will be producing and using in the marketplace. Because of the length, the entire report is not reproduced, but the excerpts show the students' complying with formal report writing and adopting a tone and style anticipatory of professional writing. My editorial comments appear in brackets.

FINAL REPORT

HAL ONE

AN INDEPENDENTLY OPERATING ROBOT DOG

INDUSTRIAL SPONSOR:
STUDENT ASSOCIATION

INDUSTRIAL ADVISOR:
B AND M CONSULTANTS

FACULTY ADVISORS:
DR. BLANDFORD
MR. MITCHELL

PROJECT ENGINEERS:
THOMAS J. STEPHENS
BRADLEY W. POLLEN

DATE: MAY 17, 19XX

UNIVERSITY OF EVANSVILLE, EVANSVILLE, INDIANA

[The title page is spaced attractively and contains the specified information. Full names and initials should be given for advisors. The authors could have chosen different type for some items instead of using all capitals. All capitals make it appear that all information has the same weight; yet the date, for example, is probably not as important as the title.]

ACKNOWLEDGMENTS

WE WOULD LIKE TO THANK THE FOLLOWING PEOPLE OR

GROUPS OF PEOPLE FOR THEIR VALUABLE HELP IN

CONSTRUCTION OF THIS PROJECT:

MR. MITCHELL

DR. BLANDFORD

STAFF OF THE ELECTRICAL ENGINEERING STOCKROOM

BARRY MULLINS

KELLEY CAMBELL

ELIZABETH LILLEY

KIMBERLY WELKER

GREGG JOHNSON

DEBBIE BOTTORFF

GOD

ALL OUR OTHER FRIENDS WHOM

WE HAVE NOT SEEN FOR SO LONG

[It is not necessary to have an acknowledgment page, but it is not uncommon.
This one shows both appreciation and wit.]

[Photograph of Hal One, the robot dog.]

TABLE OF CONTENTS

[The table of contents is detailed and accurate according to the page given. The format is functional. Subtitles listed under major subjects should be in lowercase.]

TABLE OF FIGURES

[The figures are identified specifically, which is good. The figure number could appear before the identification. The title of this page should be ''list'' rather than ''table.'']

[The "introduction," "applications," and "mechanical design" follow one another and give the reader necessary background, the scope of the project, reasons for doing the project, and a description and drawing of the final design. The reader is then prepared to read farther in the text.]

INTRODUCTION

The design objectives of Hal One were to build:
1) a small mobile robot controlled by a microprocessor
2) ultrasonic sight allowing Hal to see his world
3) speech synthesis enabling Hal to communicate directly with humans
4) acoustic input enabling Hal to respond to human commands
5) low power sensor enabling Hal to sense his hunger
6) contact switches enabling Hal to feel objects he does not see

[The list should be parallel in structure. Numbers 2–6 are. One way to correct number 1 is to include it in the opening statement: Hal One, a small mobile robot controlled by a microprocessor, was designed to meet these objectives:]

Not all of these objectives were competed. Many of the project divisions worked independently but were not successfully integrated into a whole. This report presents our answers to the design objectives, what we did, and how we did it.

APPLICATIONS

Because Hal One is a small, self-contained mobile robot, he could be the basis for several different types of applications. The robot can be easily modified (usually only a software change) to form a versatile tool in the elimination of tedious or dangerous tasks.

Since the robot has the ability to sense motion (by noticing changes in his sonic environment), he could be used as an automated security guard. Hal One could be programmed to follow the perimeter of an area or to choose a random patrol pattern. The robot would then periodically stop and examine his surroundings for any signs of movement which would be an indication of a intruder. He could then sound an alarm (not necessarily audible) to alert an authority to the presence of the trespasser.

A second application of this small robot is in message or mail delivery. The robot could travel down a hall (following a wall) and stop at the appropriate doorways along the way. The robot then would signal that it was there. Hal One's sonic sight would be able to sense doorframes and corridor branches. A software change would be needed for each building or floor that the robot serviced. Letters could be placed in a box on the back of the prototype, or a much larger frame could be designed so the robot could handle all types of package and mail delivery.

With modifications to the body of the robot, Hal One could be used as the basis for automated cleaning. Hal One's brain and sensing devices would form the basis for the control center of a "smart" cleaning system. As a vacuum cleaner or floor buffer/waxer, the robot would follow a systematic pattern through a room or hall, cleaning as it went. Hal One has the ability to avoid any obstacles he encounters and with the proper programming to cover completely a designated area.

MECHANICAL DESIGN

OBJECTIVES:

1) Test grounds: provide a dynamic test for real-time control systems programming
2) Mobility
3) Durability
4) Appearance

[To be consistent in format and information, items 2–4 should also have a comment following them.]

FINAL DESIGN

The final design layout is illustrated in Figure 1. The body is six inches wide, twenty-six inches long, and twenty inches high. The entire body, wheels, and pulleys are made of clear Lexan. Black rubber O-rings are used for tires and fan belts.

The brainboard is attached with DB-25 connectors mounted on the front and rear.

A small DC motor ($\frac{1}{35}$ hp) drives one rear wheel through a pulley and belt speed reduction made with Lexan, pressed bearings, and O-rings. The motor is controlled through a power transistor and relay mounted directly above it.

The front wheel is turned by a gear reduction driven by a small DC motor. Positional sensing is accomplished with optical sensors.

A negative five-volt supply and a positive five-volt regulator are mounted on the rear wall. The reset button, on/off switch, and fuse for the regulator are also located there.

Most of the body is made of ¼-inch Lexan sheet with ⅜-inch blocks in the corners. The brainboard is covered with a .040-inch piece of Lexan bent in a five-inch radius. The wheels are machined from ½-inch Lexan with black rubber O-rings as tires.

For design alternatives, details, and drawings see Appendix A.

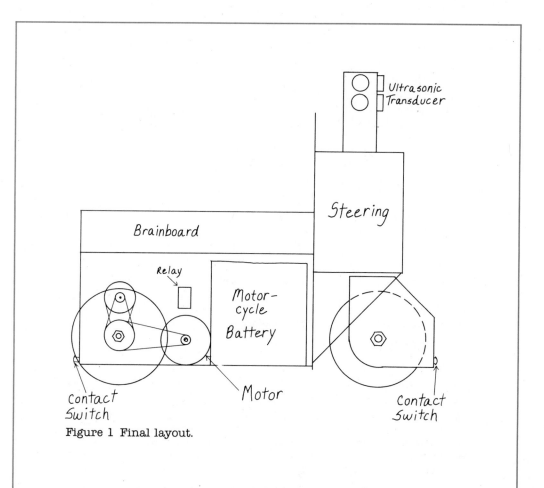

Figure 1 Final layout.

[The "Steering Control" and "Steering Positional Feedback" sections illustrate the report's detail and the writers' care in explaining what was done, as well as telling why certain things were not done or what happened if they were. Notice that readers are told more information is available in Appendix C.]

STEERING CONTROL

OBJECTIVES

1) Turn front wheel left or right on command
2) Use two or less I/O lines
3) Minimize cost
4) Maximize power supplied to the motor

FINAL DESIGN

The final design (Figure 5, next page) switches the polarity of the motor with four transistors driven by open collectors, not gates. One side of the motor is grounded through a saturated NPN transistor. The other side is connected to six volts by a saturated PNP transistor. PNP transistors were used because the load could then be put in the collector circuit, thereby holding the transistors in saturation better.

The PNP transistors were tied high through a one amp fuse to protect the circuit if both control bits go low. A small resistor was not used because of the loss of power it would entail to the motor. The small resistance of the fuse affords some limit to power surges when switching from one direction to another.

Alternate designs and resources: see Appendix C

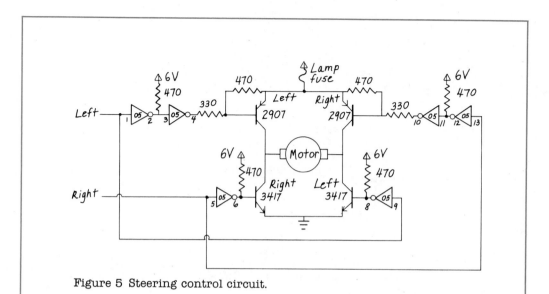

Figure 5 Steering control circuit.

[Each function of the robot dog is explained in a section like the following on Hal's ability to see.]

ULTRASONIC SIGHT

OBJECTIVES:

1) The ultrasonics must be able to detect the proximity of items that could lead to possible collisions with the robot.
2) The circuit must provide an ultrasonic pulse and be able to receive a returning echo.
3) The circuit must also be able to determine the relative distance to the object from the robot.

FINAL DESIGN

Functionally the ultrasonic tweeter outputs a sound pulse, and a similar ultrasonic tweeter receives the reflection off an external object. The distance from the external object is proportional to the time between the transmitted signal and the received signal (see Figure 14).

$$\text{Distance (in feet)} = \frac{1080 \text{ ft./s} * t}{2}$$

Speed of sound = 1080 feet per second
Divide by two because sound has to travel there and back.

ACOUSTIC COMMAND INPUT

OBJECTIVES:

1) Receive and decode acoustic input
2) Minimize processor time

PRESENT SITUATION

This area still needs research in both theoretical approach and hardware/
software implementation.

The present command grammar has each command consisting of five tones.
The first tone will serve as a reference, and the succeeding four will be compared to it. If the tone is higher than the reference tone, it will represent a
logical one. If it is lower, it will represent a logical zero.

The most favorable approach generates all the tones with the human vocal
cords. Variations on this approach would use different devices to generate
the tones. The more accurate the tone is, the shorter the tones can be. Possible tone generation devices are dog whistles, tuning forks, or a hand electronic tone generator (possible from an old television).

If vocal tones are used, each tone should be at least one second in length. If
other devices are used, the tones could be shortened. It is hard to relinquish
the flexibility of vocally issued commands.

The hardware/software division will be difficult to draw. At minimum, the
hardware would present a frequency number to the processor every two-
tenths of a second. A possible solution would be to use an additional four or
eight bit processor to sample constantly the acoustic input.

[When functions were not completed or successful, the authors simply say so
and explain. No apology is necessary or given since the project is understood
to be research with time as a factor in its scope.]

FINAL BUDGET

POWER SUPPLY	COST
6 volt 24 amp-hr motorcycle battery (Wisco H-1)	$ 36.30
Battery charger (transformer $5.69)	$ 15.00
5 volt 1 a/2 amp regulator	$ 6.00

Mechanical	
Drive motor (Dayton 2M273)	$ 9.63
Steering motor	$ 3.00
Wheel bearings Genbearco BR7714 3 @ $2.65	$ 7.95
Pulley bearing Shatz BR7704	$ 2.49
Pulley bearing Shatz TR1r4 2 @ $3.54	$ 7.08
Front steering thrust bearings Aetens E-1 2 @ $4.74	$ 9.48
Front steering bearings Hoover R377	$ 5.41
O-rings for tires 3 @ $1.55	$ 4.65
O-rings for pulley drive	$ 3.09
Bolts, nuts, axles	$ 10.00

Electronics	
DPU Motorola 6802	$ 8.95
Memory chips Intel 2716 2 @ $6.95	$ 13.90
I/O ports Motorola 6821 3 @ $3.50	$ 10.50
Counters, ttl, op amps, etc.	$ 28.35
P & B relay	$ 9.00
Ultrasonic transducers 6 @ $9.65	$ 62.95
DB-25 connectors 6 @ $7.00/pr	$ 21.00
Wire, pc boards, heat sinks, chip sockets	$ 60.00
Transistors, diodes, resistors, 4 meg crystal	$ 11.00
TI TMSK202 speech development kit	$ 60.00

Total $405.73*

Proposed budget $516.08

*Lexan not included

FINAL RESULTS

PROJECT DIVISIONS	STATUS
Processor w/memory & I/O	Working
Mechanics	Working
Voltage regulator	Working
Motor controllers:	
Drive	Working
Steering	Working
Steering feedback	Working
Speech output	Software errors
Acoustic input	Not working
Contact switches (interrupts)	Working
Ultrasonics	Working: limited 1 foot max.
Low power sensor	Working
Software	Control modules work separately limited Integrated, but not working

FUTURE PLANS

Brad Pollen will continue to work on this project this summer. The minimum goal for the summer is a working program using contact switches as sensors. The second goal will be the bench operation of the ultrasonics by a microprocessor and then the operation of ultrasonics within Hal's already operating program. The remaining unfinished parts (low power sensor, speech output, and speech input) will be dealt with in that order by both project engineers in the fall.

[The concept of bringing the report to a conclusion is good.]

[The following is an example of information presented in the appendix.]

Motor Sizing

Force to Overcome Slope

Weight \ Incline	20 lbs	25 lbs	30 lbs	35 lbs.
10°	3.47 lbs	4.34 lbs	5.21 lbs	6.08 lbs
20°	6.84 lbs	8.55 lbs	10.26 lbs	11.97 lbs
30°	10 lbs	12.5 lbs	15 lbs	17.5 lbs

Acceleration

Speed \ Distance for Acceleration		2'	1½'	1'	½'
½ mph = .73 $\frac{ft}{s^2}$		.134 $\frac{ft}{s^2}$	.179 $\frac{ft}{s^2}$	.269 $\frac{ft}{s^2}$	.538 $\frac{ft}{s^2}$
1 mph = 1.46 $\frac{ft}{s^2}$		.538 $\frac{ft}{s^2}$	.717 $\frac{ft}{s^2}$	1.08 $\frac{ft}{s^2}$	2.15 $\frac{ft}{s^2}$
1½ mph = 2.2 $\frac{ft}{s^2}$		1.21 $\frac{ft}{s^2}$	1.61 $\frac{ft}{s^2}$	2.42 $\frac{ft}{s^2}$	4.84 $\frac{ft}{s^2}$
2 mph = 2.93 $\frac{ft}{s^2}$		2.15 $\frac{ft}{s^2}$	2.87 $\frac{ft}{s^2}$	4.30 $\frac{ft}{s^2}$	8.60 $\frac{ft}{s^2}$

Force to push a given weight up a given slope.

Acceleration when given the final velocity and distance covered.

Table 2

[The report mirrors a real report in industry in its thoroughness and use of figures and tables to support text. The students took care with organization and presentation. They were limited by the university's meager word processing capabilities and lack of graphics software. As a result, the students' submitted hand-prepared drawings; these should have been more carefully drawn. Nevertheless, the engineering faculty was pleased with the students' work.]

Student Example 2: Humanities/Business Report

The report is typical of research written in the humanities. Notice that few headings are used. In their place are strong, clear topic sentences. One can very easily glance through the report reading topic sentences and know the outline of ideas, which are just not extracted and presented as headings. Many writers in the humanities prefer this style and write sections or chapters without internal breaks. They expect their readers to read through a section of information and understand it from introductory remarks, topic sentences, transitions, numbering items within paragraphs, and other rhetorical devices. In contrast, writers of technical writing anticipate that their readers may need to read only parts of the report or refer again to certain sections. As a result they prefer headings to make reading and referencing easier. In this example, consider the good organization and clear writing of the report.

536 Lodge Avenue
Evansville, IN 47714

December 4, 1986

Dr. Laura Weaver
English Department
University of Evansville
Evansville, IN 47714

Dear Dr. Weaver:

With this letter, I am enclosing my research report on the OPEC (Organization of Petroleum Exporting Countries) topic you approved on September 4, 1986. Directed at an audience with a general interest in economics and international affairs, my report discusses the Organization's role as an oil price-setter.

Seeking to viably judge the cartel as it acts in this capacity, my paper shows that OPEC's pricing influence is being undermined by three factors: (1) the internal dissension among cartel members, (2) the energy adjustment strategies of major oil importing countries, and (3) OPEC's declining position as a supplier. Tension between member nations is making compromises on pricing policies difficult to reach. Furthermore, France, West Germany, and the United States are employing energy policies which have allowed them to greatly reduce their dependence on high-priced OPEC oil. This factor, in addition to the increased energy supply by non-OPEC oil exporters and alternative energy sources, has forced the Organization to lower prices to remain competitive in world markets.

I hope you find my report interesting and well researched. If you need to discuss it with me, please call me at 424-8628.

Sincerely,

Andrea Jones

Andrea Jones

Enclosure

OPEC'S DECLINING INFLUENCE IN SETTING WORLD OIL PRICES

Andrea Jones

Composition 210

Dr. Laura Weaver

December 4, 1986

TABLE OF CONTENTS

LIST OF ILLUSTRATIONS

ABSTRACT

The Organization of Petroleum Exporting Countries' (OPEC) ability to set global oil prices is being undermined by three significant factors: internal dissension, energy adjustment strategies, and OPEC's declining position as a supplier. Tension, stemming from the needs of individual members and the cartel's power structure, is making compromises on output and pricing policies difficult to reach. In addition, France, West Germany, and the United States, major oil importing nations, are employing energy adjustment strategies to significantly decrease their dependence on high-priced OPEC oil. Furthermore, non-OPEC suppliers and alternative energy sources have forced the cartel to lower prices to remain competitive in the global market. Today, the Organization's ability to monopolistically establish and maintain world oil prices is largely ineffective.

FOREWORD

The world today faces the challenge of the coming energy transition. Evidence shows that in 1979 the known recoverable global oil resources were 1102 billion barrels of oil (BBO). At the 1982 consumption rate of 20 BBO per year, oil resources would be depleted by the year 2034 (Ivanhoe 167). As oil resources are exhausted, the rich industrial nations, dependent on cheap oil as their major energy source, and the poor developing countries, until recently looking forward to their own entry into the petroleum era, will have to seek alternative major energy sources. With less than a half-century's oil supply remaining, the global challenge is to change energy forms before being forced to do so.

Furthermore, this paper stems from the premise that the energy transition will not respect national boundaries. The long-term demands for energy are great, and the political and economic linkages between nations are so strong that, as a practical matter, the competitive search for new energy sources may give way to international cooperation in conservation, research, and development. Any contribution to the global energy supply will be of general benefit.

In sum, the Organization of Petroleum Exporting Countries (OPEC) can aid in the energy transition. In order to do so, however, its ability to set world oil prices must be enhanced and stabilized. Recognizing the complex implications of OPEC's actions, as they affect international politics and economics, this paper seeks to viably judge the cartel in its role as an oil price-setter. For, in this role, OPEC's significant contribution can be to gradually deplete oil without significantly disrupting international relations or monetary structures. Although non-OPEC nations claim the cartel's ability to set prices is not waning, this paper proves that it is. On the basis of the problems undermining OPEC's ability to set world oil prices, corrective action can be taken to stabilize global prices and outputs, ultimately facilitating the energy transition. The world challenge can be met much more readily if sovereign countries, including the cartel's thirteen member nations, cooperate, allowing the cartel to use its knowledge and ability to regulate production, outputs, and prices.

INTRODUCTION

In 1973, with the initiation of the first oil embargo, OPEC (Organization of Petroleum Exporting Countries) finally realized the pricing power it had sought since its formulation in January 1961. Acting as a cartel, with the objective of limiting competition to charge high prices, the governments of thirteen nations monopolistically set world oil prices higher than they had ever been. Political and economic changes arising since then have, however, affected the cartel's ability to set collective pricing policies and influence global prices. Pricing plans, made on the basis of unanimity, are becoming increasingly more difficult to make because of the membership's internal dissension. Also, major oil importing nations are adjusting their energy strategies to decrease their dependence on high-priced OPEC petroleum. Finally, the cartel's position as an energy supplier is being undermined, forcing OPEC to lower its prices to remain competitive in world markets. Thus, when judging the Organization in its role as a price-setter, evidence shows that the cartel's influence in establishing world oil values is declining.

DISCUSSION

Internal Dissension

    To act most effectively in their role as a unilateral price-setter, OPEC members must function collectively. In theory, therefore, the OPEC cartel should act as a business enterprise which limits competition and monopolizes the supply of its resource. This would allow it to set prices at a level which maximizes current and future revenues. The optimal price for oil should be high enough, so that when profits are distributed, each cartel member is convinced it is better off remaining in OPEC. Members should also perceive that it is in their best interest not to undermine the established price (Wyant 91).

    In practice, however, this is not the case. OPEC consists of the governments of thirteen nations with divergent and different political strategies, revenue needs, and orientations in regional and international politics. The actions of each government must be based on two objectives: (1) to maintain the independent interests of their sovereign nations and (2) to maintain the collective strength of the cartel on which their nation's economic development and revenue needs depend. The incompatibility of maintaining both objectives simultaneously creates tension. Individual OPEC countries must consider factors like: their respective nations' level of economic development, absorptive capacity, population size, development plans and priorities, resources, political pressures, and the possibilities for trade-offs and compromises they could offer or sustain, when the cartel sets collective price levels (Choucri 109). To further their sovereign interests (regarding the factors mentioned), individual OPEC members take actions incompatible with cartel goals. Consequently, because members with different domestic interests must compromise to set prices, the cartel, as a collective group of nations, suffers stress.

    To illustrate this point, the OPEC membership can be divided into two general groups, low reserve, densely populated countries and high reserve, sparsely populated countries. By examining the political and economic objectives of both groups, the basis for cartel stress and for the membership's dissension when formulating pricing strategies becomes evident. First, analysis of low reserve, densely populated nations, like Venezuela, Algeria, and Indonesia, reveals that they support relatively high price levels. Recognizing that oil is an exhaustible resource, they must weigh the depletion rate of their calculated reserves against their immediate needs for oil revenues. Depletion is a primary constraint in their policy calculations (Choucri 110). At some marginal point x, each of these countries will suffer from internal strain because it cannot remain indifferent to a revenue loss resulting from low prices, production cutbacks, spare capacity, or other means used by the cartel to maintain prices. A loss in oil revenues will be equated with a sacrifice in security needs, social programs, economic infrastructural development, etc. (Moran 3). When domestic strain occurs, the governments of these countries will seek more revenue by (1) insisting on larger market shares, thus forcing other OPEC members to absorb more idle capacity to maintain the established price, or by (2) cheating, thus expanding exports by shaving prices (Moran 4). Unless the cartel can reallocate the market shares and reduce the temptation to cheat, OPEC's established price will be undermined. Thus, when domestic policies are diametrically opposed to the established price policies, as in this case, internal cartel dissension results. The inability of the sovereign nations in this group to compromise their independent interests undermines the Organization's collective interests, including its ability to unilaterally set world oil prices.

In contrast to low reserve, densely populated OPEC nations, high reserve, sparsely populated OPEC nations have different policy constraints. For example, Libya has depletion concerns. The Libyan government wants the cartel to engage in long-range resource planning to protect OPEC's resources from rapid and unplanned exploitation. Also, Kuwait and Abu Dhabi encourage cooperation and counter moves that are not in the cartel's interests when policy is made. All high reserve, sparsely populated countries want to maintain relatively stable prices. Price changes should be smooth and gradual, based on the depletion rate of the cartel's reserves.

Problems between the two groups arise when high reserve, sparsely populated countries exert pressures in market allocation. High reserve countries are more flexible in absorbing production cutbacks than their counterparts. They also have the revenue base to maintain idle capacity. If market share reductions are allocated to low reserve, densely populated countries, which cannot reduce their revenue or moderate their production rate, dissension occurs. For example, a total OPEC quota of 14.5 million barrels per day (mbd) is needed to stabilize the market, but countries like Venezuela cannot cut current production levels. Saudi Arabia, the highest reserve country, views the low reserve countries' refusals to make concessions as a sign that OPEC no longer has the collective discipline to observe national quotas (Vielvoye 50). If quotas are not observed by OPEC members, too many barrels of oil reach the market. This drives prices downward and affects the profit distribution and the revenue needs of all of the OPEC nations. Thus, for OPEC to function as an effective cartel, it is necessary for these two groups to overcome the divergent political and economic needs which overshadow the cartel's collective priorities. The locus of convergence must be a collectively set and collectively maintained price level. By focusing on this common objective, OPEC can maintain cohesion and established prices and facilitate the future energy transition.

In addition to the internal dissension created by groups of nations in OPEC, some stress is created by the differing bargaining power individual members have in relation to the cartel. As the following examples show, when individual members obtain great bargaining power because of the carterl's asymmetrical power structure, OPEC's ability to collectively set prices is undermined. To illustrate, Saudi Arabia, with a small population, relatively low oil revenue needs, and one-third of the world's oil reserves, is the cartel's most significant member. The Saudis can unilaterally change prices overnight (Choucri 109). According to Sidney Alexander, Saudi Arabia is so large an actual and potential supplier that if it holds marker crude (light Arabian 34°) at an established price, the real price of oil can be held constant (41). In addition, Alexander also maintains that "output is not explicitly allocated by the cartel, but, essentially, it is governed by scaling the prices of all other crudes to the current price of Saudi Arabian marker crude" (qtd. 44). Recognizing this, Saudi Arabia's policy has, in the past, been to maintain prices at established levels and avoid rapid, precipitous price increases or decreases. It was willing to cut back on production and use its absorptive capacity to effectively allocate market shares among cartel members. Its objective was to stretch out the life span of oil reserves. Traditionally, "it has [also] been the Saudi objective," asserts Edward Morse, "to maximize its own freedom and to constrain that of its OPEC partners. Similarly, it has been the goal of virtually all of Saudi Arabia's partners in OPEC to enlarge their own freedom to produce and price oil and to keep Saudi behavior predictable and constrained" (799). Thus, prior to the 1980s, the Saudis' use of production constraints supported prices. They acted as a swing producer, cutting back production to make demand and supply match.

During the summer and fall of 1985, however, the Saudis were no longer content to play this role. They were losing their allocated market shares as other members cheated on quotas and Saudi Arabia absorbed the slack. To push world prices down fast, they flooded the oil market with exports and established the policy of netback pricing. . . .

Another example of individual nations making it difficult for OPEC to create unified price strategies is found in the ongoing argumentative relationship between Iran and Iraq. Iraq has unilaterally decided (without OPEC support) that its production policy will be governed by its ability to export. By continually increasing production since its pipeline to the Red Sea opened, cartel established quotas have been undermined. Furthermore, Iran recognizes that any move granting Iraq larger output quotas will give that country more oil revenues to use to finance the current war. Iran, therefore, adamantly opposes any increases in Iraq's allocated shares, claiming it will increase production by two barrels for every one awarded to Iraq (Vielvoye 50).

In conclusion, it is evident that the nature of the power structure in OPEC affects the cartel's ability to collectively set world oil prices. When the needs of subgroups or individual members are incompatible with the Organization's policies, these subunits instigate domestic policies which undermine cartel established prices. Internal dissension, therefore, occurs. As a result, it becomes difficult for OPEC to reach compromises concerning future price levels which satisfy all thirteen nations.

Energy Adjustment Strategies
Although the economic linkages between oil exporting and oil importing nations remain relatively strong, the relationship between OPEC, as a supplier, and the Western industrialized nations, as buyers, has changed. OPEC effectively set world prices during the embargoes. Following the 1973 and 1979 oil shocks, however, Western importing countries perceived the need to maintain independent control over their oil-dependent, industrialized economies. They began fostering independency from high-priced OPEC oil by pursuing the following energy goals: (1) diversification of oil sources away from the cartel's Persian Gulf nations, (2) diversification of energy sources away from oil, and (3) instigation of conservation measures to lower the levels of energy consumption (Ikenberry 107). By advancing toward these goals using different energy adjustment strategies, Western na-

tions affected the world oil market. The West's policies decreased total petroleum demand. Consequently, as the theory of supply and demand would indicate, the cartel was forced to lower oil prices to maintain its revenue levels. OPEC's position as a powerful price-setter was undermined by the French, German, and American application of the following energy adjustment strategies.

After 1973, the French government addressed the problem of national control over foreign energy sources by closing off imports and moving to meet its energy needs through domestic production. Using state institutions and state-owned enterprises in petroleum and nuclear energy for the foundation of a national program, the Socialists directly involved the government in energy production. . . .

Paralleling the French strategy is the West German strategy. Although the German energy strategy revision did not involve the government as an energy producer, it involved the government as a negotiator. . . .

Instead of acting as a producer or negotiator, the United States government acts as a facilitator to employ its energy adjustment strategy. Its policy is based on the idea that if market forces are allowed to work freely, oil import dependence may ultimately be lowered as substitutes and competitive energy forms, at cheaper prices, are introduced. As oil prices rise, the production of alternate energy forms will be stimulated and consumption will fall. Conversely, if prices fall, the government actively engages in decontrolling regulatory and price obstacles.

Two other methods of undermining OPEC's price-setting ability have also been suggested for incorporation into American strategy. Both methods would reduce OPEC prices on United States oil imports. First, an import quota action would involve a monthly auction of oil import entitlement tickets under sealed bids. The government would continuously adjust the number of tickets offered and sell tickets with different maturities, keeping enough in circulation to meet the needs of domestic refiners. By encouraging front companies and a secondary market for the tickets, OPEC exporters could increase their market shares by discounting. Cartel members would have trouble policing prices because of the sealed bids (Moran 83–85). A second method for reducing prices is an import tariff. Assuming that OPEC maximizes prices to maximize revenues and cohesion, the tariff would create a monopsony for American buyers. Pricing power would be transferred from OPEC to the U.S. government. If OPEC increased prices to offset the revenue loss from decreased exports, the cartel's profit would be reduced more (because of the tariff), resulting in internal dissention (Moran 81).

In sum, an examination of several Western countries' energy adjustment strategies reveals that OPEC's ability to set prices was undermined because its position as a supplier declined. Industrialized countries recognized the need to decrease their dependency on OPEC oil. World oil demand shrank as importing nations restructured their energy programs. Because of reduced demand, the cartel had to lower prices to maintain their established revenue levels.

OPEC's Position as a Supplier Undermined

In a way similar to that mentioned above, the Organization's ability to set world oil prices was also undermined by an increase in the number of non-OPEC suppliers. In the early and mid-70s, the cartel could maintain its price hikes because other oil producers could not take up the slack when the embargo was instigated. Since that time, however, oil prices have collapsed because non-OPEC members increased their oil production significantly, and OPEC could not agree to cut their output in corresponding amounts in order to keep prices high (Nulty 88).

Moreover, for OPEC to successfully maintain monopolistic market management, it would have to limit the number of major suppliers (Morse 196). Non-OPEC nations have slightly more than half of the world's known oil resources, as the following table shows:

Table 1.		Known Oil Resources
	Location	Known Oil Resources as of 1-1-79 in Billions bbl
OPEC:	Arabia and Iran	523.0
	Venezuela	54.8
	Libya	30.0
	Nigeria-Cameroon[a]	20.5
	Algeria-Tunisia[a]	11.3
	Indonesia	9.0
TOTAL OPEC RESOURCES		648.6
NON-OPEC:	Soviet Union	100.8
	United States	117.9
	Mexico	47.1
	Joint U.S.-Mexico field	18.4
	UK-Norway-Denmark	20.0
	Canada	16.3
	China	8.5
TOTAL NON-OPEC RESOURCES		329.0

Source: Adapted from Ivanhoe, L., "Potential of World's Significant Oil Provinces," p. 167.

[a]Cameroon and Tunisia are not OPEC members, but they share the Niger Delta and Triassic oil provinces with Nigeria and Algeria, respectively.

With these resources, noncartel countries have become significant oil exporters. For example, Britain and Norway, with the discovery of the Northern North Sea Province, entered the market as recently as 1983 (Morse 795). In addition, the Soviet Union has begun exporting to non-Communist nations. Mexico has the potential to produce at levels equal to Saudi Arabia (and may become a secure source for one of the world's largest oil importers, the United States) (El Mallakh 45). The ability of these "new" suppliers to export, taking up the slack which OPEC refuses to supply so it can maintain high cartel prices, has caused the price of oil, on the world market, to drop. Consequently, OPEC's Chairman, Arturo Hernandez Grisanti of Venezuela, was prompted to call "on non-OPEC member countries, including Britain, Norway, and the Soviet Union, to co-operate with the organization. He warned that oil prices would plummet further if these countries refused to assume responsibility for a stable market and persisted in increasing output and exports, while reducing their prices" (qtd. in Yen 13).

In summary, the cartel's ability to set prices is dependent on its ability to control its resource. But, OPEC has little influence over the exports of independent suppliers. Consequently, supply is exceeding demand, and prices are declining. Until OPEC regains control over the amount of oil that reaches the market, its ability to unilaterally set world prices will remain ineffective.

In addition to non-OPEC exporters, alternative energy forms, now being developed and used, are undermining the cartel's supply and price-setting functions.... Even though most of these alternatives are not yet utilized at their full potential, coal, natural gas, and nuclear power are already making significant contributions to the world's energy supply. As the following paragraphs show, they have allowed petroleum importing nations to decrease their energy dependence on OPEC's high-priced oil.

Because oil is an exhaustible resource, coal's importance as a fuel source has increased in domestic and manufacturing use, particularly in power generation and iron and steel production. And, according to Al Sowayegh, coal reserves total "more than ten times the level of proven oil reserves" causing "many energy experts (to) consider coal to be the nearest available resource for oil" (186). Much of the world's estimated total coal reserves of 8960 billion metric tons is located in the industrialized countries. For example, almost 18% of the estimated total is located in the two highly industrialized countries of West Germany and the United States,[b] as Table 2 shows.

Table 2.	Estimated Coal Reserves (billions of metric tons)		
Country	Proven Reserves	Estimated Reserves	Total
West Germany	62	—	62
United States	81	1425	1506
World total estimated coal reserves (including Communist nations)			8960

Source: Al Sowayegh 187

Another plausible substitute for oil is natural gas. Since the means of transporting it over long distances in pipelines and special tankers has made gas available to many areas, its use has increased to meet a significant part of the world's energy demands. In 1980, the four major producers of natural gas, the United States, the Soviet Union, the Netherlands, and Canada, were non-OPEC nations. They accounted for 75% of the total gas production during that year. The largest non-Communist producer was the United States. Accounting for 37% of the world's gas production, America fulfilled 27% of its total energy requirements for 1980 by using gas. This

[b]Again, while researching alternative energy sources, I found the information and statistics to be generally the same, irrespective of the source. Therefore, the material for this section is taken from Al Sowayegh's book, *Arab Petro-Politics*, because he presents it in a clear and simple manner.

percentage is equivalent to 492 million tons of oil and is expected to double by the end of the decade. Likewise, the Soviet Union, the largest Communist gas producer, accounted for 29% of the world's production in 1980 (Al Sowayegh 187–188).

Finally, in addition to coal and natural gas, nuclear energy use has also increased dramatically since the first oil embargo. In 1973, 107 nuclear reactors were producing slightly more than 40,000 megawatts of electricity. Seven years later, 253 nuclear reactors had an output slightly less than 136,000 megawatts of electricity (Al Sowayegh 189). The advantage of using nuclear energy is that it gives large energy outputs for relatively small energy inputs. It is not as readily exhaustible as other energy forms, like the fossil fuels (oil, coal, etc.). This factor may also account for the increasing number of nuclear power stations world-wide, as nations seek to make the transition from oil to other energy forms.

Thus, as oil importing countries decrease their dependence on OPEC oil by using alternative energy forms (like coal, natural gas, and nuclear energy), OPEC will be forced to seek additional buyers to retain its current level of earnings. Otherwise, the cartel would have to absorb the amount of slack equal to the amount of energy generated, in alternate forms, by non-OPEC members. If it absorbed more slack, the Organization would not meet its current revenue needs. OPEC members would want to raise prices. This would, however, stimulate increased production of substitute energy forms in other nations. Consequently, as OPEC's position as a supplier is undermined, its ability to monopolistically set prices decreases.

CONCLUSION

Since it first gained the power to monopolistically set world oil prices, in 1973, OPEC's ability to continue doing so has been undermined by several significant factors. Internal dissension is making it difficult for the cartel to collectively set output and pricing policies. Non-OPEC countries are subverting the Organization's price-setting ability, too. French, West German, and American energy adjustment strategies have allowed these importing nations to significantly decrease their dependence on high-priced OPEC oil. Finally, non-OPEC suppliers and alternative energy forms have forced the cartel to decrease prices in order to remain competitive in the world market. Thirteen years after the first precipitous price hikes were instigated, the cartel's ability to unilaterally establish and maintain global prices is much less effective.

WORKS CITED

Alexander, Sidney S. *Paying for Energy: Report of the Twentieth Century Fund Task Force on the International Oil Crisis.* New York: McGraw-Hill, 1975.

Al Sowayegh, Abdulaziz. *Arab Petro-Politics.* London: Croom Helm Ltd., 1984.

Cateora, Philip R. *International Marketing.* Homewood, IL: Richard D. Irwin, Inc., 1983.

Choucri, Nazli. *International Politics of Energy Interdependence.* Lexington, MA: Lexington Books, 1976.

El Mallakh, Ragaei, ed. *OPEC: Twenty Years and Beyond.* Boulder, CO: Westview Press, 1982.

Ikenberry, G. John. "The Irony of State Strength: Comparative Responses to the Oil Shocks in the 1970s." *International Organization* 40 (Winter 1986): 105–137.

Ivanhoe, L. F. "Potential of World's Significant Oil Provinces." *Oil and Gas Journal* 83 (18 November 1985): 164–168.

Moran, Theodore H. *Oil Prices and the Future of OPEC: The Political Economy of Tension and Stability in OPEC.* Washington: Resources for the Future, 1978.

Morse, Edward L. "After the Fall: The Politics of Oil." *Foreign Affairs* 64 (Spring 1986): 792–811.

Nulty, Peter. "How to Keep OPEC on Its Back." *Fortune* (26 May 1986): 87–88.

Vielvoye, Roger. "OPEC Inaction Undermines Oil Price." *Oil and Gas Journal* 84 (31 March 1986): 50–51.

Wyant, Frank R. *The United States, OPEC, and Multinational Oil.* Lexington, MA: Lexington Books, 1977.

Yen, Ren. "Trying Hard to Prevent a Price War." *Beijing Review* 29 (6 January 1986): 13.

Publishing Your Student Work

Later, in your professional life, publication may be tied to your success—even required to survive. However, you need not wait until you have graduated to submit articles, and any success you have in being published will be impressive when you begin job hunting.

Students normally are humble about their possibilities to be published. You will be surprised at the many opportunities available to you if you will investigate. Take advantage of them. As an undergraduate, everything you write and publish does not need to be in your major subject area. You certainly do not have to be published in a major journal. Ask one of the English teachers at your school what opportunities exist on campus for writing awards or publishing. My school, for example, has a campus-wide writing contest. To the English faculty's frustration, sometimes students in engineering, the sciences, business, and other areas walk away with all the prizes. Every winning essay, story, and poem is published in a booklet that certainly qualifies as a legitimate entry under "publications" on a résumé. You also can select topics for classwork that will make likely articles. Popular periodicals are good possible publishing sources. I do not suggest scholarly journals because it would be very unusual for an undergraduate's work to be accepted for publication in such journals; most undergraduates do not have the depth of understanding, the background, and a writing style necessary to qualify. However, the same is not true of publishing in a popular journal on a subject you know something about, on your major area of study or on a hobby. Visit the public library. It will have more popular periodicals than scholarly journals. Find the page where it tells about the editor and subscription rates, and see what it says about manuscripts. Periodicals that accept submissions will publish their publication requirements. The statement will tell where to send materials, how to send them, if they are returned, and usually how to prepare the manuscript (paper, margins, spacing, number of copies, and so on).

Decide what magazines you want to write for. Analyze the kinds of articles published. You may already know enough to write a general article, or you may decide to use a class assignment to gather information that would make an article. A few years ago one of my students had a project in her computer system design course. Her hobby was weaving. She wrote a software program that used the computer to design weaving patterns. She also wrote an article about the project, sent it to one of the popular sewing magazines, and succeeded in having it accepted and published. You can do the same.

Find out who is publishing among your teachers. Tell them you want to try to have some papers published as an undergraduate. Ask them if they will read and constructively criticize the work that you are considering sending and if they know of any opportunities for you. Ask the reference librarian to show you works like *Writer's Market* that set forth publishing opportunities. I think you will be surprised at your success. If you carefully analyze the source and send only material that is suitable to the source you are asking to consider your work, you should succeed. Most people, even as professionals in a technical field, do not publish because they never make the effort to ready an article for publication, remain too shy or insecure to believe that anything they write would ever be published, or incorrectly analyze the periodical they are submitting to, and therefore have no chance at the beginning for success. If you do your research, make yourself do the writing, have someone go over the writing before you send it, revise it to be as effective as possible, be diligent, and send material off more than once if rejected, you will succeed. Seeing your writing in print is personally gratifying. In today's "information age" publishing demonstrates your ability to communicate— an important trait in the technical and professional fields.

Practice Exercises

1. Your instructor will decide if a formal report is appropriate for the work you are doing. He or she may decide to assign a group project, in which case you will write only a section of the formal report but will be part of a working group. Together you will make editorial decisions about the whole report and act as critics for each other's writing. Group work is often found in industry, so such a situation is good practice. It often works well in the classroom because a report can be accomplished in a shorter time. If word processing is available, use it to its fullest capabilities to write and edit.
2. Your instructor will make available a group of formal reports or assign you the responsibility of finding a report to critique. Using this chapter, write or present orally a critique that says what is strong and weak about the report from the reader's point of view. Offer specific suggestions for improving the weaknesses.

3. Your teacher can make a class assignment, or you individually can decide that you want your writing published. Search for magazines that publish in an area of your interest or knowledge, or use resources in the library to identify publishing opportunities. Make a selection, then analyze its writing style and subject matter. Afterward, research and write a piece that you think is like what your chosen source will publish. Your teacher will act as editor. Together, make the writing as good as possible and write as much as possible in the style of the source you have selected. Prepare the piece for publication according to the specifications set by the publisher. Send it off. Good luck!

Chapter 11

Working Reports

All companies require reports. Everyone in technical professions writes them, but not everyone writes them well. Some reasons for this follow: "reports" written in college are not actually like those required in industry, so the college "practice" is not directly helpful; the kinds of reports written are numerous and varied, so preparing for every writing situation is difficult; different reports are not necessarily standardized within professions or even among companies, so writers have no reliable source of reference, and some people consider report writing second-class work, so they give it less attention and care than other work. This chapter cannot cover every type of report, but it does provide a useful approach and guidelines for several common reports and will teach you to write any report more effectively.

Guidelines for Writing Effective Reports

Have a Good Attitude

Many people consider the report something that has to be done in addition to real work, the more important activity. They write reports in haste, at the end of the day when they are tired, or as a group when the writing can no longer be put off.

Schedules and workloads are legitimate reasons for delaying paperwork, but putting reports aside because you dislike writing or consider reports unimportant is not acceptable.

Understand Why Reports Are Important

A report functions as a record of work performed by the company. People change jobs, leave, die, forget, or remember wrongly. To offset the unreliability of human recollection, written reports record the history of how, why, when, or by whom something was done. They capture problems and successes of work in progress. For example, if a question is raised by anyone for any reason sometime after footings were poured, or laboratory tests were performed, or a machine was tested, the answer is sought in the project's documentation. If it is complete, accurate, and clearly written, the answer is easily given. If the report system is haphazard, casual, incomplete, or so cryptic that it is unintelligible, no satisfactory answer is possible which can be serious, particularly in situations involving liability.

Identify Purpose and Audience before Writing

Nothing is as irritating or as useless as a report that does not provide the information requested and, as a result, cannot be used. For example, suppose the salespeople in an oil and gas company ask the geologist to prepare a report on a certain land block that has formations of an age conducive to generating either or both oil and gas. They specify that the potential buyers are more interested in finding gas than oil. The geologist does not listen, or does not pay attention, or does not care and writes a lackluster report highlighting the oil possibilities and mentions gas finds as a secondary interest. The report is not the one requested, but worse, it is not functional for the purpose needed. The writer in no way misrepresents information—lies—or omits damaging facts. He or she simply does not write a report that serves the purpose. To write useful reports, know the audience and why the report is requested.

Use or Develop a Standard Form

Many professions publish model report forms common to their disciplines. For example, the American Institute of Architects (AIA) makes such forms available to members. Architectural companies simply print the form on paper displaying their company's logo. Using the professionally approved form is easy, makes the company's methods part of the larger professional group, and makes information easier to understand when shared among architects of different companies because the method of presentation is consistent. One architectural firm adapted the following simple but useful form from those provided by the AIA for on-site visits:

```
┌─────────────────────────────────────────────────────────────────┐
│                                                                   │
│              COMPANY NAME, LOGO, AND ADDRESS                      │
│                   ON-SITE VISIT REPORT                           │
│                                                                   │
│   LOCATION:                                                       │
│   DATE:                                                           │
│   TIME:                                                           │
│   TEMPERATURE:                                                    │
│                                                                   │
│   COMMENTS:                                                       │
│                                                                   │
└─────────────────────────────────────────────────────────────────┘
```

Under "comments," the architect whom I interviewed sometimes uses headings such as "problems," "work on schedule," "work behind schedule," "material questions," or "specifications questions." Other times, she writes without divisions. She simply records observations as she walks around the site.

If you find yourself in a company with no standard formats for reports, develop your own. Whatever the situation, do not write information one way one week and another way the next. Not only do you appear inconsistent, but the information is difficult to collate.

If you find yourself designing a form, think how the report is used. For example, in one company where I consulted, managers told me that originally there was no form for reporting information given in the weekly progress and problem meeting. Managers from every department in this large plant reported at each meeting. The recorder noted what was reported, in the order it was reported, and distributed the report the next day as a running commentary on the meeting. The problem was that every supervisor had to read every part of the report to find if there was anything he or his people needed to do, plan for, or check. When something was found, the supervisor either highlighted or underlined it and afterward made his own list of relevant items to his particular department. The reporting was inefficient. The managers together met and produced a useful form that listed each department. As each supervisor made his report, the recorder assigned what was said to the proper department. The next day when the report was distributed, the maintenance supervisor, for example, could look under the heading "Maintenance" and find all that affected him and his people. He could schedule and begin tending to problems without having to sift through the whole report. Readers needing an overview could read the rest of the report.

Put Report Formats on the Computer

With word processing, you do not need to type report formats over and over. You simply can type the format once, bring up the format when needed, copy it to another file, and fill out the report. The original format is saved to use again in the same manner when you need to write another report using that same form.

Create an Effective Filing System

You need to keep and be able to retrieve copies of letters, memoranda, and reports you write and send. Situations arise where you need proof of original statements made about things agreed upon: orders, deliveries, work, deadlines, specifications, costs, and the like. When questions or disagreements arise, copies of the original paperwork can resolve many situations. Without them, people have to rely on memory or what they understood to have been said. Thus the possibilities for differences increase, and the possibilities of solutions decrease.

The copy is only worthwhile if it can be located. Having to ask someone to wait while you look for your copy or having to admit that you cannot find it is embarrassing. Decide early in your career to be organized and to discipline yourself to attend to housekeeping chores, such as returning phone calls, filing, writing letters, writing reports, or whatever. You will then be judged as someone who gets things done. Acting efficiently is a desirable trait in business and industry.

Types of Working Reports

Working reports are informal reports. They may be complete in a few sentences, a paragraph, or several pages. You will write and use such reports often because they communicate daily business among people and within and between companies. You must learn to prepare and write them quickly. Normally, they include little, if any, background information, have no front matter such as title page, table of contents, or abstract, and are written as memoranda or letters or by using a prepared form.

For every report you write, remember to identify the report completely. Have written on it somewhere the company's name, receiver, sender, subject, date, and a distribution notice if others are to receive the report. Use headings, drawings, charts, tables, or other visual aids to clarify the meaning. Write everything required for the reader to be able to understand but omit everything else. Write using correct English, punctuation, and spelling. The following section discusses informal reports common to business and industry:

Reports giving technical information
    Description
    Process and procedure
    Laboratory notebooks
Reports about work performed
    Progress
    On-site or field
    Trip
Reports about people and things
    Evaluation
    Recommendation

When you need to write a different type of informal report from those previously mentioned, use the guidelines given at the beginning of this chapter and whatever principles are useful from the following discussion on individual types. In every case, be organized and practical.

Informal Reports Giving Technical Information

Description Reports

A technical description tells about an object, substance, organism, mechanism, location, or system. The purpose of the description depends on the subject and audience. The purpose may be to describe the parts of a bird feeder to the general audience who will purchase the feeder, or it may be to describe how a storm becomes a hurricane to the general public who watch the evening television news, or to describe the same subject to a professional audience of meteorologists. The language and amount of technical detail used in the description differs depending on the purpose and audience, but all description needs to be organized carefully, written objectively, and tailored to the audience and their needs.

A description may be the subject of the report itself or part of a larger report. For example, a publicity piece about new car models describes certain technical differences, but it also includes writing that is not description. Likewise, an announcement of a change in procedure to workers who must enact the procedure may give the background and reasons for the change as well as a description of the new machine and the location where it will be placed within the plant. The description could also include how the change alters the whole production system. The following guidelines help you organize and write effective descriptions:

1. *Know the readers.* What do they need to understand from the description: How something works? What it does? What effect it has on something else? How to use it? Do the readers need background information in order to understand the description? Do they need the description to be an overview or to be detailed? Must they make decisons (whether to purchase, give approval) based on the description?

2. *Ask yourself questions that the reader will want answered*: What is being described? What is its purpose—its appearance? How does it work? What does it do? What is distinctive about the whole (size, shape, texture, weight, or density)? What is it made of? What is distinctive about the parts? How do the parts make the whole?

3. *Be objective.* Leave your feelings out of the description. See whatever is described without prejudice. Leave nothing out. Do not color the description to reflect your attitude. Instead, record faithfully and accurately what you see or understand.

4. *Describe in an orderly manner.* Begin with the top and move to the bottom. Describe from left to right or vice versa—from inside to outside or vice versa—from general to specific—from start to finish—from background necessary to understand to a detailed description.

5. *Use accurate language.* It may or may not be specialized. The audience will determine whether you describe using technical terms or more common words. Regardless, be precisely accurate. The color, texture, shape, condition, material, or production method should be correct and complete. If not, the reader may misinterpret or misunderstand. To say something is "big," or "slow," or "soft," or "in good condition" is not being precise.

6. *Use visuals to aid the description.* Often a picture will communicate better than language. The choice of visual depends on the subject described. It can include photographs, drawings, contour maps, diagrams, blueprints, or any other visual that will clarify. When preparing visuals, scale them to the space where they appear. Place them so the written description and the visual can be seen together. Decide if a visual of the whole should be shown first, followed by a cutaway or parts of the whole shown in detail. Put yourself in the reader's place and show whatever is needed to allow the reader to form a correct mental picture and understanding. Review Chapter 7 for advice about preparing illustrations.

A very common use of description is to describe a mechanism. As always, the purpose and audience help determine what to include and how to organize. The following sections often appear:

Introduction: accurately name the mechanism; identify the larger class into which the mechanism belongs; describe the function of the mechanism, and explain how the mechanism accomplishes its purpose.

Body: partition the mechanism and discuss the parts in relation to the whole. Discuss each part in the same order and cover the same topics. Some common topics include

    physical description of each part
    functional description of each part
    relationship of parts to the whole
    out-of-the-ordinary features
    an analysis of strength and weakness

Conclusion: briefly summarize the mechanism's function, primary parts, and major features.

Process and Procedure Reports

Process and procedure reports are often confused. A process tells how something works; a procedure tells how to do something. The first is an explanation. The second is a set of instructions. Both explain actions in sequence and in chronological order.

Before writing, know your audience and purpose. Both reports must give enough details either to understand the process or to do the procedure. Before writing either report, know the subject inside-out; know everything that makes it work, every step anyone needs to do, everything that can go wrong. Decide where or if you need visuals and what kinds of visuals are best. Outline the process or procedure in order to check for completeness and accuracy. Follow these writing suggestions:

PROCESS

- Write an accurate, limited, and inclusive title.
- Identify the audience and the purpose for writing.
- Plan to use visuals wherever they will assist the explanation.
- Follow an outline like the following:

  Introduction
  - —Introduce the process and identify the purpose of your explanation.
  - —Identify the intended audience. Tell any special qualifications the audience needs to understand the process.
  - —Give a brief description of the process and any background information.
  - —State the principle(s) necessary to understand the process.
  - —Give any special conditions needed for the process to occur.
  - —Define technical terms; if necessary, explain technical information in plain English.
  - —List, in the order you plan to present them, the major steps of the process.

  Middle
  - —Explain each step in sequence.
  - —Structure each step alike. If in step 1, you define, state the purpose, explain individual parts, and so on, you must order the information in step 2 the same way.
  - —Include substeps if applicable. They should also be presented in sequence and written alike.

  Conclusion
  - —Summarize the major steps and discuss a cause-and-effect relation between the steps and the process, or place the process in some larger system or action and say how it relates.

PROCEDURE

- Write an accurate, limited, and inclusive title.
- Begin by telling why the procedure is done.
- Define special terms. Tell all the materials, tools, or other equipment needed.
- Say how long the procedure itself takes. Note any unusual timing of individual steps. For example, if someone needs to wait 2 hours between steps 3 and 4, say so before having the person start the procedure.
- Divide the procedure into steps. Number the steps. Present them chronologically and in words the reader can understand.
- Explain in detail how to do each step. Do not assume the reader will know how to do something a certain way.
- Write accurately and precisely. For example, do not write "fold" the oil into the flour when you mean "beat" the oil and flour together.
- Provide pictures whenever they make instructions easier to understand.
- Include warnings, cautions, and notes when needed. Place them so they are seen before any accident, harm, or damage occurs.
- Write in active voice: "turn," "rotate."

- Use parallel lists for writing instructions. If you begin a list with an active verb, begin all lists the same way.
- Use white space to divide steps. Make the page easy to read and make it easy to find your place again after doing a step in the procedure.

Example of Difference between Process and Procedure: Blood Pressure Measurement

Process: *How the measure occurs.* The writer might begin by explaining how the process measures the blood vascular system. As part of the explanation, the writer may explain that the cuff causes pressed air to compress the artery. When air is released, the person taking the measure can listen through a stethoscope to the sound in the artery. The sound determines a measure of hemodynamics, is displayed on the dial attached to the cuff, and lets one measure the blood pressure.

Procedure: *How to take a blood pressure measure.* The writer may begin by identifying the equipment and preparation needed to take a blood pressure. The instructions will include how to apply the cuff: apply it to bare flesh over a brachial artery; position the arm (if that is the area having the cuff) at heart level—not above or below, and so on.

     The process tells about the process; the procedure tells how to do an action related to the process.

Procedure Example: Student Work

The information on pages 277–278 was handed to students as background material for writing a set of instructions telling someone how to build a small aquarium. After reading the information, students were to prepare questions about what else they needed to know before writing. To find out about materials and hobby building kits, they sought answers through reading, telephone interviewing, and visiting hobby and hardware stores. A sample of a student's questions along with excerpts from his set of instructions is shown on pages 279–281.

Making a Tank*

Should the beginner wish to make his own tank, the first choice of metal for the framework is angle-iron. If this is not available, then a strong wooden frame may be constructed, especially if he has some knowledge of the wood joints used in carpentry. Hard woods, such as oak, should be used.

One of the best glazing cement formulae (if making up, and not buying a ready made mixture) is, two parts whiting putty, one red lead and one white lead, all mixed together with gold size so that a workable mixture without lumps will adhere to the glass and frame. (The cement should only be used when freshly made up.)

The iron frame should first be freed from rust and then painted with at least two coats of aluminum paint, then one undercoat of flat white paint and finally two good coats of enamel paint of the preferred colour. [Colour, like honour, tyre, fibre, etc., is British spelling.]

While the framework is drying, consider the kind of glass necessary to glaze the tank. It stands to reason that if the tank is a small one, thin glass may be used, but for the large one, a much thicker and stronger kind is necessary. The deeper and wider the tank, the greater the strain. For example, a tank 24″ long by 12″ wide by 12″ deep, requires two sheets for front and back of heavy drawn clear sheet glass, and the ends of 32 oz. sheet. The ideal choice for the base, which takes all the weight, is slate, but as this is, unfortunately, practically unobtainable, a good substitute is ¼″ wired plate glass.

A much larger tank, say 72″ × 36″ × 36″, would require ½″ toughened plate glass, which is very strong. A tank in between these two proportions mentioned would require plate glass. Toughened plate is five times more resistant than plate. The bases should always be much stronger because of the weight of the whole tank of water plus that of rockwork, compost, etc. Aquarium base glass should be of wire polished or figured plate from ¼″ to ¾″ according to size.

(continued)

*Derrick Latimer-Sayer, *Teach Yourself Indoor Aquaria*, (London: The English Universities Press Ltd., Published by Hodder & Stoughton, 1965), pp. 15–16.

When working out the exact sizes of glass to be used to fit a frame it is a good idea to cut out sheets of cardboard to the exact size and give them with the glass to the cutter.

Let us imagine that we are going to glaze a 24″ × 12″ × 12″ frame. The base will be the first to be positioned and should measure 23½″ × 11½″. The front and back will consist of two pieces of heavy drawn glass 23½″ × 11½″, and the ends of two pieces of 32 oz. sheet glass 11″ × 11¼″. It will be seen that the measurements allow for a cushioning layer of cement about ¼″ in thickness all round.

The lengths of the base glass and the back and front must be the same, but the latter must allow for the thickness of the base, and also for the layers of cement top and bottom. They should be about ⅝″ shorter than the internal height of the frame. The end panel measurements should be about 1″ shorter than the internal width and the same height as the back and front. One or two pieces may be cut for partitions across the inside of the finished tank for later on they will be found very useful during breeding activity, and perhaps for isolation purposes for some fishes.

Glazing a 24″ × 12″ × 12″ Tank

Use a putty knife to spread the soft cement mixture evenly into the frame angles about ¼″ in thickness. (The amount of cement required in this case will be about 2¼ lb.) Pockets of air should be pressed out. The base should be pressed gently but firmly into positon; then the back and front, and finally the two ends. All excess cement must be removed by trimming off with the knife. There should be perfect contact between glass and cement. The glass should be clean during this work. Place weights on the base plate and use wooden struts to hold the other glass in position. The tank should now be left for three days, except perhaps for another finishing coat of glossy paint on all frame sides.

In due time the supports should be removed and the tank filled with water and allowed to soak for at least twenty-four hours. Then thoroughly clean all glass surfaces and the tank is ready.

Problems	Solutions
How to cut angle iron?	If you do not have your angle-iron cut at a metal shop, you can use a hacksaw to cut the angle-iron. It is very important that you are careful to make your cuts straight.
How to cut glass?	If you do not have your glass cut at a hardware store, you can use a commercial glass cutter. To use a glass cutter you need a straight edge to make a straight cut. After you run the glass cutter across the glass at the required length you pick up the glass and tap it gently along the cut to receive a straight cut.
How thick should the glass be?	For a 24" x 12" x 12" aquarium, the sides should be made out of heavy clear sheet glass. The base should be made of slate or 1/4" wired plate glass.
How is the aquarium held together?	The glass and the angle-iron are held together with a glazing cement that can be purchased from a hobby shop. The glass should be very clean before applying the cement. The cement should be about 1/4" in thickness. Weights should be used to apply pressure while the cement is drying.

AQUARIUM CONSTRUCTION

The instructions provided list a step-by-step process which can be easily followed by any active hobbyist. The completed aquarium will measure 24″ × 12″ × 12″ and hold a little less than 15 gallons.

Tools and Materials Needed:

PROPANE TORCH
SOLDER
METAL SAW
TAPE MEASURE
SMALL WHEEL GLASS CUTTER
C-CLAMP
WAX PENCIL
STRAIGHT EDGE (YARDSTICK)
PROTECTIVE EYEWARE
2-74″ LONG SECTIONS OF ⅝″ BRASS ANGLE
1-50″ LONG SECTION OF ⅝″ BRASS ANGLE
36″ × 35½″ PLATE OF DOUBLE THICK WINDOW GLASS
2½ LBS OF SILICON IN A SQUEEZE TUBE
METAL PRIMER
ENAMEL PAINT OF DESIRED COLOR

1. Cutting the Glass

WARNING: Glass cutting is a simple technique when done according to proper procedure. However, regardless of your expertise, protective eyeware such as goggles should be worn to minimize injury should splintering occur.

A. For a $24'' \times 12'' \times 12''$ aquarium, you should start by laying the large sheet of double thick glass on flat, solid table-top. Using the wax pencil, mark the cut lines according to Figure 1.

B. Now the glass needs to be "scored." For this the glass cutter and straight edge will be needed.

Important: Complete steps 1B and 1C for each cut *in order* (cut 1, cut 2, ...) as shown in Figure 1.

To start, align straight edge with wax mark at cut 1. With light but firm pressure, start at one end and "etch" the glass in a continuous, non-stop motion the entire length of the line. It is imperative that you *not* double back and re-etch. If your effort did not leave a sufficient score, turn the glass over and etch at the same mark.

C. To break the glass, hang the smaller half over the table by aligning the score mark with the table's edge. For cuts 1, 2, & 3 you will need an assistant to help you break the glass after scoring. Now lay the straight edge on the glass at the table's edge—essentially sandwiching the glass at the score mark, see Figure. 2. Have your assistant apply steady, even pressure on the straight edge while you, holding the overhand, apply downward pressure twisting toward the table. At this point, the glass should snap, and the result be a nice clean cut.

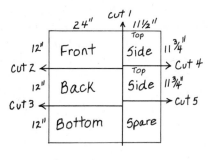

Figure 1

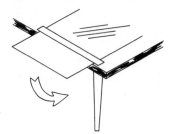

Figure 2

Laboratory Notebooks

Information gathered from experiments and first-hand observations is recorded in laboratory notebooks. It is sometimes hard to realize that personal notes themselves will ever be of value. Although notes are often the source of other writing and not writing that stands alone, the laboratory report or notebook is the primary record in patent law, the complete record of ongoing work, the source of procedures not explained in other publishing about an experiment or project, and a primary source of work subjected to litigation.

What to write is always a challenge. Basically record all information that will explain final data. Errors or trials that lead to final information need also to be included. Any reference to equipment, time, place, weather, resources, or any other contributing condition should be complete so that future readers can understand without the author being present to explain. Write thoughts completely and in words that others will understand or that you will understand months or years later when the laboratory experience is not fresh in your mind.

One key to clarity is organization. If you do not use a printed form, develop a format so you can record information the same way each time. Besides helping you to gather the same information each observation, the method makes collating the information easier.

For notes leading to patents or to prove experiments were made, or to detail any other demanding experimental work, follow these rules:

1. All entries should be made in indelible ink on pages that cannot be removed.
2. Pages should be numbered in advance, entries should be consecutive, and each page should be filled before going on to the next. If for some reason space on a page is skipped, one should draw lines through any part of the page left blank.
3. Each entry should be dated, signed, or initialed by the person entering the data. Some companies require that entries be signed or initialed by a qualified witness who is not part of the work, but someone who understands its premise.
4. Any changes should include an explanation for the change, be dated, and be initialed by the person making the change. Correction fluid or pasteovers should not be used.

Informal Reports about Work Performed

Progress Reports

A progress report tracks activities, problems, and progress made on a certain job. In large jobs where things happen quickly, the progress report is the means for identifying problems and avoiding continuing them without solutions. Such reports are required daily or at some other regular interval. The larger and more complicated the project is, the more often progress is monitored. Such tracking is especially needed when different crews are working simultaneously or in locations apart from one another. When writing progress reports, remember the following:

1. Use a consistent form for a series of reports on a specific job. Include project

identification, location, date, work completed to date, work in progress, work to be completed, problems, solutions, name of person writing the report. Example:

```
                    Progress Report
Project:                              No.
Location:
Report Date:
Report Writer:
Work Completed:
Work to Be Completed:
Problems/Solutions:
```

2. Send copies to all involved parties. For example, a progress report on a commercial building under construction would be sent to the contractor, others directly involved in the construction, and also to the architect, the owner, the owner's lawyer, and the bank financing the project.

On-Site or Field Reports

The on-site or field visit ensures progress is occurring and that the contractor is following specifications. One normally thinks of inspecting things under construction, but the inspection could just as well be for manufacturing, testing, the building of a data processing system, or any other situation requiring work performed according to specifications.

Know what to look for when making the inspection. One person interviewed suggests making the inspection alone if possible. If the job superintendent accompanies you, he or she may distract your attention, either innocently or intentionally, away from something you should see. This interviewee also suggests asking for submittals if you have any questions about materials or specifications. In other words, rely on the original written agreement, rather than on what the superintendent orally tells you is acceptable. She also recommends sketching illustrations of problems or questions. Often the picture communicates faster and better than the word. Her notebook for on-site visits is filled with freehand drawings. The notebook remains intact for future reference, but the secretary often makes a copy of a sketch to include in the typed on-site report distributed to interested parties.

Trip Reports

A trip report is primarily a record of expenses incurred in traveling on company business. It either justifies monies charged to the company or details monies to be reimbursed. Most companies have forms for this report, and they are simple to complete. The main responsibility for the person who will be writing a trip report is to maintain an accurate record during travel. Business supply stores sell many forms or books for this purpose. You can simply record expenses on a sheet of paper as they occur. Always obtain receipts whenever possible.

Some companies also ask for the purpose of the trip and, if applicable, the most valuable information gathered or accomplishment made on the trip. Remember that a report is often read by people other than the person to whom it is sent. As in many other writing situations, you need to write accurately and correctly because people of influence may read something of yours and as a result form an opinion of you.

Informal Reports about People and Things

Evaluation Reports

Early in your career, you will write self-evaluations, but as you advance, you will be responsible for quarterly, semiannual, or annual evaluations of those who work for you. Some companies provide forms that ask you only to check ratings and write a summary comment. Other companies ask you to construct the form as well as write the report. The primary goal is to be specific. New employees are often bashful about "tooting their own horn," but if they do not, possibly no one will hear about them. The balancing act is to write confidently but without sounding pompous about what you have accomplished or are doing. Whether you are writing about yourself or someone else, be concrete. Everyone is "sincere," and "hardworking." Find the individual trait that you or others possess. Mention and document it. One or two concrete examples to illustrate a characteristic are more impressive than a general overview that says nothing specific. If you or the other person finishes work on time, document it. If you or the other person is a good team worker, tell how.

Recommendation Reports

Recommendations can be about a person, product, process, company, or almost anything. They appear as part of numerous reports, but they can also be the subject of the report itself. A good approach to writing recommendations is to study the subject, decide the proper course of action, and make a straightforward recommendation. Some points to consider are the following:

1. Analyze the audience and do not risk offense. You may know that the primary reader is absolutely in favor of the subject, yet your study tells you not to recommend or to recommend with reservations. Write your findings truthfully but with caution. Do not offend by saying the idea is foolhardy or ill-advised or anything else that may insult the person who supports the idea. Your reputation will be built on your ability to analyze problems correctly, to communicate, and to get things done, but it will also depend on your skill in not offending or embarrassing others. The smart aleck does not go over well in industry. Learn to be diplomatic.

2. Present all the facts and be sure that your opinion is sound when you make the recommendation. You do yourself no favor by presenting an opinion and having someone later find information you omitted, ignored, or did not locate. Be careful in your research. Walk a tightrope; research the topic well, but do not be the one who never stops the study and produces the results. Learn to

know when you have enough information to be well informed, then move forward to get things done.

3. Prepare a well-organized report—one that is easy to read and understand. One standard pattern of organization is the following:

Introduction
    Problem statement
    Recommendation statement
    Statement of the report's organization and scope
Explanation of source and reliability of data in the report
Explanation of the recommendation
Discussion of the advantages of the recommendation
Discussion of the disadvantages of the recommendation
Summary of conclusions
Restatement of the recommendation

You may not need all sections. You may want to reorganize the information. Do whatever will produce the most effective report but organize and format so the report looks good and is easy to use.

Practice Exercises

1. Collect a group of report forms from local businesses and discuss with others in the class how you would use the forms and what their good and poor points are.
2. Select a subject that can be discussed both as a process and a procedure. Write both kinds of reports.
3. Select a project you are doing this quarter or semester. Write a series of progress reports on work in progress.
4. Write a self-evaluation of your strength and weakness as a technical communicator or as a future professional in your discipline.
5. Keep a laboratory notebook on a laboratory project or a design project or a modeling project or anything appropriate.
6. Write a technical description. Include visuals suitable to the audience and purpose.

Chapter 12

User Documentation

Wherever we go—banks, shops, schools, libraries, travel agencies, government offices, hospitals, and factories—we find business and industry converting to computer systems and workers using a keyboard and TV-like screen.

In the short memory of those involved, this way of working seems ordinary. Older people marvel at it; middle-aged people strive to understand it; young people cannot imagine working any other way. But work was done differently before, of course. It was done manually for years and centuries before the computer. We need to realize that of all the changes a computer system brings, none is more important than the change in the nature of work.

The worker becomes a computer "user" who relies on user documentation first to understand what a computer system is and what it means to the worker's responsibilities, then to learn how to do the job, and later to review forgotten procedures, learn new ones, or correct errors.

Since users are directly related to the productivity of a computer system and thus to their own productivity, it seems logical that anyone developing or writing user documentation would do so in a way that best serves users. Such logic does not always prevail. Too often the documentation is confusing, poorly written, overly long, or inadequate, and users are offered little training or support. Those who have time to adapt or who naturally relate to the computer become satisfied and proficient users. Others despise the computer but manage to work at minimum efficiency. Still others never master the machine or the documentation and quit.

In your careers, many of you will either use, help specify, or write user documentation. You, therefore, should recognize documentation that is well written, be able to say what is needed in documentation being developed, and, if applicable, write accurate and understandable documentation. To that end, this chapter identifies different types of user documentation, lists contents, and offers writing tips.

Types and Standards of User Documentation

User documentation primarily divides into two groups: introductory documentation and software documentation.

Introductory Documentation

Introductory documentation publicizes the software and is written mostly by professional writers within a software company or in an advertising company hired to promote the software product. Most of you will not write such documentation; however, many of you will make decisions about buying computer software. Therefore, the following discussion talks more about evaluating introductory documentation than about writing it.

The audience of introductory documentation includes:

buyers of software
managers of departments affected by the computer system
in-house or consulting data processors who will install or service the computer
    system
accountants responsible for the financial well-being of the business using the system

Such documentation has certain general characteristics:

Purpose: Provoke interest in or sell the software
Audience: Anyone thinking of buying software or comparing different software
          programs
Writer: Software developer or professional writer
Style: Eye and mind-catching; clear and easy-to-read; nontechnical language
Format: Easy-to-read; enticing

Introductory documentation appears in many forms: advertisements, brochures, letters to prospects. But whatever the form, its purpose is to attract the user to this software and away from the hundreds of other similar products competing for the user's attention. In today's world of mass advertising, trash mail, and telecommunication marketing, catching anyone's attention is an enormous job. For this reason, the eye or mind-catching concept is sometimes as important as the content. A Charlie Chaplin character or a variety of apple has nothing to do with computers, but talented writers have used them to create wonderful ads for IBM and APPLE.

Besides catching the user's attention, introductory documentation should say what the software is, does, and requires, so that users can decide if it is relevant and can prepare questions to ask the software's representative. The documentation is prepared often as a series of writings. Different pieces give different levels of detail. Some intend only to capture the user's attention. Others are for users who are already interested and want details. They are now comparing software products or deciding whether to buy. The following is a checklist of what should be included in introductory documentation or considered by the user before making a software purchase. Not all information will appear on a single publicity piece, but all should be available somewhere in the complete sequence of publicity information. If you do not understand certain terms, ask someone about them or consult the word list on pages 19–22. Do not, however, seriously consider software without knowing about the topics listed.

Introductory Documentation Checklist

1. Name the software.
2. State the purpose of the software.
3. Describe what the software can do and what options are available.
4. Identify necessary hardware and other necessary prerequisites.
5. List available manuals.
6. Indicate if any training course is available and, if so, the cost.
7. State the cost of the software.
8. Specify the computing mode. If terminals and communication equipment are needed, say what is needed. Some systems will require telecommunication software as well as equipment.
9. Explain storage requirements.
10. Identify the required master files: main title, subtitles, number, size, and media.
11. Identify the required working files: number, size, and media.
12. Identify the operating system under which the software is designed to run.
13. Indicate what language(s), compiler(s), and other items are needed to run the software.
14. Indicate how one recovers from failure.
15. Explain the processing controls.
16. Give the timing of a sample run on a specific configuration.
17. Explain about data security and protection.
18. Date the information.
19. Give an address or phone number or the proper way for users to inquire further about the software.

Software Documentation

Software documentation introduces users to computer programs, answers questions users have later while using the software, and remains a major reference throughout the time users work with the software.

The most common user is someone who uses the software to work. The documentation should serve this user well, for real losses are at stake. If the user cannot use the documentation satisfactorily, the result can be a reduction in the user's productivity, a poor job performance, a loss of self-esteem, and even loss of employment. Given the seriousness of these results, no other factor of a computer system is more important to the user than good software documentation. A few of you may write software documentation, but all will be "users." The following discussion defines content and gives suggestions for style. From this, you should know how to write effective documentation or what to expect in the documentation you purchase or use.

The audience of software documentation includes:

users
education directors, training directors, and seminar leaders who train users
supervisors of those who work using the software

Software documentation has certain general characteristics:

Purpose: Instruct users to work successfully and independently with the software
Audience: Users, trainers, supervisors
Writer: Software developer or professional writer
Style: Simple, clear, accurate, complete; communicates with visuals
Format: Easily updated; easy-to-read

Software documentation includes training materials, quick reference information, and instructions for enacting the software. We will quickly discuss the first two, then concentrate on the major writing type, the user manual. Training materials are supplied by both software producers and trainers who write the materials themselves. The materials should be tailored to the individuals being trained. Although good training depends largely on the person doing the training and on some methods not directly related to writing, the written materials used in training should have all the good features of a manual (see pp. 290–293) to be effective.

Quick reference documentation is the user's review notes. People use it when they know what to do but cannot remember a sequence of action, what key to strike, or some other factor that blocks them from performing the software function. The reference gives the key to remembering. The following are some tips for creating quick reference documentation or for evaluating the reference included in the software you are considering purchasing or are using:

1. Create a medium that will last. Use heavy cardboard, a plastic overcoat, or something that will withstand lots of handling. If the documentation is something the user peels off and sticks somewhere, check the quality of adhesive. Make sure it will hold for a long time and that it does not make the front side of the documentation also sticky.
2. Design the documentation so it is easy to handle or display. Include a way to hang it, stand it up, or attach it to a surface.
3. Select a type size suitable to the design. If the documentation is to stand near the keyboard or hang on a wall, estimate its distance from the user and print it in a type size readable from that distance.

4. Pare away all but the essential information. Offer no explanations, only a key to remembering what the user understands but has forgotten.
5. Imitate how users organize. Their notes put commands together that have to do with one task. They place commands together that they perform frequently. Writers should do the same. Break the quick reference into tasks and title the tasks by what users call them, followed by the software command title.

Software documentation for program instruction appears in either computer-readable or paper form. Computer-readable means that the documentation appears on the terminal screen or on keys the user strikes to execute certain software functions. Only professionals can write or code this form of software documentation. Since this book is about writing, it will focus on paper documentation, the mainstay of which is the user manual.

Tips for Writing Software Documentation—Mainly User Manuals

1. *Prewriting*
   a. Conduct audience analysis. Before you begin writing, observe users doing their work. Talk with them. Gather a feel for their language and attitude. Record conversations when possible. Note the words they use to describe what they do. Plan to use those words in writing documentation about the same work. Writing manuals is the perfect place to use readability indexes (see pp. 85–86).
   b. Write a small sample. Let users try it. Sit with them and notice where they stop, puzzle, ask questions. If someone asks, "Do I type Return now?," you know the documentation needs to be clearer. If someone does not know the meaning of "abort," you should ask the programmer, if possible, to modify the language in the program; you should certainly change it in the manual.
   c. Schedule time and resources for writing. Do not schedule a year for developing and programming a program and three or four weeks for writing documentation. Do not assign the writing task to whoever happens to be available or automatically to the person who writes well. That person may not have been in contact with the program or the users. Unless the "good writer" has time to educate himself or herself, the writing should be done by someone familiar with the software.
2. *Organization*
   a. Organize by user behavior rather than by the behavior of the machine. Break documentation into task categories or prepare little books of documentation on individual tasks. The shipping clerk, for example, may not need the documentation related to taking inventory.
   b. Eliminate the "big" manual. Many users barely read the newspaper; it is foolish to hand users a 200-page manual with every page filled with words. Thick and wordy manuals suggest the software is difficult and complex. The users are overwhelmed before beginning.

3. *Style*
 a. Write accurately and clearly.
 b. Use a consistent, nontechnical vocabulary. Using the same word over and over for the same meaning is a virtue. Mixing terms or using several words to mean the same thing confuses the user.
 c. Write instructions in a logical or chronological order. Give instructions as commands: "Do," "Load," "Insert." Make instructions easy to read. Use lists, numbers, headings, different typeface, underlining, color—anything to make clear the different steps of the instructions. Such a presentation lets the user do a step, then look back at the manual and quickly find the next step.
 d. Avoid passive voice. It can omit who does the action.

 Example:

Passive voice: "After scrolling to the beginning of the text, the file was saved."
The user does not know who "scrolled" or who "saved" the file.

Active voice: "After the operator scrolled to the beginning of the text, she saved the file."
Clearly, the operator "scrolled" and "saved" the file.

 e. Replace words with pictures or other visuals when possible and effective. Place the visual on the same or facing page with the information it illustrates. Having to flip back and forth from the visual to the text annoys users. Besides, users normally do not look ahead, so they may not know a picture is provided.

4. *Contents*
 a. Front matter
  • Prepare a title page.
  • Name the software.
  • Include the version number of the manual.
 b. Overview
  • Identify the user. Say what background or requirements the user must have to use the software.
  • State the purpose of the documentation. Tell how it achieves the purpose.
  • Give any tips for effectively using the manual or software.
 c. Table of contents
  • Title chapters and sections within chapters to say what is included. A clever title is fun but rarely useful in reference.
  • Make the contents a good reference by including topics within chapters.
 d. Software functions: For each function, specify the following:
  • Input
   Input needed
   Format
   Medium
   Samples of input

- Processing
  - Effect of input
  - Error detection: How can errors be corrected
  - Date security and protection
- Output
  - Format
  - Medium
  - Accuracy
  - Options
  - Interpretation and use of output
  - Samples of correct output

e. System specifications
- Identify the functions the software can perform.
- Give the method of performing the functions.
- Describe the system, including component programs and modules.
- Give hardware requirements.
- Give software requirements.
- Explain method of access.
- Tell about data security.

f. Management information
- Tell whom to contact for additional help or further information.
- Tell how and when the manual is updated.
- Tell how and to whom to report errors discovered in the manual.
- Tell what user training is available.
- Tell what other documentation is available.
- Give the date of publication.

g. Glossary
- Define technical terms in words a new user will understand.
- Alphabetize the entries.
- Format so the term being defined stands out.
- Print the term in an easy-to-find way (different color, typeface, boldface).

h. Index
- Name items in the index by user's task.
- Cross-reference software procedures with user's task.
- Compile the index by using index cards. Enter one item per card. Afterward, alphabetize the cards, then take all cards with alike items, and compile them into one index entry (see the discussion on indexing, pp. 232–233).
- Review cards for accurate page numbers.

5. *Test*

a. Have actual users test the manual. Note where they cannot read the manual and perform the software function on the first try.
b. When testing, do not stand by to prompt. Observe from a distance or leave users to themselves. Ask them to make notes about problems.

6. *Production*

    a. Number to show if the manual is the first issue or a later one. Within the manual, number each page to show its sequence in the manual and to show the issue number (p. 8, 4).

    b. Design in loose-leaf or some other form that makes amending and updating easy.

    c. Use tab cards or some other effective way to separate sections.

    d. Make pasteups before printing so you can judge how the information will look on the page. Proofread carefully.

    e. Insist on the best printing available. Poor quality printing makes the manual hard to use and says that you did not care enough to insist on first quality work.

A Professional's View of User Documentation

Research for this book brought me in contact with an analyst supervisor of the Data Processing Department of a large manufacturing company of home appliances. When I asked her view of user documentation, she answered, "User documentation in the data processing community has been and is atrocious." When I asked her why, she replied without hesitation, "Analysts despise doing it. They feel like they're not accomplishing anything (programming is their challenge), and it's a pain to do. But in my area, none of this matters. My analysts, who also do the writing, know that I expect good documentation. Without it, a system is in trouble from day one." Later in the interview, she gave a number of things she does to cause better documentation. I share her comments with you as a checklist for improving user documentation.

1. Involve the supervisor.

> I review every program documentation written by my people. If it is on-line, I sit down at the terminal, put myself in the user's place, and run the program with the author of the program or the documentation sitting next to me. Every time I have a question or encounter a problem, the author makes a note and afterward revises the documentation to eliminate these trouble spots. Afterward I look at the revisions. The big problem is that writers often do not know what users will understand and what they will not, and they don't make the effort to find out. The more I role-play as a user, the more I make my writers aware of how they have misjudged what the user will understand.

2. Define the problem before programming.

> I insist that my analysts define the problem and solution in English before they begin designing programs. Many times a user thinks a program problem is a system problem, when really the fault lies in the user documentation. If analysts are forced to explain problems in language that users can review and understand, they

clarify issues for themselves, avoid some problems, and have a good start on a writing style to use in user documentation.

3. Have users share the responsibility.

We, at this company, make users assume an interest and responsibility in systems and documentation we develop for their departments. After an analyst interviews users to determine need and writes the system specifications, that document goes back to the users who read and sign it, signifying that the specifications describe a system that will do what the users need. I will not let my people begin programming until we have that signed document back in the shop. Before we asked users to sign, we would show them the document, and they would, without question, agree that it was all right. Or they would not read it and then complain after the system and documentation were in place. Once they had to sign their names, they found plenty of time to read and think seriously about the specifications.

4. Learn from users.

We work hard at learning from users. It used to be that analysts would write the programs and the documentation, go to the users' area for implementation, leave the manuals with the users, and never see the manuals again. We have started a program of collecting user manuals whenever we are planning a documentation update. We look at what users have written in the margins, what notes or examples they have added, what they have crossed out, and we incorporate their improvements into the update. More important, we work at determining why their comments were necessary, and we try to avoid making the same mistakes in future documentation. Needless to say, this kind of project cannot be done without management's blessing. Those in charge must be willing to allot the time and to show support for the work.

5. Be consistent.

We are striving for consistency. In our company "plant" means one thing, "division" another. Some writers in their documentation used to write "plant" and use the "division" code. Is it any wonder that users make mistakes? In my shop, we have the same word mean the same thing for every transaction.

6. Treat documentation and programming alike.

If analysts would treat user documentation just as they treat programming, the documentation would improve. Someone trained in computer science learns to tell the computer everything. Curiously enough, no one resents doing so. Yet the same data processor does not want to tell the user everything. Supervisors should capitalize on this work habit used in programming and help analysts transfer it to writing user documentation.

7. Cut down on abbreviations.

Writers use too many abbreviations in user documentation. The user either does not know what they stand for, or the abbreviations make the documentation awkward to use, since the user must consult a glossary for every unknown term.

8. Make documentation easy to read.

Often the analyst creates documentation that is oversized when programming. When it comes time to include that documentation in a manual, the analyst should redraw it to scale for the size of the page. Too often the analyst simply reduces it on the copier so that it will fit on the page. The result is unreadable documentation because the printing and other information are too small to read.

9. Design documentation to help the user.

We had an example where every hour a person on the plant floor needed to enter a defect count: a record of the number of parts that were discovered defective within that hour. Our first on-line design was not user friendly. We had one screen for the parts codes and one, multiple-line screen for entering multiple entries of defective parts.

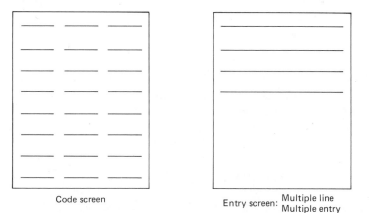

Code screen   Entry screen: Multiple line
                                          Multiple entry

The problem with this design is that users could not remember the codes, so they constantly had to go back and forth from the code screen to the entry screen. Some users solved the problem by making lists of the codes and pasting the lists on the terminal. When it came time to update, we redesigned these screens so the user could enter on the same screen where the code appeared. On a twenty-four line screen, we listed code on 22 lines and left 2 lines for entry. The user can scan the screens until one comes up with the correct part and code listed. When this happens, the user makes an entry at the bottom of that screen.

Code

Entry lines

This solution worked in this case because the code and quantity fit the line length, and the entry is small enough to fit into the display. A solution is not always this easy to come by, but writers can do much to help users if they will think from the user's point of view.

10. Take all documentation through one focal point.

The only way I know to gain consistency and maintain standards is to have all documentation reviewed by one person. In our department, I am that person. I purposely assumed this responsibility because I wanted my people to know that I will be reading what is produced. I wanted them to see that I am willing to give time to improving documentation. If I am willing to make the effort, they had better be.

Practice Exercises

1. Collect several manuals. Evaluate their strength and weakness. Plan revisions to correct weakness. Share your plans in writing with the teacher or verbally with the class. Give your reasons for making the changes.
2. Find a manual that presents a procedure in language that could just as well or better be presented in pictures. Redesign the section using visuals to present the same information. Write or tell why you think the revision is better.
3. Gather a group of introductory documentation about a particular software program. Use the checklist on page 288 to decide what the documentation tells you and what information is missing. Prepare questions for the software representation based on the information given or omitted. Judge the documentation. How effective is it at catching your attention? in being easy-to-read? clear?
4. Design an introductory piece of documentation for a software program you know. Use the tips on pages 287–288.
5. Choose a procedure—it can or cannot be computer related—and write a user's manual. Use the guidelines on pages 290–293.
6. Your teacher may arrange an assignment between your technical writing class and a class of computing science majors working on developing a system. Your

class will be the users. The computer scientists will explain to you the system, then present to you their system specifications. Decide if you understand them. Ask questions about things you do not understand. Later in the project, your class can test the user documentation. How clear and complete is it? What problems does it present? Share the challenges; suggest solutions for effectively presenting technical information.

7. If word processing is available to you, use it when applicable to prepare these assignments.

Part 4

Oral Presentation

Part Four discusses the oral presentation of technical information.

Chapter 13: Speaking Effectively
- identifies different types of speaking
- gives suggestions for speaking effectively
- discusses visuals appropriate for oral presentation
- gives advice about interviewing
- provides practice exercises

Overview

The public watches and listens more than it reads. This habit increases your
need to speak effectively. People see and hear good communicators on television
and in public forums. As a result, they expect other speakers to be poised,
confident, and prepared. They are less tolerant of poor speakers. Part 4 of this
book helps you become an effective presenter.

Chapter 13

Speaking Effectively

Throughout your career, you will speak with managers, secretaries, clients, draftsmen, technicians, the public, and your colleagues. To a large extent, your effectiveness will depend on your ability to communicate with all these people—upward, downward, and laterally.

This chapter talks about different types of speaking, gives suggestions for speaking effectively, discusses visuals appropriate for oral presentation, and gives advice about interviewing.

Types of Oral Presentations

You will use all three of the traditional types of speaking in your technical profession: impromptu, extemporaneous, and manuscript.

Impromptu

Impromptu is an unplanned, unpracticed presentation. Any situation when you are called upon to speak without notice requires an impromptu response. Such an occasion can occur in a meeting, a one-to-one conversation, on the telephone, and in any number of other situations. These responses are not "presentations," so you cannot prepare for them, but you can practice and improve your response to questions or invitations to give your opinion. The goal is to be clear. Listen to yourself. Do you go on and on? Do you digress? Do you fumble with words? Or, do you pause, answer directly, and speak only about the subject under discussion? Listen to others. Imitate ways of answering that you admire and understand because the answers are so simple, yet so accurate. A clear answer suggests a clear thinker. Set about learning to speak simply and precisely when you are unexpectedly asked to comment.

Extemporaneous

Extemporaneous is a planned, practiced presentation that is not memorized or read. This type of presentation is common and one most of you will often make. For example, you will report the progress of a project in a meeting, or explain about environmental matters at a public hearing, or present a project or product to a prospective client, or instruct a group about a new procedure. At different times your intent will be to inform, persuade, or instruct; sometimes you will combine intentions. Always you must know your purpose and audience before planning your presentation. The same type of analysis you do for writing is applicable for speaking. Review the strategies on pages 28–31.

Just as organization is important to writing, it is equally important to speaking. Plan an opening, development, and close. (See the ideas for content that follow the discussion on manuscript presentation on pp. 302–303.)

Because the presentation will be extemporaneous, you will not write the complete text, but you should outline the talk and make notes about facts or ideas you wish to make or want to say accurately. Prepare notes on 8½ by 11-inch paper rather than on note cards. It is disconcerting to see speakers shuffle a pack of note cards. The audience often becomes more interested in watching the stack go down than in listening to what is being said. Notes prepared on regular sized paper can be placed within a folder or notebook. The writing or typing can be large so that it is easy to see. Special thoughts or facts can be highlighted by underlining or in color or in some other way. You can easily turn the pages and stay organized, particularly if you arrange the pages consecutively in a loose-leaf ring binder.

Practice. At the actual presentation, you will say things differently from how you say them in practice. But by practicing, you will discover where you have trouble saying what you mean, good phrases that you want to use in the actual presentation, and whether you can say what you want to within the time allotted. Make a rule for yourself always to stay within the time specified. If you are asked to speak for 5 minutes, do it. If you have 20 minutes, be finished within that time or sooner.

Manuscript

Manuscript is a completely prepared presentation that is read. Most of the time, you should avoid reading speeches. Only a very practiced reader does not need to look mostly at the text, can read in a conversational way, and can appear to be speaking rather than reading. Too often the reader loses eye contact with the audience, and the audience loses interest. However, when information is technical, legal, or complicated, reading from a prepared text is sometimes necessary. When you do so, practice. Know the material well enough to look at the audience.

Organization of Oral Presentations

An oral presentation is basically organized the same way as a good report. It has an opening, development, and close. Some points to consider for each section follow:

Opening

Open your remarks courteously. Thank whoever invited you or say something about your pleasure in giving the presentation. Make the remarks relative to the situation and personal so the audience will feel you are sincere. Think carefully before beginning with a joke. If the joke is relative to the presentation and in good taste, you may want to establish a relaxed tone and catch the audience's attention. But if you are telling a joke just to appear clever, forget it. Too often, jokes fail to be funny. If the joke has no application to your topic, the audience may wonder why it was told. You are not helping yourself when this happens.

Clearly state the topic and purpose of your presentation. You may wish to say how the talk will develop. You may want to qualify your research, methodology, or the factual basis of the ideas you will present. You may want to say at the beginning what you want from the audience—approval, action, consideration, a purchase, or understanding.

Development

Organize to maximize understanding. Remember that comprehending through listening is more difficult than through reading because the listener cannot go back and relisten or stop and think about a topic and proceed at his or her own rate of understanding. Use techniques that help listeners comprehend. Begin with something they know and relate it to the unknown you are presenting. Begin with the simple and move to the complex. Organize by one of several traditional patterns: comparison and contrast, classification and division, chronology, cause and effect, space, or priority. Use transitions to move the listener along with you: "Now that we understand that . . ."; "After the third step, . . . occurs."; "As we move around the object to the left, we see . . .."

The most important point to remember is not to cover too much information. Keep the number of ideas to a minimum. If the topic is big and complex, select the most important or the two crucial ideas and present only those. Use the time to develop, explain, and illustrate rather than to pile ideas upon one another.

Close

Do not end with "That's it." Summarize; ask for action; tell the audience what they should now do or understand. Remember to thank them for their attention.

Impressions Influence Oral Presentations

First Impressions

Whenever you speak, the impression of you begins before you open your mouth and utter words. The audience observes as you get up from your chair and approach the podium or prepare to speak from your seat at a conference table. What they see influences their expectations. If you are confident, poised, courteous, well dressed, and well coordinated, people anticipate a good delivery and can even decide that you are knowledgeable before you say anything to back up that opinion. You do not need to go to charm school to acquire an effective manner. Observe those who speak. Notice what impresses you. Imitate such actions. Practice. For example, if you answer in class, enter a class discussion, or speak in a committee meeting, assume the posture, manner, attitude that you judged effective in others. When you later make a formal report in one of your major classes or in the workplace, you will have practiced and be comfortable with the style you wish to acquire.

Mannerisms

Speaking involves being seen, so mannerisms are important. Have you ever seen yourself speak? If possible, do so. Evaluations by fellow students and the teacher can mention that you sway back and forth or never look at the audience or turn your back every time you use a visual, but the truth of how you appear will be more dramatic if you see yourself perform. Explore the possibilities of seeing yourself on videotape. If your school offers a speech class that videotapes class presentations and lets students see themselves, consider taking the course. If the school has a service that lets you videotape other class presentations or practices and review your work, take advantage of the opportunity. Even if there is a small charge for the service, it will be worthwhile. If video equipment can be brought to the classroom, your teacher can arrange for this opportunity. Be willing to see yourself objectively. To improve, you must want to be better. It takes practice. Just like in a sport, you cannot mentally decide that your tennis serve must improve and have it do so without work. The same applies to physical characteristics related to speaking. The following is one guide for self-analysis of your presentation:

Name: _____

   After viewing yourself on videotape answer the following:

Did I communicate my message clearly? How?

Was it difficult to *listen* to my presentation? Why?

Did my physical appearance detract from my oral message? If so, how or why?

Was the language I used appropriate? Why?

Did my delivery and manner of presentation complement the message I was trying to share? Why?

If I were to present this speech again, how would I change it?

Equipment

It destroys the audience's confidence in your authority or competency if you do not know how to use the slide projector, dim the lights, or adjust the microphone. Any time you are to speak, be familiar with the room you are to use and test the equipment. Every action should be an informed one. Know how loud you must talk to be heard by anyone sitting in the back. Know about sight lines for any visuals you plan to use.

Personal Appearance

Clothing and personal appearance count. For class work, you do not need to don a suit or a dress to give a report, but you should be neat and appropriately dressed because your appearance communicates an attitude. In business, if your appearance suggests that you do not care about yourself, the audience may not either. As a result, your performance may be rated poorer than it actually was.

Sensitivity

Be sensitive to human conditions. If the room is beastly hot, the hour is late, the audience has listened to others for hours prior to your talk, be responsive. You may want to offer the opportunity to stand for a minute or to take a short break. You may need to cut short your presentation and present only highlights. People can listen for just so long. Be aware of this.

Visuals for Oral Presentations

There is a saying: "One picture is worth more than ten thousand words." While it literally may not be worth that many words, truly visuals can reinforce and make ideas clearer. Software graphics packages, sophisticated printers, plotters, and slide generators offer new opportunities for artistic expression and experimentation, but traditional types of visual aids can be just as effective as computer-generated ones. Whatever medium you choose, create the visual with the audience and place of presentation in mind. The following are some guidelines:

- Create visuals that people can easily see, understand, or read. Size of print and image should be governed by the size of the audience and the room where the presentation will be made.
- Do not put too much on one visual. A good rule is to put only one concept on each visual.
- Use only one color for the typed or lettered information unless you want a single word to stand out. If you choose a type size and kind, select one that is easy to read.
- Be aware of the effect of color on the audience. Generally subdued colors create a mood of trust; bright colors cause a mood of surprise (hence, caution); too many colors create confusion.
- When you use an overhead, do not leave the visual on the screen after you are through using it. People can continue to consider it instead of what you are saying. Do not turn and talk to any visual; keep yourself turned toward the audience.
- When your visual is a handout, think carefully about when to distribute it. If you do so at the beginning, the audience can consider or read it rather than listen to you. If the audience is large and you stop to distribute the visual at the appropriate time in your presentation, the distribution may take too long for everyone to have a copy. As a result, you must pause too long and lose the audience's attention, or you begin talking about the visual before everyone has a copy. If the handout has several parts that you want the audience to refer to at different times in your presentation, then their reading everything is difficult to control. Sometimes they continue to read while you are talking and wanting their attention. Handouts are useful when you want the audience to take the information with them but consider presenting the same information on a chalk-

board, flip pad, transparency, or slide. You can control when each of these is or is not visible to the audience.

Informal Presentations

Not every presentation is a stand up situation. You need to evaluate, plan, and practice whatever types of public speaking you do. One common situation is to be seated at a table and talk from that position. You may be part of a meeting, making a point, even reporting on a project. Often the audience in this situation is more relaxed. You may feel free to make a comment to someone sitting alongside. People in this situation often have paper and pencil with them, and they may write while you are talking. You are never sure whether they are taking notes on what you are saying or working on their own interests. All these conditions make it difficult to feel good about your effectiveness. One way to do your best is to gain control. Speak with authority. Be organized. Move through information with competence. If appropriate, use handouts or visuals to keep their attention. Ask questions. If you cannot see the people, stand up or move your chair so you can see everyone. Do not be shy. After all, it is your time, and you are being graded by your teacher, employer, or peers. Why feel hesitant about doing your best? People respond to effective speakers. Make them respond to you.

Another common informal presentation is to make an introduction. When you do so, be prepared. Do not make an introduction off the top of your head. Do not give every credential and everything the speaker has ever done. Do not steal the essence of the speaker's topic. Instead, say something about the reason for the occasion, remark why this particular person is well suited to address the subject or group, welcome the speaker graciously, and quit.

Another informal speaking situation is talking on the phone. Just as most people have never seen themselves speak, many have never heard their voice as it records. Arrange to do so and listen to its timbre. You may have the impression that you sound melodious and full-voiced when, in fact, your voice records high and thin. You can change your voice tone through practice. Inexpensive tape recorders allow almost anyone to practice recording and to eliminate annoying voice habits or sounds.

Teleconference calls are now commonly replacing face-to-face meetings, and you need to consider how to be effective without a personal appearance. Everything said about being prepared, being clear, and being brief applies. In the future, more use will be made of calls that include visually seeing other callers over a TV screen. Everything about impressions applies.

The Personal Interview

Arrive prepared both mentally and physically. Remember that your appearance and manners make a first impression and that the way you express yourself and the quality of your questions and answers will reveal your mind. Know as much as possible about the company before you arrive. Know why you have an interest in joining this organization or in working to produce its product. Write a list of questions that you think the interviewer may ask you. Have someone role-play the interview with you. The person will ask the questions; you will respond; the person may throw in an unexpected response; how do you handle it? Do not talk too much about yourself personally. It is fine to mention that you like skiing if the interview is in Denver but do not go on and on about your passion for the sport. The interviewer may think that your real reason for wanting the job is to ski. Do not talk a lot about your husband or wife or children. Keep the discussion on professional topics. Remember that you are there to find out if you want to join this company if offered the job, and they have invited you to find out if they will make the offer.

Once you have interviewed, keep a journal of your impressions of your performance. What do you want to improve? How can you work to be better at the next interview? What questions surprised you? What do you wish you had asked or said? Review the journal before going to the next interview.

Practice Exercises

1. If possible, videotape yourself as you practice for delivering an oral report. Write a critique of your practice performance. Have the actual report presentation videotaped. Review both tapes and evaluate your improvement.
2. Keep a journal for a set period of time in which you record observations of speakers you observe. Decide what to imitate and what to avoid. Apply your intentions. Record your own impressions of your progress in becoming a more effective speaker.
3. The teacher will create a committee situation. Each person will give a brief report and comment on the reports of others. The rest of the class will observe and record the effectiveness of each speaker. The situation should have some problems: perhaps people talk while another is speaking; perhaps the speaker cannot see the audience. Have the participants handle problems and let them be judged and judge themselves on their effectiveness.
4. The teacher will arrange mock interviews. If possible, the teacher will have a guest interviewer visit class and interview students. Reactions from the interviewer, the persons interviewed, and the audience will be discussed in class.
5. The teacher will assign introductions. Rather than having members of the class make a long series of individual introductions, the teacher will intersperse the introductions with other classwork over a period of time. As the introduction exercise proceeds, the class members should benefit from discussing good and weak points and from seeing successful and not so successful examples.

Part 5

Handbook for Grammar and Punctuation

Part 5 covers the basic rules of grammar and punctuation:

Overview

Writers and those who evaluate writing need a common vocabulary for communicating. As both a comfort and a curiosity, language for talking about writing is the same whether we are attending seventh grade, high school, vocational school, college, graduate school, or working in a profession. The comfort is that once learned, the terms or rules are applicable throughout our writing career. The curiosity is why does it take some of us so long to master the rules or why do we forget to apply them even though we have studied and practiced them before? Educators do not know why grammar and punctuation rules are not readily learned or retained. Yet, we all know from giving our work to an editor (a teacher, supervisor, friend, or professional critic) that after a careful reading, the person will probably find errors.

This handbook covers the basics. It gives proper names for the parts of speech and common writing errors. It identifies common ways to correct errors. It encourages you not to fall back on old excuses like, "I never did learn the parts of speech," or "I never was any good at grammar," or "I don't know the rules for commas. I just put one in whenever I pause." Like any other body of knowledge, the rules of English can be learned, and you must learn them to be educated and competent. No one is going to be impressed with your written or spoken presentation if it contains glaring errors in common language usage.

Grammar

The Sentence

The sentence is the basic unit of expression. It can be long or short, simple or complex, but it always contains a subject and predicate and expresses a complete idea.

Subject

The subject is the word or group of words that tells who or what performs or experiences the action of the verb.

The park protects nearly a thousand buffalo.

"The park" is the subject that performs the action of "protecting."

The manager sent a memo to all employees in the division.

"The manager" is the subject that performs the action of "sending."

The experiment was completed by the end of the semester.

"The experiment" is the subject that experiences the action of "was completed."

Predicate

The predicate is made up of the verb and any words that modify it. Most frequently the predicate tells something about the subject.

The park protects nearly a thousand buffalo.

"Protects" is the verb that tells what the "park" does.
"Nearly a thousand buffalo" is the direct object receiving the action of the verb.

Nearly a thousand buffalo were protected by the park.

"Were protected" is the verb phrase that tells what the "buffalo" experience.

Every sentence must have a subject and predicate. You need to understand how to write these elements correctly.

Writing the Subject

The subject can be a noun, a noun phrase, a pronoun, or a verbal noun.

1. A noun names one or more persons, places, things, conditions, ideas, creatures, or activities.

    noun/thing
    ↓
    [Railroads] eventually replaced steamboats for carrying freight.

    noun/condition/activity
    ↓
    The [snowmelt] helps make a good harvest in the northern plains.

2. A noun phrase is a group of words made up of a main noun and words that describe, limit, or qualify it.

    main noun---words that describe it--------------
    ↓
    [Uncertainty about farming on the semiarid plains] evaporated as railroads forged west.

3. A pronoun is a word that takes the place of a noun.

    noun
    ↓
    The [tribes] were under assault from smallpox and white

    pronoun/takes the place of "tribes"
    ↓
    settlements. [They,] nevertheless, continued to farm, trade, and defend themselves.

4. A verbal noun is a word or phrase formed from a verb and used as a noun. The two types are the gerund, which ends in "ing," and the infinitive, which is usually introduced by "to."

    gerund/noun/subject
    ↓
    [Fighting] insects is the farmer's constant battle.

    infinitive/noun/subject
    ↓
    [To write] well is satisfying.

Writing the Predicate

The predicate must contain a verb, and the verb is one of three types—linking, intransitive, or transitive.

1. A linking verb is followed by a word or word group that identifies or describes the subject. The most common linking verb is a form of "be" ("is," "are," "was," "were," etc.) Other linking verbs include "seem," "become," and verbs that convey the senses, such as touch, sound, taste, smell, and sight.

```
subject              predicate
  ↓                     ↓
noun                linking verb   describes the subject
  ↓                     ↓
Westminster      was              first a palace.
```

The word or word group that follows the linking verb is called a subject complement. It "completes" the meaning of the subject. If it is a noun, such as "palace," it is called a predicate noun. If it is an adjective, such as "majestic," it is called a predicate adjective.

```
subject    verb
  ↓          ↓                   subject complement
pronoun   linking verb           predicate noun
  ↓          ↓                         ↓
He         seems         a good student.

       subject       verb    predicate adjective
          ↓            ↓            ↓
   The surveyor    looked    tired
```

2. An intransitive verb names an action that has no direct impact on anyone or anything named in the predicate.

```
subject  predicate
  ↓         ↓
noun    intransitive verb
  ↓         ↓
Fish     swim.

subject          predicate
         noun          intransitive verb
           ↓                  ↓
Metal tools   often rust.
```

3. A transitive verb names an action that directly affects a person or thing mentioned in the predicate. The word or word group naming the person or thing is known as the direct object.

```
subject  predicate
  ↓         ↓
noun     verb                      direct object/receives the
  |        |                              ↓
  |        |                       action of being misjudged
  |        |                              ↓
Custer   misjudged the Indians'   strength.
```

Sometimes you want to use an indirect object to show for or to whom the action of the direct object was done. You can do so by placing it between the verb and direct object.

noun   verb   indirect object   direct object
↓   ↓   ↓   ↓
Custer gave the soldiers encouragement.

Types of Sentences

1. The simple sentence contains a subject and predicate that make sense and can stand alone. The subject and predicate may be modified, but the sentence must remain one clause, a group of related words that contains a subject and a predicate.

          subject   predicate
   noun   verb
   ↓   ↓
[Tepees of a huge Indian village] [stood for miles along the river.]

2. The compound sentence contains two or more independent clauses (each with a subject and a predicate) that can stand alone as sentences. The clauses/sentences can be joined by a comma (,) before a coordinating conjunction ("and," "but," "or," "nor," "for," "yet," "so"):

Sentence 1   coordinating   **Sentence 2**
                   conjunction
                    ↓
[The meeting is scheduled for Tuesday], but [it needs to be rescheduled.]

by a semicolon (;) when the thoughts of each sentence are closely related:

Sentence 1   semicolon
                             ↓
[The short herring season was exceedingly sweet]; [$6.5 million dollars

Sentence 2 (continuing the same thought)
worth of herring was loaded into boats at the season's end.]

by a semicolon before a conjunctive adverb ("however," "nevertheless," "consequently," see p. 318 for a complete list):

Sentence 1
[A herring is a small, nondescript fish];

Sentence 2 conjunctive adverb
                ↓
however, [it may well be the most abundant species of fish in the sea.]

3. The complex sentence contains two or more clauses, but all are not equal in importance, nor can they all stand alone as sentences. Those that do not make a complete statement are called dependent clauses; they need the other clause to make a complete statement. Those that can stand alone are called independent.

Dependent clause	*Independent clause*

noun   verb phrase   pronoun   verb phrase
 ↓   ↓   ↓   ↓
[Since parchment is stretched animal skin,] [it   can mold
even after being treated in a lime solution.]

Sentence Modifiers

The skeleton of the sentence is the subject and predicate, but the flesh and personality come from additional, modifying elements. They describe, limit, or qualify words within the sentence. Common types follow:

1. Adjectives and adjective phrases modify nouns. An adjective describes or limits a noun or pronoun. Adjective phrases begin with a preposition ("with," "in," "of," "at," "by," "before," etc.)

                    adjective noun   adjective phrase/modifies "bucket"   adjective noun
                        ↓   ↓   ↓   ↓
Hank carried a 5-gallon bucket of gasoline out of the   machine shop.

        noun linking verb predicate adjective   predicate adjective
         ↓   ↓   ↓   ↓
The   result is   formidable   and productive.

            Adjective   adjective adjective noun   adjective phrase/modifies "beetles"
               ↓   ↓   ↓   ↓
Tough-looking,   purple,   dung   beetles   with fanciful horns

verb   direct object
 ↓   ↓
use   the horns   in courtship rituals.

2. Adverbs and adverb phrases modify verbs, adjectives, other adverbs, and whole sentences. They specify how, when, where, why, to what degree, and for what purpose. Adverb phrases begin with a preposition ("with," "in," "of," "at," "by," etc.). Normally you form an adverb by adding "ly" to an adjective.

        noun   verb   adverb phrase/tells where
         ↓   ↓
The   dog   scratched   behind his ear. (Modifies a verb)

        adverb/tells how adjective noun
             ↓   ↓   ↓
The   disturbingly   silent   man remained in the room.
  (Modifies an adjective)

adverb/tells degree   adverb   adjective noun
↓   ↓   ↓   ↓

The very   disturbingly silent   man remained in the room.
(Modifies an adverb)

adverb/tells degree
↓

Realistically, the whole project is off.
(Modifies the whole sentence)

3. Comparatives and superlatives compare one person or thing with another or all others in a group of three or more.

   The comparative is formed by adding "er" or "more" to the word; the superlative is formed by adding "est" or "most" to the word. Do not use both means of forming the comparative or superlative with the same word ("most wisest").

   Diamonds are harder than emeralds.
   (Two things compared)

   Among the group members, Bill is the wisest.
   (More than two compared)

4. An appositive is a noun or noun phrase that immediately follows and identifies another noun, noun phrase, or pronoun. If you need it to understand the sentence, do not set it off with commas; if it adds information, but is not necessary to understanding, set it off with commas.

   noun   appositive/necessary
   ↓   ↓

   Russia's leader Gorbachev met with the American leader in Iceland in 1986.

   noun   appositive/not necessary
   ↓

   Gorbachev, a seasoned politician, met with the American leader in Iceland in 1986.

5. A participle is a word formed from a verb and used to modify a noun.

   participle noun
   ↓   ↓

   The running dog overcame the thrown stick.

   A participle phrase is a group of words based on a participle.

   noun   participle phrase
   ↓

   The dog,   running to overtake the stick, leaped with joy.

Participles are present, past, or perfect.

a. The present participle adds "ing" to the basic verb form and describes a noun as acting.

```
     participle   noun
         ↓          ↓
The   melting    lava raced down the hillside.
```

b. The past participle often adds "d" or "ed" to the basic verb form and describes a noun as acted upon.

```
                      participle  noun
                          ↓         ↓
The family feasted on baked      turkey on Thanksgiving.
```

c. The perfect participle adds "having" to the verb and describes an action that has been completed before the action named by the verb.

```
     participle                                                    verb
 ⌒‾‾‾‾‾‾‾‾‾‾‾‾⌒                                                     ↓
Having discovered a blood test that will reveal cancer, the scientists anticipated a Nobel Prize.
```

6. An infinitive is "to" plus a verb and modifies a noun, adjective, or verb.

```
     noun   infinitive/modifies "need"
       ↓      ⌒‾‾‾‾‾⌒
The   need  to eat    is basic to humankind.
```

```
                    adjective  infinitive/modifies "excited"
                        ↓          ⌒‾‾‾‾‾⌒
The child was   excited    to witness the arrival of Santa Claus.
```

```
          verb  infinitive/modifies "eats"
            ↓      ⌒‾‾‾‾‾⌒
Garfield  eats   to live.
```

Common Sentence Errors

A handbook cannot discuss every kind of sentence structure or reason for error, but people who evaluate writing regularly agree that most errors occur because of a small number of mistakes. The following list is based on that understanding. If you write and speak error-free of these problems, you can be confident that most of your communication is grammatically acceptable, and you are recognized as someone who knows how to use the language correctly.

1. *The Fragment:* an incomplete sentence. It lacks either a subject or predicate (noun or verb) or it fails to make complete sense by itself.

Being unprepared. (fragment) Another reason for not doing well is being unprepared. (sentence)

Because you hand work in late. (fragment: The dependent clause contains a pronoun [you] and a verb [hand], but it does not make sense by itself.)

Because you hand work in late, you never receive full credit for what you do. (sentence)

2. *The Run-on Sentence:* two or more sentences run together with no punctuation.

Sentence 1	Sentence 2

run-on
Micronesia is a group of islands on the move they float.

The error can be corrected many ways, and each is as good as the other. The choice depends on the surrounding text and the author's style.
   Examples of corrections:

Micronesia is a group of islands on the move. They float.

The period divides the two sentences.

Because they float, Micronesia is a group of islands on the move.

One sentence is made into a dependent clause.

Micronesia is a group of islands on the move; they float.

Two sentences on the same idea can be joined by a semicolon.

3. *The Comma Splice:* two or more sentences joined by commas. The comma alone cannot join sentences.

comma splice
A summit is not any meeting between two heads of state, the rulers must be equal and capable of making major decisions on the spot.

A number of ways exist to correct the comma splice. The choice depends on the relationship you wish to show between ideas. Some possible corrections follow:

You can separate the two sentences with a period. No particular relationship is shown. The two ideas exist independently.

A summit is not any meeting between two heads of state. The rulers must be equal and capable of making major decisions on the spot.

You can also join the two sentences with a semicolon if the ideas in both sentences are closely connected.

> A summit is not any meeting between two heads of state; the rulers must be equal and capable of making major decisions on the spot.

You can make one of the clauses dependent.

> Because the rulers must be equal, a summit is not any meeting between two heads of state.

You often can join the sentences with a comma followed by a coordinate conjunction ("and," "but," "or," "nor," "for," "yet," and "so"). The connector shows the relationship.

> A summit is not any meeting between two heads of state, for the rulers must be equal and capable of making major decisions on the spot.

You often can join the sentences with a semicolon followed by a conjunctive adverb ("however," "nevertheless," "also," "moreover," "hence," "instead," "therefore," "likewise," "thus," "indeed," "furthermore," "consequently," "otherwise"). The connecter shows the relationship.

> A summit is not any meeting between two heads of state; instead, it is one wherein the rulers must be equal and capable of making major decisions on the spot.

4. *Lack of Subject-Verb Agreement:* a mixture of singular and plural. If the subject is singular the verb must be singular; if the subject is plural, the verb must be plural. Be careful of the following circumstances:
   a. Pronouns like "everyone," "each," "anybody," "somebody," "either," "neither," "everybody," and "no one" take singular verbs. The error most likely occurs when the subject pronoun is separated from the verb by a prepositional phrase with a plural noun.

singular pronoun	prepositional phrase	singular verb
	preposition plural noun	
↓	↓ ↓	↓
Everyone	of the members	sends a contribution.

   b. The subject is not always placed at the beginning of a sentence nor is it always the first noun in the sentence.

verb	noun/subject
↓	↓
There are 30,000	students attending this university.

c. Compound subjects can be joined by "either . . . or" or "neither . . . nor." The verb agrees with the closer subject.

plural   singular singular
↓   ↓   ↓

Neither the dogs nor the cat   is   a good car traveler.

singular   plural plural
↓   ↓   ↓

Neither the cat nor the dogs are good car travelers.

d. Collective nouns such as "union," "group," "navy," "team," "committee," "board," "pride," take either a singular or a plural verb depending on the intended meaning.
Use a singular verb when you speak of the group as a whole.

The pride of lions rests after the hunt.

The singular verb ("rests") tells you the writer considers the pride as a whole.
Use a plural verb when you speak of the group as individuals.

The committee have voted to postpone the decision.

The plural verb ("have") tells you the writer considers the committee as individuals.

e. A relative pronoun ("who," "which," "that") takes either a singular or plural verb, depending on the word to which it refers.

relative pronoun
refers to reports plural verb
↓   ↓

Please hand me one of the reports that   are on the desk.

relative pronoun
refers to report singular verb
↓   ↓

Please hand me the report   that   is on the desk.

5. *Lack of Pronoun-Antecedent Agreement:* a mixture of singular and plural. A singular pronoun must have a singular antecedent and vice versa.

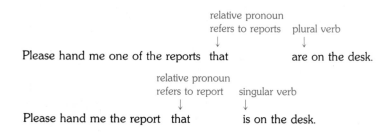

singular/antecedent   singular pronoun
↓

No   student was going to keep his or her book after the semester.

6. *Faulty Pronoun Case:* a mismatch between the case (subjective, objective, or possessive) of the pronoun and its function in the sentence. The form of the pronoun must be the same as the pronoun's use in the sentence.

   subject complement (subjective)
   ↓
   It was he who went to the movie.

   indirect object (objective)
   ↓
   The school gave him the option of work-study or a scholarship.

   possessive pronoun (possessive)
   ↓
   It is our belief that writing is important.

7. *Dangling Modifier:* lack of correct reference for the modifier. Dangling modifiers make the sentence incorrect or confusing.

   While cooking the turkey, the baby played in the kitchen.
   (It appears as if the baby cooked the turkey.)

   While the mother cooked the turkey, she let the baby play in the kitchen.
   (The meaning is correct.)

8. *Misplaced Modifier:* incorrect positioning of a modifier. The modifier should be placed as close as possible to the word it modifies; otherwise, the meaning can be confused.

   The man has been trying to get a contract for five years.
   (The reader does not know whether the man has been trying for five years to get a contract or trying to get a five-year contract.)

   Correction: For five years, the man has been trying to get a contract.

9. *Faulty Parallelism:* inconsistent grammatical presentation in a series. Any two or more elements of the same importance should be structured alike. A common place to use parallel structure is in a list. For example, if you begin the first item in the list with a verb, start all other items with a verb; if you begin with a prepositional phrase, begin every item the same way.

   Correct Usage
   Before using word processing do the following:

   Turn on the computer
   Insert a diskette
   Bring up a word processing program

(Each item begins with a verb.)

Correct Usage
Common forms of exercise are running, jogging, swimming, and bicycling.

(Each form ends in "ing.")

Punctuation

Most of the time when a piece of writing is marked with many punctuation mistakes, an analysis will show that only two or three repeated errors are being made. Punctuation is not difficult to learn. If you have not mastered the basics, decide to do so during this course. You need only to learn the following rules to eliminate the most common errors. Train yourself to proofread carefully in order to correct errors yourself before the reader sees them.

Apostrophe (')

1. The apostrophe shows possession. Add an apostrophe plus "s" to singular nouns and indefinite pronouns.

    boy's bike   one's notebook   everyone's

   Add an apostrophe plus "s" to plural nouns that do not end in "s." Add only an apostrophe to plurals that end in "s."

    children's   rats'

   Add an apostrophe or apostrophe plus "s" only to the last member of the group to show joint possession.

    Bill and Jack's tripod.

   Add an apostrophe plus "s" to each member of the group to show individual possession.

    Bill's and Jack's tripods.

2. The apostrophe shows omission of one or more letters or figures.

    can't = cannot   '89 = 1989

3. Do not misuse the apostrophe in "it's" and "you're."

    it's = it is;   its = the possessive of it, not it's nor its'
    you're = you are;   your = the possessive of you, not your's

Brackets ([ ])

1. Brackets enclose the author's comments or explanations inserted in a quotation.

   "The purpose of the island's [Kwaj] development is far from frivolous."

   "Housing starts were slow last month [November '89]."

2. Sic (Latin for "thus" or "so") within brackets means the error in the text is not yours.

   "The American Revolution began in 1876 [sic]."

Colon (:)

1. The colon is a convention in salutations, citations, time, and titles.

   Dear Mrs. Stephens: Dear Professor Higgins:

   Personal Computing 87 (February 1988): 13

   3:30 P.M.

   Technical Writing: An Aid to Better Communication

2. The colon correctly introduces a list or series when the words before the colon are a complete sentence. Do not use a colon when an incomplete sentence precedes the list or series.

   The spice cinnamon is often used in the preparation of various foods: coffee cake, spice cake, tapioca, stewed fruits, pumpkin, ham, and broiled grapefruit. (complete sentence before the colon)

   The cook regularly uses cinnamon, nutmeg, garlic powder, rosemary, and Italian seasoning. (incomplete sentence before the list)

3. The colon introduces a quotation (particularly if the quotation is more than two lines or is indented and set apart in the text). A sentence should precede the colon.

   The Dutch seek to protect the southwestern corner of their country with a colossal hydraulic-engineering project described as follows:
       "The project is a vast complex of dams, dikes, and channels that barrier. . . ."

4. The colon also is used in sentences leading into a graph or table or rule or standard.

   Figure 1.2 shows the general flow of energy through the generator:

   A basic policy of this agency is as follows:

Comma (,)

1. The comma before a coordinate conjunction ("and," "but," "or," "nor," "for," "yet," and "so") correctly separates two sentences.

> The electricity went off, but Sarah did not lose what she was typing into the computer.

2. The comma is a convention in dates, numbers, addresses, informal salutations, and titles or degrees.

> May 22, 1990
>
> (but 22 May 1990   or   May 1990)
>
> The report was prepared on January 15, 1988, and forwarded to the Dallas office the next day.
>
> 12,438,102
>
> 7200 Monroe Avenue, N.E.
>
> St. Petersburg, FL 33710
>
> My home is in St. Petersburg, Florida, which is located on the West Coast. [The comma sets off an address or date from the following sentence elements.]
>
> Dear Ray,
>
> Jane Shaw, M.D.

3. The comma separates items in a series. Follow each item, except the last one, with a comma.

> Before I can go on vacation, I must go to the bank, wash and iron my clothes, pack, have the car serviced, and arrange for someone to care for the pets.

4. The comma separates introductory phrases and clauses from the main sentence.

> Whenever I have a lot to do, I get very irritable and short with other people.

You sometimes need a comma to keep the reader from reading past where he or she should pause.

> Because the floodwall blocks viewing, the river is not seen by anyone driving on Southlane Avenue.

Without the comma, the reader easily can read: "Because the floodwall blocks viewing the river. . . ." The reader will realize that this reading is not right, but he or she must back up and begin again. You do not want to cause your readers to do this.

5. The comma sets apart from the rest of the sentence nonrestrictive modifiers (nonessential elements in the sentence). Restrictive modifiers (essential elements to the meaning of the sentence) are not set off by commas. Sometimes the question is one of which is which. The only one who can really decide is the writer, and even then that is a personal decision. The best way to decide is to ask yourself: Is this information essential to the meaning of the sentence? If it is, do not use commas. If it is not, set the information apart with commas.

The specifications [for the Turnville Tunnel] were drawn up by the firm of Turnbull and Turnbull. (restrictive/necessary for meaning/no commas)

The specifications[, which were very well presented,] were drawn up by the firm Turnbull and Turnbull. (nonrestrictive/not essential to the meaning/use commas)

6. Some people use too many commas or use them incorrectly. Avoid the following comma errors.

   subject   verb
     ↓   ↓
   a. The most common punctuation error,   is the comma.
      Do not place a comma between the subject and verb.

   final adjective   noun
         ↓   ↓
   b. The long, hot, dry, wasted, summer is almost over.
      Do not place a comma between the final adjective and the noun.

   verb   direct object
     ↓   ↓
   c. The boys raked, leaves.
      Do not place a comma between the verb and direct object.

                  coordinate conjunction
                          ↓
   d. Bill is going to participate in both golf,   and baseball.
      Do not place a comma between two words linked by a coordinate conjunction.

   last subject   verb
         ↓   ↓
   e. Art, literature, and music,   are my favorite studies.
      Do not place a comma between the last subject in a list and the verb.

Dash (—)

1. The dash is a mark that abruptly separates items. It often replaces the comma or parentheses. Be careful not to overuse it. To type a dash, type two unspaced hyphens with no space between the words before and after the dash.

I like to do lots of things—go to plays, visit museums, attend concerts—that involve the arts.

2. Do not use the dash to join two sentences.

Ellipsis (. . .)

1. The ellipsis is three periods in a row used to indicate something omitted from a quoted passage. Use four periods when the omission comes at the end of the sentence. The fourth dot stands for the period of the sentence.

   "Well-written documents are carefully thought out . . . and organized so that they read easily."

   "No single solution can be a cure-all for the many problems of effectively documenting a computer system. . . ."

2. What you leave out should be supplemental material, not anything essential to meaning. Sometimes you find a quotation that would be just right for what you are writing except it has some contradictory information within in. Do not use the ellipsis to omit what you do not want your readers to see. Such practice is unethical and irresponsible.

Exclamation Point (!)

1. The exclamation point follows an emotional statement. In technical writing, you should use this punctuation sparingly.

   Four minutes after liftoff, the spaceship exploded!

2. If your typewriter or word processor does not have this punctuation mark on the keyboard, type a period, backspace, and type an apostrophe over the period. Do not use more than one exclamation point at the same time.

Hyphen (-)

1. The hyphen is used to break a word at the end of a line and carry the rest of the word to the next line. The break must come between syllables. If you do not know the syllables of the word, check the dictionary.
2. The hyphen is used in all words beginning with self:

   self-assured   self-appointed

3. The hyphen is used in fractions and ratios that function as adjectives preceding a noun.

   four-fifths   five-to-one odds

4. The hyphen is used in compound numbers from twenty-one through ninety-nine.

   thirty-two chickens   eighty-nine people

   Technical writing prefers numbers over 10 to be in figures (32, 89).
5. The hyphen can create compound modifiers.

   The hand-addressed envelope makes the letter look more important.

Parentheses ( )

1. Parentheses insert parenthetical information within a single sentence or between sentences. Use no punctuation before the first parenthesis. Place after the second parenthesis any punctuation usually required after the last word before the first parenthesis. Punctuate and capitalize normally any sentences within the parentheses.

   Even though Sid already knew about the error (John says Sid knew from the very beginning), he disclaimed any responsibility.

2. Place acronyms within parentheses the first time you introduce them. Place the acronym after the words it represents.

   The next location for the annual meeting of the National Council of Teachers of English (NCTE) is San Antonio, Texas.

Period (.)

1. The period is an end punctuation. It signals the stop of a complete thought.

   Matisse repeatedly painted his same room in Cannes but changed appointments like table coverings or decorative screens.

2. The period also is used in the following ways:
   To end an abbreviation: Mr., Inc., etc., dept.
   To serve as decimal points for figures: .2245, $8.35, 13.2%

Question Mark (?)

1. The question mark ends a sentence that asks a direct question.

   What change occurred to the leaf texture during the experiment?

2. Do not use a question mark after an indirect question.

Incorrect Usage
The students asked how the reduction in student aid would affect their out-of-pocket expenses?

Correct Usage
The students asked how the reduction in student aid would affect their out-of-pocket expenses.

Quotation Marks (" ")

1. Quotation marks indicate the exact words quoted from another speaker or writer. At the end of a quotation, the period or comma is placed inside the quotation mark.

   Garfield said, "Lazy people are to be admired."

   In Kealsey's essay on Thomas Mann, he remarked that Mann "never believed anything he wrote would be a success."

   Place the colon or semicolon outside the quotation mark.

   The brochure tempts you with a "winter get-away": a trip to the Riviera.

2. If what you are quoting is more than three lines, introduce the quotation with a grammatical structure calling for a colon, drop to the next line, indent ten spaces from the left-hand margin, and single-space.

   In the material on graphics, Stuart makes the following points about charting:
   > The line chart is a necessary visual aid for scientists and engineers because it best plots behavior or trends of two or more related variables. The independent variable is usually plotted horizontally and the dependent variable vertically. Common independent variables include time, distance, voltage, stress, and load. Common dependent variables are temperature, money, current. . . .

3. Quotation marks identify titles of works that are shorter than book length: magazine articles, poems, short stories, essays, and the like.

   My favorite short story is Conrad's "Heart of Darkness."

4. Words can be set apart by either italics or quotation marks.

   In word processing, a "bug" means a problem in a program.

Semicolon (;)

1. The semicolon can join two closely related sentences.

To do well in school requires effort and discipline; these qualities are also necessary to do well in one's profession.

2. The semicolon used before a conjunctive adverb can correctly join two sentences.

My check was delayed this month; consequently, I will be late paying my bills due at the first of the month.

3. The semicolon is used to separate items in a series when at least one of the individual items themselves has commas.

I want to take the following with me on my trip: my new, expensive, fast-exposure camera; my down-filled, green parka; and my downhill skis.

Slash (/)

The slash separates elements in dates, indicates a fraction, and replaces "per."

12/12/25 . . . . December 12, 1925
4/5. . . . . four-fifths
/request . . . . .per request

Capitalization

Some unusual situations call for unusual capitalization, and some companies, as part of policy, capitalize words that are not ordinarily capitalized, but for the most part, the rules of capitalization are standard. Capitalize the following:

People's names and initials:

Laura H. Stuart

Civil, military, religious, and professional titles that are a part of the name and immediately precede the name or are used to refer to a specific person:

Representative Scott
Colonel Tom G. Patton
Professor Smith
The Judge will render a decision today.

Academic degrees:

The Ph.D. is a final degree in a field of study.
The B.A. degree can be given in education.

Place names:
   Parts of the world or a country: Capitalize "north," "south," "east," and "west" when they officially designate that part of a country, continent, or other geographical area.

   the Midwest   the Orient   South America

   Countries, states, cities, counties

   Canada   Florida   St. Augustine   Pinellas County

   Rivers, lakes, islands, mountains, plains, hollows, keys—any topographic location

   Mississippi River   Lake Huron   Death Valley   Skunk Hollow

   Public place, buildings, monuments

   Washington, D.C., Mall   Empire State Building   Washington Monument

Organizations:
   Institutions, companies, associations, governmental and judicial bodies

   National Council of Teachers of English   Sears   Duke University
   Supreme Court   Department of Education

Archaeological and cultural periods:

   Iron Age   Romanticism

Laws, acts, treaties, and government programs:

   Embargo Act   Bill of Rights   Magna Carta
   Social Security   Medicare

Astronomical terms and geological terms and names of genus, family, order, class, and phylum:

   Big Dipper   Jupiter   Jurassic   Arthropoda

Proper names attached to laws and principles:

   Kepler's first law

Awards:

    Caldecott Children's Book Award

Calendar and time notation:

    April   Tuesday   Easter

Brand names:

    Buick   Jello   Anacin

Titles:
    Key words in titles of books, periodicals, pamphlets, newspapers, movies, television programs, musical works, artworks

    Journal of Physical Science   *Portrait of a Woman in a Red Hat*

Do not capitalize in the following situations:
Words derived from proper nouns

    pasteurize   bohemian   bacchanal

Time periods designated numerically

    seventeenth century   twelfth

Seasons

    autumn   spring

College classes

    sophomore   senior

General groups

    senior citizens   welfare recipients   yuppies

Titles that follow a proper noun

    John Smith, mayor   (but Mayor John Smith)

Common plant and animal names

    periwinkle   house sparrow   thistle   tortoise

For a more complete discussion of proper capitalization for scientific terms, consult the *Council of Biology Editors Style Manual* and the U.S. Geologic Survey's *Suggestions for Authors.*

Numbers

The rule to remember always is to be consistent once you choose how you are going to enter numbers in the text.

Generally write a number as a figure in the following situations:
Addresses

6333 Oak Hill Drive, St. Petersburg, FL 33710

Dates

February 23, 1920   20 February 1920

Time—with A.M. or P.M.

10:00 A.M.

Sums of money with the $ or ¢ mark

$21.50   63¢

References to pages, figures, illustrations, and the like

Page 9   Illustration 12

Units of measurement

13 feet   12 tons   2380 rpm   12.4 milligrams   1″ × 2″

Identifying numbers

Social Security number: 122-02-3278
Account number: 133 9889 4587
page 13

Decimals

4.7 liters

Percentages

82 percent
82%

"Percent" should be used with numbers only. When no number is expressed, "percentage" is used.

Fractions connected to whole numbers

62½

Tables
All numbers in tables are written as figures

Mileage figures

23 miles   65 MPH

Often in your writing, you have a choice of writing a number as a figure or word. The following guidelines will help you choose.

1. Write in words any numbers under 10; write as figures any numbers over 10.

Henry VIII had six wives.
I planted 48 new tulip bulbs this year.

If numbers under and over 10 are linked together in a series, write all as figures.

The city has 12 parks, 1 zoo, 1 ice rink, 26 tennis courts, and 3 swimming pools.

2. Write in words any numbers that begin a sentence.

One hundred and forty people came to the yard sale.

3. Write the hour in words when used with o'clock.

nine o'clock

4. Write one number as a figure and one as a word when two numbers function as a compound adjective.

five 100-foot rods
2 four-lane roads

Abbreviations

Normally you do not abbreviate in formal writing, so use abbreviations carefully. The lack of an all-inclusive industrywide list of abbreviations is another reason to use abbreviations cautiously. The following, however, are accepted and standard:

Titles before and after names

Mr.   Ms.   Mrs.   Dr. Smith   Raymond Koppel, Jr.
(Do not write: The Dr. visited Mary and gave her medicine.)

Time when used with the actual times

900 B.C.   6:30 A.M.
(Do not write: My A.M. class in literature is a bore.)

For a more complete reference of proper abbreviations, consult the *Abbreviations Dictionary*.

Summary

This handbook for grammar and punctuation does not purport to be a complete guide to grammar and usage. For a more comprehensive coverage of grammar, punctuation, capitalization, numbers, and abbreviations, I refer you to *The Rinehart Handbook for Writers* by Carter and Skates (Holt, Rinehart and Winston, 1988).

Index